FINANCIAL FACTS OF LIFE
PERSONAL PROSPERITY
IN 30 EASY LESSONS

Bob Rosefsky

John Wiley & Sons, Inc.
New York ▪ Chichester ▪ Brisbane ▪ Toronto ▪ Singapore

Library of Congress Cataloging-in-Publication Data:

Rosefsky, Robert S.
   Financial facts of life : personal prosperity in 30 easy lessons / by Bob Rosefsky.
     p.   cm.
   Includes bibliographical references.
   ISBN 0-471-58729-X
   1. Finance, Personal. I. Title.
HG179.R648 1995
332.024—dc20   94-16686

Printed in the United States of America

10 9 8 7 6 5 4 3 2 1

About the Author

Author and educator Bob Rosefsky has had an extraordinary career spanning more than thirty years in gathering and dispensing financial wisdom. From his original professional background in law and banking he expanded into writing, teaching, broadcasting, lecturing, and consulting.

His activities have included a nationally syndicated newspaper column distributed by the Los Angeles Times Syndicate; eleven books, including a college textbook, *Personal Finance,* which is one of the top selling texts in the field; two educational television series: *You and the Law* and *Personal Finance,* the latter having been nationally distributed by PBS since 1978; and nine years as a commentator and call-in radio host for ABC's Los Angeles TV and radio affiliates.

Honors and awards have kept pace. The *Personal Finance* telecourse won an Emmy as Best Instructional Series, and Bob himself won Emmys as Writer, Host, and Instructional Designer of the series. He has won the John Hancock Award for Excellence in Financial Journalism; the Golden Mike Award from the Southern California TV News Directors Association, and the Greater Los Angeles Press Club Award for his specialized commentaries. He has served on the Board of Governors of the Society of American Business and Economic Writers and the Board of Advisors for the Meredith Corporation/Better Homes and Gardens Family Network.

His own personal life bears testimony to his successful use of the wisdom he has accumulated. He and his wife of thirty-five years, Linda Sue, a psychotherapist, have four grown children and, as of this writing, two young grandchildren. By following his own financial advice, Bob was able to accumulate enough resources by age 52 to enter semi-retirement. He and Linda Sue now reside in Palm Springs, California. They spend about three months of each year as guest lecturers on cruise ships around the world.

This book is a compilation of valuable lessons that Bob has learned from both his own life and the experiences of others.

Contents

INTRODUCTION   xi

One   **And This Little Piggy Stayed Home**   1
A vivid childhood memory prompts the question:
Who decides how you should spend your money?

Two   **You Can Fool Alot of the People Alot
of the Time**   5
The first encounter with Snake Oil Sam and one of
his myriad con games.

Three   **We Aim to Please**   9
Danger ahead: Earning and spending money to
satisfy other peoples' expectations.

Four   **Getting a Head Start**   13
An early lesson on living with debt.

Five   **With Friends Like That . . .**   17
My guru, Rod Serling, introduces me to the
Twilight Zone of starting a career.

Six   **Me? A Co-Conspirator?**   23
The perils of getting conned, and how we each can
innocently lead others into making costly financial
mistakes . . . and vice versa.

Seven   **There's No Such Thing as a Sure Thing**   29
To dispel your frivolous fantasies, a bizarre case of
how a 100% absolutely positively can't-miss
proposition backfired.

Eight   **Put Your Money Where Your Knowledge Is**   33
             A frightful tale of what can go wrong when you sail
             into uncharted waters, and how to steer a safe
             course.

Nine   **Lend Me Your Ears**   41
             A sampling of horror stories that a banker heard
             from customers, and lessons to learn from them.

Ten   **The High Cost of High Anxiety**   55
             Examples of the unhappy fate awaiting anxious
             sellers and anxious landlords. Don't let it happen
             to you.

Eleven   **You'd Think They Should Know Better**   61
             Bankers can make mistakes too, even whoppers,
             and you can learn from their folly.

Twelve   **Behold the Turtle: It Makes Progress
             Only when it Sticks its Neck Out**   69
             Trials and errors in becoming an entrepreneur.
             Ordeals to be survived and lessons to be learned.

Thirteen   **Success, the Bitch Goddess? Bitch Back!**   87
             Who, and what, determines your success? And the
             benefits of bitching back at those who attempt to
             control your fate.

Fourteen   **A Most Disabling Problem**   93
             A terrifying insurance experience that can happen
             to anyone, and how to protect yourself.

Fifteen   **Rosefsky's Rule #738b:
             You Don't Ask, You Don't Get**   97
             A positive attitude to see you through the financial
             glitches and denials of life.

Sixteen   **I Owe, I Owe, So Off to Work I Go**   **105**

When work becomes drudgery you may want to make a change. You need the right skills and the right attitudes to see you through. Lessons from life.

Seventeen   **The Bigger They Are, the Harder You Fall**   **119**

Is bigger better? Pros and cons of big versus small companies for you as an investor, an employee, a customer, a lender, a supplier. And when all is said and done, who really can take the best care of you?

Eighteen   **Quid Pro Quo**   **127**

Who's scratching whose back? Legal lessons on contractual fundamentals that affect your money.

Nineteen   **Decisions, Decisions**   **135**

Guidelines to help you make some of the tough financial choices, and how they worked for me.

Twenty   **A Chemistry Lesson**   **143**

What can make a business relationship work, or fail? Of entrepreneurs and corporate folks.

Twenty-one   **Got You Covered?**   **147**

Will your employer stand behind you through thick? Or only through thin?

Twenty-two   **Talk-Radio**   **151**

Behind the scenes of radio call-in shows, and how I got there myself.

Twenty-three   "You're on the Air . . .
                How Can I Help You?"   159
                Of the 10,000 times I asked that question during
                the years of my call-in show on KABC Talk-Radio
                in Los Angeles, these represent *the twelve most
                frequent and troubling areas of financial concern of
                the public.*

Twenty-four   Jests and Jibes   211

Twenty-five   Going Broke by Going for Broke   219
                Enthusiasm is wonderful in a business venture, but
                beware of an excess of it. Lessons for
                entrepreneurs, investors, lenders, employees,
                suppliers, and others whose financial well-being
                is at stake.

Twenty-six   Ego Trips Have High-Priced Tickets   233
                How ego can get in the way of sound financial
                decisions, and how that can hurt you

Twenty-seven   "How Could You Believe Me when I Said I Loved
                You when You Know I've Been a Liar
                All My Life?"   245
                You're in for heartache if you place too much trust
                or reliance on the wrong people

Twenty-eight   Getting this Kids Off the Payroll   255
                Why some parents never seem to be able to stop
                shelling out money for the kids, and some workable
                ideas to help solve the dilemma

Twenty-nine   That Was Then, This Is Now   263
                Looking back on some major decisions regarding
                life insurance: how the concerns of twenty- and
                thirty-somethings impact on the financial well-being
                of fifty- and sixty-somethings

Thirty   **A Fitting Ending   269**

Do's and don'ts of estate planning: An array of case
histories that had unhappy endings, and what you
can do to keep that from happening to you

Introduction ⎯⎯⎯⎯⎯⎯⎯⎯⎯⎯⎯⎯⎯

Financial Facts of Life? Here's one small sample: You never heard anyone laying on their death bed saying, "I wish I had spent more time at the office."

But I'll bet these moanings are familiar to you:

"My money problems run my life."

"I wish I had spent more time with my kids."

"I work so hard to make money that I never have time to enjoy spending the money I'm making."

"I take my work home with me, if not for real, then in my head. And it stresses me out so much that I can't enjoy the free time that I do have."

"No matter how much money I make, it's never enough to impress my spouse/parents/friends."

"We just live from paycheck to paycheck. Can't we ever get just a little jump ahead?"

And so it goes.

All too often we let ourselves believe that the Financial Facts of Life are embodied in such things as articles which promise "Six Hot Stocks That Could Triple Before Sunset!" Or in investment brochures that offer a "Sure-Fire Wealth Formula That Will Let You Retire Next Year!" Or in happy hour banter that rings with the lure of "I can get you in on a good deal . . . trust me."

In short, we fail to distinguish sales pitches from facts, illusions from reality. And that can be a costly mistake.

This book offers reality. If you're looking for common sense, for valuable lessons from life's experience, for a chance to learn from the mistakes of others, for motivation to examine and improve your attitudes towards money, for information that will be as valid in a decade or a century as it is today, you've come to the right place.

And what about *Personal Prosperity?* It's not simply money in the bank, although too many people think that's the only measure of success in life.

Personal Prosperity can have many parts: the glow that comes from a sense of self-esteem . . . the satisfaction of being self-sufficient . . . the ability to control acquisitive impulses . . . the discipline to set and achieve realistic goals . . . the ingenuity to live within one's means with pleasure and dignity . . . and, perhaps most important, the capacity to enjoy the beautiful things in life unsullied by money demons.

It's my hope that this book will set you on a course toward Personal Prosperity. Oh, yes, there are also a lot of specific tips on investing and borrowing and budgeting and taking risks. But they're the stocking stuffers. My most important objective is to get you to think realistically, productively, and positively about how you want to get along with your money. Will it be the force that controls your life? Or will you seek your own comfort zones, and then have your money be the means that allow you to enjoy your chosen comfort zones? My own preference is for the latter. But most folks, I've found, get trapped in the former. Let this book get you out of that trap.

*
**   *
**   *
**

Authors often put quotations at the start of their books—frequently they are mystical or symbolic references that purport to distill the essence of the book into a sentence or two. They leave it up to you to figure out what the quotations mean. Well, we can do better than that. Here is an assortment of quotations, each with my comment as to its relevance to Personal Prosperity, and to life in general.

*"The world is too much with us. Late and soon,
getting and spending, we lay waste our powers.
Little we see in nature that is ours."*
—William Wordsworth

Wordsworth, my favorite poet and anti-yuppie, is warning us that we're so caught up with obtaining *things,* from morning til night, that we're wasting our humanity.

*"It's no trick to make a lot of money . . . if all
you really want to do is make a lot of money."*
—Herman Mankiewicz and Orson Welles
Citizen Kane

This famous film depicted a man obsessed with money and the power that comes with it. The pathos of the story, the real humanity, is that his obsession stunted the rest of his life. He may have been a financial giant. But he was an emotional runt.

ॐ

"Experience is not what happens to a man. It's what a man does with what happens to him."
—Aldous Huxley

The true value in learning is in putting the learning to work.

ॐ

"If a man empties his purse into his head, no one can take it away from him. An investment in knowledge always pays the best interest."
—Benjamin Franklin

This is true whether you're trying to fill your bank account or fulfill your life.

ॐ

"There is more to life than increasing its speed."
—Mohandas K. Ghandi

If this needs explanation, you're reading the wrong book.

ॐ

"People are always blaming their circumstances for what they are. I don't believe in circumstances. The people who get on in this world are the people who get up and look for the circumstances they want, and, if they can't find them, make them."
—George Bernard Shaw

I've lived a lot of my life by these words, as you'll see when you read this book. Perhaps you'll be inspired too to reach out for something you thought was beyond your reach.

*"I've never been afraid to fail. That's something
you have to deal with in reality. You're not
always going to be successful. I think I'm strong
enough as a person to accept failure. But I can't
accept not trying."*

—Michael Jordan

The retired basketball star, on embarking on a baseball career, gives evidence of a simple yet powerful trait. Henry Thoreau said, "Most men live lives of quiet desperation." Jordan's words serve as inspiration to prove Thoreau wrong.

❧

*"Gone? Love is never gone.
As we travel on, love's what we'll remember."*

—Edward Kleban

And all the money in the world can never buy it.

❧

*"You can always go out and make more money.
But you can never go out and make more time."*

—Bob Rosefsky

I rest my case.

Please do come back and browse among these sayings. Let them give you cause to better your life.

Chapter One

And This Little Piggy Stayed Home

A vivid childhood memory prompts the question: Who decides how you should spend your money?

A few rare childhood memories are vivid: This one is as clear in my mind today as it was when it happened over half a century ago. At the time I barely knew the difference between a nickel and a dime, let alone having any awareness of financial matters. I learned a lesson that has stayed with me; it may have been a tad cruel, but it has helped me maintain a realistic attitude about money.

I was five years old and had just made my first major life-altering decision: I was going to run away from home. The reasons for doing so escape me, but I remember making my announcement to my parents at the dinner table. (I must have already been a well-disciplined child. Most kids who purport to run away just do so. They don't announce it in advance.)

Having announced my intent, I left the table and went to my bedroom to pack my worldly possessions, including my piggy bank, in a suitcase. Minutes later, suitcase in hand, I stomped past the dining room and toward the front door.

"Where are you going to go?" my mother asked, barely able to contain her bemusement.

"I don't know," I responded defiantly.

"What are you going to use for money?" my father asked.

"I have my piggy bank packed in my suitcase." I had no idea how much money was in the piggy bank. And if I had known, I wouldn't have had a clue as to what it would buy, but that ignorance wasn't going to deter me.

"Where did you get the money that's in your piggy bank?"

"I got it from you," I answered my father.

"Well," he responded forcefully, "you can't use money that you got from me to run away from home."

I pondered that bit of parental mandate. My little mind could not dispute it. I had thought the money had been given to me, but now I was being told that there were strings attached. It was my money, but only if . . . .

The fight went out of me. I put down the suitcase and returned to the dinner table a sad, perplexed, and chastened little boy. I would run away from home another day.

I don't think my parents ever knew how that incident affected me. I recall only that many years later, on retelling the story as a humorous moment of my childhood, my mother was particularly amused at how neatly I had packed the suitcase, a trait long since lost.

*
**   *
**   *
**

Strings attached to *my* money?

Not really *my* money to do with as I please?

Others can lay claim to *my* money?

These may seem like bitter pills to swallow, but all these statements are true much of the time all throughout life. Oh, yes, there are givens: bills to pay and toys to be bought and future plans to be realized with the money that you earn. But there will always be other, often unexpected, claims to that money.

Most simply put: The more firmly you believe that your money is exclusively yours and that no one else has any right either to the money itself, or to tell you how to spend it, the more painful it will be for you when you can't spend it the way you wanted to. I got my first inkling of that lesson the night I tried to run away from home, and somehow it stuck with me.

On the opposite side: The more you define and recognize any possible claims to your money other than what you plan to do with it, the easier it will be for you to maintain peace of mind and financial stability.

Here is a very small sampling of some of the dreadful sounds you may hear—or may have already heard—telling you that your money may have to be spent in ways other than you had planned.

* "Pat needs braces."
* "We got a notice from the IRS today questioning some items on last year's return."
* "Our rent/mortgage payment will be going up next month."
* "But I was only going five miles an hour when I hit him from behind . . . it couldn't have done that much damage!"
* "He's my brother. I know he's a jerk sometimes, but if he doesn't get a loan from us, he'll be in real trouble."
* "We're your parents. We broke our backs to get the money to send you to college. If it weren't for us, you wouldn't be in the position you're in today. Have we ever asked you for anything before? Is it too much to ask you to help us buy a little condo in Florida?"
* "No, the insurance policy deductible is $1,000, not $250. We owe the other $750."
* "Sorry, but you're not covered for that."
* "The prom will cost how much?"
* "Your mother called today. Your father has to go into a nursing home, and they can't afford it. And your brother and sister haven't a penny to spare to help them."
* "It's about that partnership investment you made last year. I'm afraid I've got some rather bad news for you."

What experiences have you already had that you can add to this list? As the ever-skeptical Roseanne Roseannadanna used to say, "It's always something."

No, you don't have to be paranoid, and you don't have to forego spending for your own needs and pleasures. This is an attitudinal matter: It would be helpful to set your mind to the possibilities and contingencies that could have an impact on your regular spending patterns.

Once you've anticipated those potential budget-busting events, the next step is to figure how you can minimize the traumas. For example: Is your insurance program (life, health, disability, dwelling, auto) up to date and as comprehensive as possible? Are there gaps that need to be closed, and that can be closed cost-effectively? Do your parents have good nursing home insurance and medicare supplemental insurance to protect themselves, and indirectly to insulate you from exposure?

Are there events in your future for which it would be wise to start a savings plan today? Weddings? College? A stake to use to go into your own business? Retirement?

The more you can anticipate any such future events, and the more you take concrete steps to be ready for those eventualities, the more you'll be able to use your own piggy bank for the things you want.

Now for the very important flip side of this issue: Could *you* be, in any way, the direct or indirect cause of interference with *someone else's* future spending plans? Parents? Children? Relatives? Friends? Or do they think/fear that you might be? If so, do you want your cloud to continue hanging over their heads? It's your move.

You Can Fool Alot of the People Alot of the Time

The first encounter with Snake Oil Sam and one of his myriad con games.

How old were you the first time someone pulled the wool over your eyes? Was it a childish prank (a "gotcha!"), or was it in adulthood when you were victimized by some scam or consumer abuse? The sooner you learn about the wiles of Snake Oil Sam, the better you'll be able to protect yourself from him; but you'll never be completely immune from his tricks.

I was eleven years old, and my parents had taken me with them on a visit to New York City from our hometown, Binghamton, which was about two hundred miles northwest. It was summertime, near dusk, and we were strolling along Fifth Avenue in midtown Manhattan after dinner.

We saw a small cluster of people gathered around a darkened doorway, and we stopped to see what was attracting their attention.

A well-dressed and well-spoken man was demonstrating a toy in the recessed doorway. It was a doll whose arms and legs were made out of accordion-folded crepe paper. You've seen the kind—they make wiggly-jiggly skeletons and ghosts at Halloween.

He held the doll in front of him and jerked it up and down, making the arms and legs quiver as if the doll was dancing. I can still almost hear his clever spiel: "As you'll see, ladies and gentlemen, these are no ordinary dolls . . . these dolls don't need me to help them with their dancing . . . these dolls can dance on their very own!"

Then, lo and behold, he leaned down so as to let the doll stand *on its own* on the sidewalk. And the doll *did* stand on its own! And it wiggled and jiggled up and down, doing an eerie dance without any visible means of support!

My eleven year old eyes were astonished, but my brain, steeped in the mysteries of my then-current hobby, magic tricks, said, "Wait just a minute."

The pitchman was now offering to sell the dolls to the gathered crowd. They came in packages that were very tightly wrapped so they couldn't be easily opened on the spot. The doll kept dancing as the pitchman handed out the packages in exchange for the dollar bills that the eager crowd was all but throwing at him.

In the midst of the pandemonium I sneaked around the side of the crowd and I saw the secret, which was obscured by the twilight and the darkness of the doorway. There was an accomplice who stood facing the audience with his hands behind his back. Tied to one of his fingers was a dark thread. The other end of the thread was tied to a hook on the opposite wall of the doorway, and it was drawn taut but couldn't be seen unless you were right on top of it.

The dancing doll had a tiny pin taped to the back of its head. When the pitchman set the doll down to dance, he simply slid the hidden pin over the invisible thread, thus seemingly suspending the doll in midair. When the accomplice twitched his finger—as I saw him doing—the thread twitched with it and the doll danced accordingly.

Alot of the people in the crowd bought the dolls, but I was amazed that no one opened their package right there to see if the doll really could dance. They all went along their way, thrilled with the prospect of giving this miraculous toy to their children and grandchildren, and never thinking how they'd get their money back if their doll didn't dance. Oh, dear.

My parents passed on this opportunity of a lifetime. But a few years later they went on a vacation in the Caribbean (without me). They returned home laden with gifts for family and friends. In particular, they had bought a number of small bottles of Chanel No. 5 perfume at an astonishingly low price. They had bought it from a very honest-seeming street vendor who had let them sniff a sample. It was the real thing, as were the box and the bottle.

As they unwrapped their trove I heard them utter angry shouts. The liquid in the bottle was not Chanel No. 5. It wasn't even perfume. It was kerosene. But it *looked* like perfume. Oh, dear.

*
**   *
**   *
**

I could understand how strangers on the streets of New York could get fooled. But my parents? My early warning system regarding Snake Oil Sam thus began to function. I was eventually to write and broadcast prolifically on the subject, as later tales in this book will illustrate.

I was also busy for many years on the lecture circuit talking about the dangers of consumer fraud. That's more fun than writing or broadcasting because you get to see the reactions on people's faces. I would open my lecture with some general warnings about Snake Oil Sam and his bag of tricks, and there would always be a number of faces in the audience that would be signaling, "I'm too smart to get caught by shenanigans like that!" Then, as I'd begin to enumerate the schemes in detail, those holier-than-thou faces would suddenly flash embarrassment as they realized that they had been victimized.

On the other hand, I always harbored a certain fear when I talked about Sam that I was not just warning the public, but that I was also teaching some up-and-coming scam artist yet another way to rip off people. That's a risk that comes with the job, as I've been reassured by many law enforcement people who deal with consumer fraud.

Thus the ultimate dilemma in trying to prevent what could be financial devastation for many victims: In order to warn would-be victims we are, at the same time, educating the perpetrators. This is why we can never get rid of Snake Oil Sam, and why you will someday fall victim to one of his schemes, some of which we'll explore later in this book.

"Oh, no!" you say? You're too smart to get caught? That's what I thought, too, until the incident recounted in Chapter 6.

Chapter Three

We Aim to Please

Danger ahead: Earning and spending money to satisfy other peoples' expectations.

Much of our financial life is structured around trying to please someone and trying to live up to certain expectations. To some extent that someone you're trying to please is yourself, and the expectations are your own. But inevitably there will be occasions in which you try to please someone else, or live up to the expectations of others. That can be tricky and hazardous.

My father had a tough life. When he was just three years old his father died, leaving a young and illiterate immigrant widow with five children, the oldest of whom was eight. It was Hard Knocks 101 all around. Hard work was the order of the day, seven days a week, for everyone. My father worked his way through elementary school, high school, college, and law school. "Fun" was not a word in his vocabulary, I've always been sorry to have to say. "Making money" was the magic password. Even after he had made enough to keep his own family comfortable, the "fun" part never took its rightful place in the man's life.

This was quite perplexing to me as a young lad. Because of his hard work, I didn't have to, and yet he expected it of me because that's what he had to do. (I was his first child.) At least I thought he expected it of me. I was never really sure, which is why I was perplexed. Further, his own fathering skills were relatively poor because of his own lack of fathering.

All of this began to hit home when I was about twelve, an age when the concept of self-sufficiency can start becoming meaningful if properly introduced. I was a reasonably normal, healthy, fun-loving kid. I got good grades in school. I comported myself well. I had all the normal prepubescent idiosyncrasies. But I didn't work. I got an allowance, for which I did some household chores. But I didn't have a job—a job job—and I heard about it more than I cared to.

"When I was your age I was up at the crack of dawn earning money . . . and after school I earned more money . . . and on weekends I earned still more money." That was the litany I heard constantly from him.

The most common reference to his working childhood was his job as a newspaper boy, which he claimed began at the tender age of three selling the *Binghamton Sun* starting each dawn on a designated street corner. I had been hearing this since I was three, but never knew quite what to do or say about it.

Something precipitated a heated discussion about my unemployed status. What was particularly vexing was that he never actually told me to get a job; he simply reiterated his own work status when he was my age. The tension rose to a very uncomfortable level.

The next day I resolved, on my own, to do something to satisfy my father's *apparent* expectations. I telephoned the *Binghamton Sun* and asked if they had a delivery route open in my part of town. Yes, they did, and I could start first thing Monday morning.

I couldn't wait until my father came home from work. At last I would be able to appease him, please him, maybe even make him proud of me. I counted the minutes.

When he finally arrived I could barely contain myself.

"Guess what, Dad!"

"What, son?"

"I got a job!"

"What kind of job?"

"I got a newspaper route with the *Sun*, and I start Monday morning!"

His reaction stunned me. I can still feel it to this day.

"No son of mine is ever going to have to have a newspaper route! Call up the *Sun* right now and tell them you can't do it!"

"But gee, Dad."

*   *   *
**   **   **

You work. You struggle. You earn. Who are you trying to please? Whose expectations are you trying to satisfy? Are you getting enough bang out of it? Only you can tell, and only you can do anything about it if it's not working out the way you'd hoped it would.

The most common syndrome in this area of personal financial concerns is what's called "Keeping up with the Joneses." (The phrase derives from a comic strip that was popular in the nineteen-twenties and thirties.) We all do it to some extent: having the right car, the right house, the right clothes, and so forth, to impress the right people. A lot of money gets spent in this often misguided quest—money that could otherwise be put to much more constructive use for yourself. Have you asked yourself lately, "What if I caught up with the Joneses and found that I didn't like them?" What then?

A similar plight came to my attention many years later. In my early television career I made a monthly trip to the ABC affiliates in Cleveland and Chicago to do guest spots on their morning shows. As was often the case, the staff on these shows would corner me to ask for financial advice, which I was happy to impart when I had the time. One charming lady from WEWS-TV in Cleveland told me of her dilemma.

She and her husband were in the market to buy a house. They had discovered what she called a "funky old fixer-upper" at water's edge on Lake Erie. It was available at a very low price. They'd be able to fix it up, and it would be their dream home. However, her parents and friends all insisted that they should buy an *in* house in the *in* part of the city, where everyone who was *in* lived. They didn't want to shrug off the parents and friends, but they needed reassurance just so they could do what they wanted to do.

"Whose life are you living?" I asked her. That's just a plain common sense question, not requiring any great financial wisdom. But to her it was as if I had said "Open Sesame!", and the giant rock swung away to give access to the treasure she was seeking. She bought the lakeside house, and her parents and friends loved it once they had fixed it up. I urge you to ask yourself that same plain common sense question whenever you find yourself bending your plans and your finances to suit someone else's expectations.

One quick postscript: I never really could shake trying to satisfy my father's expectations. I didn't have to work my way through college as he did because he paid the bills and gave me a monthly allowance to boot. But, perhaps more to salve my own conscience and/or to avoid having to ever ask him for extra money if I ran short, I always had some kind of job in college.

During my junior year at Yale I operated the down elevator in the Sterling Library three evenings a week. That's right, the down elevator—there were two elevators in the eight-story stacks. We were told that one only took people up, while the other only took people down. Never mind the confusion that caused among our passengers. We did what we were told.

I didn't have to do this, mind you. But I did for reasons noted above. And at the end of one pay period, my secret efforts to satisfy my father's expectations were duly rewarded: I had $40 extra to spend! Jubilant, I invited a few friends to drive with me to New York for a Saturday night on the town. ($40 would go quite a long way then.) I joyfully headed out onto the Merritt Parkway, and before we got to Bridgeport I was caught speeding—the fine: $40. We headed back to New Haven, so much the wiser.

The flip side: Shortly before my youngest child, Joshua, was to graduate high school I casually asked him what his ambitions were. "The first one," he replied, "is to make more money than you do, Dad." Even though his answer was jovial, perhaps even a bit in fun, it saddened me.

"I'm sure you will, Josh," I replied, "but don't let the money targets that I've hit be all that you aim for. There's too much more in life to be shooting for."

Just as you may be structuring your financial (and personal) plans to satisfy the expectations of others, so others might be trying to meet your expectations of them. Just as your attempts to please others can prove tricky and hazardous, it can be equally uncomfortble for others who are trying to please you.

This situation requires close, serious, and honest communication with anyone who might be emulating you, competing with you, or trying to prove something to you. A few wise words can lift huge weights off another's shoulders. All the money in the world is not as valuable as a sincere "attaboy" or "attagirl."

Chapter Four

Getting a Head Start

An early lesson on living with debt.

Debt: We can't live with it, and we can't live without it. A minor bout of bad health proved to be a lucky stroke that taught me lessons about debt when I was young, and I've put them to good use ever since.

I was thirteen when the photography bug hit me. That was back in the days when a few dollars would buy you all you needed to set up a working darkroom to develop black-and-white photos. It was an enjoyable, though smelly, hobby for teenagers.

Today we have sophisticated cameras with computer chips in them that adjust for focus, distance, light conditions and the kind of film you're using. Back then I had a little plastic box known as a "Brownie," and it adjusted for nothing. You pushed the one button and hoped for the best. You even had to wind the film yourself.

I quickly outgrew my Brownie and yearned for an affordable camera that could be minimally adjusted for distance and shutter speed. The Argus A-2 was the answer to my dreams, but the cost—$25 as I recall—put the dream beyond my reach.

Then I learned about credit. I rarely read anything in the newspaper but the comics and the sports pages, but one day I noticed an advertisement from a camera store that offered to sell cameras on a monthly payment basis.

I asked my parents how such a plan worked, and after explaining it to me they agreed to help me attain my dream. I would have to make all the payments, including the initial down payment, and they would, in effect, guarantee my debt to the store. (The owner was a good friend of theirs. I'm sure no credit histories were taken.) I was grateful for the chance, and worked hard to save up the needed $5 down payment. I soon had both my very first Argus A-2 and my very first loan payment coupon book. One dollar per week was my obligation; and I knew that if I failed to keep up my payments my camera would be repossessed. I was one motivated thirteen year old.

In the first few weeks I learned what self-deprivation was, squeezing my allowance to have the extra dollar to spare. I even went without an issue of *Captain Marvel* comics (dimes were precious then) to help assure meeting my payment plan. That really hurt, though not as much as when I learned forty years later how valuable those long-since discarded comics had become.

Then I fell ill with some minor but debilitating stomach ailment that kept me out of school and away from the corner soda fountain for almost two weeks. Despite my inability to do my household chores my parents continued to pay me my allowance (my first, albeit unconscious, hint of the value of disability income insurance).

With my allowance in hand, but with no way to spend it, I suddenly found myself in the incredibly fortunate position of being able to get *two weeks ahead* in the payment plan for the camera. Indeed, as soon as I was up and around, I took the extra money to the store and made those advance payments.

I can't describe the exhilaration I felt knowing that I was *ahead* of my obligations, but it must have been strong enough, because ever since then, whenever I've had an installment loan (car, home improvement, etc.) I've always gotten a head start by paying up a few extra months in advance at the start of the payment plan.

Months later I got my second rush when the loan was marked "Paid in Full." The camera was now mine to keep and I didn't have to make any more payments!

*   *   *
**   **   **

I've carried two nuggets of wisdom from my Argus A-2 experience. First: Whenever possible, get a head start on your installment loan payments. The difference in dollars saved or spent is not what's important. What is important is the sense of freedom and flexibility that you'll get being able to skip a payment now and then, or being able to divert money to some other need or desire when the occasion occurs, or simply finishing your payment plan ahead of time. There's a major bonus as well: This head start payment program will help assure your good credit rating.

It has pained me often in the ensuing years to hear people I'm counseling tell me that they often wait until the last possible moment to make their installment payments, and often incur late charges in the process. Indeed, many let themselves slide into the delinquent category and get into the habit of paying the late charge on a regular basis. This is not only costly, but will cause chaos with your credit history.

The second lesson is even more important: Any installment loan should be paid off before the need to borrow for that same purpose recurs. You show me someone who's in a financial bind, and I'll show you someone who bought a new car on a five-year payment plan, then traded the car in for a new one after three years, and had to add the remaining two years of payments on the old loan to the new car debt. That can be catastrophic. If you're going to trade a car after three years, don't finance it for more than three years. If I hear that you've done so, you're going to be in big trouble with me.

We'll revisit some other aspects of these debt issues later in the book, but first let's look at the flip side of this specific matter. My parents could have easily given me the money to buy the Argus A-2, or they could have made a present of it on my next birthday. But they saw an opportunity for me to learn a valuable lesson in disciplining my youthful financial concerns, so they, in effect, co-signed the loan.

You'll likely be presented with similar situations: A child, a sibling, a friend will express a desire to have something that you can afford to give them; or you can afford to lend them the money so that they can buy the item. If you want them to be able to have it, consider the wisdom of co-signing a loan for them, rather than giving or lending to them. Let the prime responsibility rest with them. It will help them establish good credit and it will insulate you from exposure. Note also that once you've co-signed for someone, and they have made prompt payments for a reasonable time, you can always ask to have your name removed as co-signer. The lender won't volunteer to do this, but they might if you ask them to. If you don't ask, you don't get. We'll revisit that lesson too.

Chapter Five

With Friends Like That...

My guru, Rod Serling, introduces me to the Twilight Zone of starting a career.

"It's not what you know, it's who you know that matters." Many young people are pushed out of their nests with that admonition: that your fortune can depend more on the personal contacts you make than on the knowledge and skills you possess.

So it was that I was sent to a highly regarded prep school at age fifteen: the Lawrenceville School in suburban New Jersey. In those days, a good record at Lawrenceville was tantamount to admission to Princeton or Yale. In our 1953 graduating class of 160 boys (the school has since become co-ed) about 40 went to Princeton and 30 to Yale.

I was programmed to study hard, behave myself, and meet the right people—not necessarily in that order. It always seemed peculiar to think of friends as "business contacts," let alone use them as such, particularly when you still have to shave only once a week. I really didn't have to worry about it: Virtually all the guys I met were ditzy, overprivileged adolescents like myself, or nerds whose only reason for existing was to be teased by us "regular" guys.

It was definitely not an environment in which the fortunes of an upcoming generation were being forged. The only one who really might have amounted to something was a guy named Reuben Batista, but he disappeared from school one day, never to be seen again. He had rushed back home to Havana because his family had a sudden emergency and needed him there. His father, Fulgencio Batista, the head of the Cuban government, was being bothered by some guerrillas led by a young chap named Fidel Castro. Well, hey, it could have gone the other way.

My good record at Lawrenceville did pay off with a ticket to Yale, and I considered myself lucky to fall in with a bunch of good friends (who remain so to this day) who couldn't have cared less about contacts. As graduation loomed, we all were cognizant of the need to get a job—a *job* job.

My father had moved beyond his law practice and into real estate development. He was also the attorney for a small bank in Binghamton. So I knew I could choose from a nice menu of law, real estate, or banking, or any combination thereof. However, I knew—and had known for many years—that I wanted to be a writer. I had to give that peculiar profession a try before I succumbed to the lure of security in one of the family trades.

I was visited by good fortune again. Binghamton's twentieth-century local-boy-makes-good was Rod Serling, the television playwright. Rod was then riding the crest of his early fame as a prolific and award-winning creator for Playhouse 90 and similar live dramatic programs. *The Twilight Zone* was still a few years away. I met Rod when he came to Binghamton to visit his family, and we hit it off very nicely. At the time he was living in Westport, Connecticut, barely an hour's drive from New Haven, and he graciously invited me to visit and talk about writing.

What more could an aspiring young writer ask for? This was the Golden Age of television, and I had a personal contact with King Midas. I drove to Westport a number of times to visit Rod. He was basically a nice guy, but brusque and often edgy. We'd chat for a few minutes in his office. He'd tell me each time that the only way to prove myself was to write, and that instead of wasting my time driving to Westport I should stay in my dorm room and write. Then he'd let me sit there for a short while and watch him while he wrote. I must have felt that that was an inspirational experience.

The day of reckoning came in the spring of 1957. With graduation day nearing, I needed to find a job. The on-campus interviews were mostly for corporate wannabes and engineers. I looked to my friend, my contact, my who-I-knew, Rod Serling, to help me gain access into the real world.

I approached him nervously with the request: Could he help me get a job at CBS that would help get me started on my professional writing career?

He phoned me a few days later: "You have an appointment with Mr. So-and-So at 10 A.M. on the seventeenth." Done! See, Mom and Dad were right. It's not what you know, but who you know. I was the hero of my dorm that night.

On the seventeenth, promptly at 10 A.M., I arrived at CBS corporate headquarters and sought out Rod's private, secret inside contact, Mr. So-and-So. I was sent to the Personnel Office, where Mr. So-and-So sat behind a desk like half a dozen other interviewers. "Wait a minute!" I said to myself, "This is just the regular Personnel Office. This is where the secretaries and the accountants and the cafeteria workers come to be interviewed. I'm Rod Serling's friend, where's the power, the clout, the inner sanctum where the really important jobs are handed out? Something is very wrong here."

My spirits brightened a bit when I sat down with Mr. So-and-So and he acknowledged that I was there to interview for what he called "The Executive Training Program." That's a little more like it, I thought.

"We'll get back to you," Mr. So-and-So said after our brief chat, and he did. I was accepted into the Columbia Broadcasting System's Executive Training Program, thanks in large part to my carefully cultivated personal contact with one of CBS's most valued and important assets, Mr. Rod Serling himself. It was the mailroom. My degree from Yale University had gotten me a job in the CBS mailroom, with $38 a week for starters.

The theory was this: By working in the mailroom you got to know where most of the offices were, and the secretaries that worked in them. As openings in any department occurred, notices would be posted on various department bulletin boards. If a given job had not been filled within a week or so, notice would then be posted on the mailroom bulletin board. Nine out of ten job offers were for secretaries and accountants. The tenth was for a cafeteria worker.

Not having become a writer-in-residence for the network within eight weeks, I quit. Glimmers of security in the family business back in Binghamton began to appear more appealing.

Rod and I would cross paths again in the years ahead. I was truly grateful for his friendship and help. I had learned a lot about the nature of one's expectations and the workings of the real world.

*
**   *
**   *
**

Yes, your knowledge and your skills and your contacts are important to you. The sum of the three shape your life's opportunities—particularly your career—and from all that springs the wealth that needs care and tending.

But if you don't maintain *reasonable expectations* with regard to your knowledge, your skills, and your contacts, you could quickly find yourself looking up out of a deep hole. One of the greatest dangers to your personal financial well-being is to have inflated expectations. My relationship with Rod Serling is a case in point: I was young, naive, and foolish. I allowed myself to believe what I wanted to believe: that Rod could somehow plug me into a magical job that would pay me well as I apprenticed to become an important writer for network television.

That's what you call a serious, if not terminal, case of inflated expectations. I had never actually asked Rod if such a possibility existed. I wanted to assume that it did, and I didn't want to hear that it didn't. If I had asked Rod flat out what kind of job he might help me get at CBS, he probably would have said, "As far as I know, all entry-level positions are in the mailroom. I'll do you a favor and make an appointment for you with the Personnel Office, or you can do it yourself. But if you're smart you'll stay home and write . . . and write . . . and write." And he'd have been right.

My inflated expectations had led me astray. Had my expectations been more reasonable I might have taken a totally different course. Fortunately, youth, and the resilience that goes with youth, were on my side. It was a case of a temporary detour, rather than going off the deep end. No harm—no regrets—just curiosity as to what else might have happened had I kept my expectations reasonable.

I was lucky. Many are not so. As some of the other case histories in this book will illustrate, inflated expectations can prompt you to take actions that can result in serious financial harm. Here are some brief and oversimplified examples:

* "I'm positive that I'm going to get a $3,000 year-end bonus, so let's take that cruise we've always dreamed about." The bill for the cruise comes in, but the bonus doesn't.

* "Nick gave me a terrific tip on the stock market/the seventh race at Santa Anita/the Florida State game. I'm going to win a bundle, so let's celebrate with a big night on the town." The horse is slow, but the credit card billing is fast.
* "Lou paid me in cash for that work, so I'm not going to declare it on my tax return. There's no way in the world that the IRS can trace the income." Lou talks. The IRS listens.

As you read how others have suffered from cases of inflated expectations, you will hopefully modulate your own expectations toward the reasonable.

The flip side: My own case of inflated expectations regarding Rod Serling was exacerbated by others who got caught up in the glamour of it all. When I told family and friends of my wonderful contact they *oohed* and *aahed* and told me how fortunate I was. I pumped them up, and they in turn pumped me up even more. A vicious circle indeed.

Inflated expectations are catchy. Are you helping to dangerously inflate someone else's expectations? If so, correct the matter before harm is done, and ask them to do the same for you.

Me? A Co-Conspirator?

The perils of getting conned, and how we each can innocently lead others into making costly financial mistakes . . . and vice versa.

It's said that the road to hell is paved with good intentions. I went there once to find out if that is true. It is. Fortunately the hellish losses were kept to a minimum. It could have been a lot worse.

My writing career, part I, came to a quick end, but that's another story. To prepare myself to work in the family enterprises—law, real estate development, and banking—I went to Syracuse University College of Law. This also would give me a student deferment from the draft, and allowed me to be near the love of my life, who was enrolled at Syracuse as a freshperson undergraduate. It all worked: By 1961 I had passed the New York Bar, had escaped the draft, and had (in 1959) married Linda Sue.

I was dividing my work days equally between our law/real estate office on one hand, and the bank on the other hand. It was a very small bank in a small city; we knew most of our customers on a first-name basis. I sat at a desk out front opening new accounts and interviewing loan customers. I was very wet behind the ears, and ripe for the plucking by the many types of con games that are played on small banks.

One day a very sharply dressed stranger came in and waited for me to serve him. I later realized that he had done this on purpose: I looked young and innocent enough to fall for his scam. The other front desk people looked too experienced to fool.

He told me that he was starting a new company in town that would employ dozens of people. He had chosen to do his banking business with us, he said, because he preferred to deal with smaller institutions where personal relationships can flourish. He was going to bring in all of his corporate accounts, and he would recommend that all of his employees and suppliers also establish their accounts with us.

I was hooked. This would be a major coup for me. It was very tough for us to compete with the big local banks. To land a major new corporate account was an extraordinary victory. And he was right there in front of me, ready to sign all of the papers!

All he wanted today, he told me, was to open a small personal account so that he could get things started. He was going to deposit $100 in cash, and within two days he would be bringing in a cashier's check for many thousands of dollars. He needed a few imprinted checks right then so he could buy some office supplies. (In those days $100 could buy a lot of office supplies. Credit cards had yet to be invented.)

We had a little check-printing machine in the back room to take care of such customers' needs. I had been well trained not to give imprinted checks to new customers until we knew that their deposits were good. Well, I thought, you can't beat $100 in cash—that can't bounce. And a cashier's check a few days from now would be as good as cash. Besides, this fellow looked so honest . . . so sincere. And I was counting the "attaboys" I'd be getting for this coup. (Inflated expectations? Yes indeed . . . danger ahead.)

Rather than risk antagonizing my new customer and possibly losing the account, I agreed to give him some checks, but cautioned him not to write more than $100 worth until his big check had been deposited and cleared. That was like telling raindrops not to wet the sidewalk. "Of course, I wouldn't write more than $100 in checks," he assured me. "How could I? I only have $100 in the account." (Ho-Ho.)

While he waited for his checks to be printed I played it safe and telephoned the local Better Business Bureau to learn what I could about this fellow and his company. "Oh, yes," the BBB told me, "he's registered with us and we have no complaints against him." I later learned that this was a very easy thing for a clever con artist to do.

At least the fellow was honest in one respect: He did use the money in his new checking account to buy some office equipment. He bought a check-writing machine—one of those gizmos that prints the amount of a check in very official-looking embossed lettering. Then he proceeded to write phony payroll checks to a variety of fictional characters who existed only on the phony ID cards he carried in his wallet, each of which bore his photo. Each check was for just under $100, which was a healthy week's salary then, and he began a check-cashing spree at local supermarkets.

He had all that the markets needed to see to cash the checks: a photo ID and an imprinted check on a local bank account that was impressively embossed with the amount to be paid.

Fortunately, the con man's intelligence did have limitations. He tried to cash two checks using two different IDs within a few hours of each other at the same market. The manager was called upon to approve the checks, and he spotted the scam. He called our bank to alert us, and we called the police and all the other nearby markets to alert them to the problem.

The police caught him a few hours later. In all, he had cashed about $600 worth of checks. No great loss to anyone involved, but the embarrassment, plus the sense of having been violated, was more stinging—and more instructive—than any actual monetary loss.

How did I get lured into being an unwitting accomplice to this petty thief? I had everything to gain—a big new account for the bank, a pat on the back from the boss, and bragging rights among my local banking colleagues. To my befogged mind at that time, I had nothing to lose either: If people cash a check that bounces, they don't have recourse against the bank.

The reality, of course, was that I had nothing to gain and everything to lose. Since the whole deal was a sham, the bank wouldn't get a new account, and I wouldn't get either a pat on the back or bragging rights. If word spread beyond our own immediate little enclave as to how I had goofed in allowing a con artist to walk out the door of our bank with a fistful of imprinted checks, I'd be covering my shame in our small town for years to come.

"Everything to gain" and "nothing to lose": two of the biggest best-sellers in the fiction category when Snake Oil Sam is peddling his wares.

* *
** ** **

I had come thisclose to being the laughing stock of the local business community. My rash actions could have proved costly to many of our local businesses, or to the bank, had we decided to cover the stores for the losses they incurred by cashing the bogus checks.

The con-man still had most of the money with him when he was caught, and it was returned to the stores. So I got off with a good scare and an expensive lesson cheaply learned.

My intentions were certainly good, but my self-interest got the best of me. The con man had played me like a concertmaster plays the violin, buttering me up, stroking my ego, prompting me to think thoughts that might not have otherwise occurred to me. I was thus on my way straight to hell.

Good intentions and self-interest don't mix well, and you don't necessarily need a con artist to roil the waters. There are many ways in which, innocently enough, you can become involved in a situation that brings financial harm to others, and possibly to yourself as well.

It's very often the case that when we make financial decisions—to buy, sell, invest, refinance, etc.—we want the approval of others. In some cases it's more than a want, it's a need. The best way we can get the approval of others is to convince them to do the same thing. "If he does what I did, then, of course, I must have been right." This is a validation, a stamp of approval, of what you have done. Examples:

* "My broker just tipped me to buy 100 shares of NPG. You'd be smart if you did the same."

* "My insurance agent says that these new double-variable universal life annuities are the wave of the future, and the best way to cut your income taxes. You ought to get in on it."

* "My lawyer told me that an *inter vivos* testamentary nonrevocable reversible trust is the one and only way to handle all of your estate planning. Shouldn't you be doing something like that too?"

These brief illustrations aren't meant to condemn the broker, agent, or lawyer. Their advice might have been perfectly right for the initial client, but it could be dead wrong for the people the client talks to at cocktail parties seeking his own form of reassurance.

Indeed there are all too many cases in which the advice is not so wise; it's a carefully structured sales pitch designed to enrich the broker, agent, or lawyer. The client who falls for it then becomes the unwitting accomplice, the co-conspirator, who can unintentionally cause financial harm to his friends.

Then, too, there are the occasional cases where the broker, agent, or lawyer offers some form of kickback to the client who attracts more clients. No innocence there—and a more insidious danger. So when seemingly well-intentioned friends or colleagues offer you a situation in which you have everything to gain and nothing to lose, you'd be wise to explore their motives for doing so before you write out a check.

The flip side: Are you, even as we speak, acting as a well-intentioned co-conspirator, doing something that could bring harm to others? You may not have thought you were, but check and double-check. It could prove costly and embarrassing.

Chapter Seven

There's No Such Thing
as a Sure Thing

To dispel your frivolous fantasies, a bizarre case of how a 100% absolutely positively can't-miss proposition backfired.

$\mathbf{F}$or about seven years I wore three career hats: banking, law, and real estate development. Virtually all of my time was spent helping people solve their financial problems. As this chapter and the one that follows illustrate, some problems defy solution. The best way to stay out of trouble is to avoid falling into the trap in the first place. The most dangerous traps of all are disguised by the victims' own thinking that they have a *Sure Thing* going for them. The simple fact is, there's no such thing as a *Sure Thing*.

The following example is admittedly bizarre, but if this can happen, anything can happen.

George had been an unwelcome customer of the bank for many years. He was a man in his forties who came from a well-to-do and well-respected family, but he himself was a ne'er-do-well and definitely unrespected. He worked only sporadically, preferring instead to leach money from his family, which he was able to do with regularity.

He had a checking account with our bank that was constantly being overdrawn. In previous years he had had loans from the bank that always fell into delinquency until the family bailed him out. When he had money in his pocket it was quickly spent on booze. He knew that the bank wouldn't lend him a nickel unless he put up a dime as collateral, but that didn't keep him from trying. (Why didn't we just throw the rascal out? In a small bank in a small town there are a lot of personal relationships that go back a long time. As long as we could put up with his relatively harmless antics there was no need to do him the potentially great harm of canceling his account.)

One day George approached me with a *Sure Thing* proposition. All of the family money, he told me, now resided in the possession of one aunt. It amounted to a few hundred thousand dollars, and was in a properly drawn trust fund. George was the sole beneficiary of the trust fund, provided that the aunt had no children at the time of her death. The aunt was in her eighties, a spinster, and in failing health. The *Sure Thing* that George was proposing was that his aunt would die without children, and that he would become sole heir of the estate in the not-too-distant future. He wanted to borrow $50,000, pledging his *Sure Thing* inheritance (many times the amount of the loan) as collateral. How far wrong could the bank go?

I put on my lawyer hat and checked out the validity of the trust agreement, which had been prepared by another local lawyer. It was 100 percent legitimate, the money was there. The terms were clear: If the never-married aunt died without children, George would be the sole beneficiary of the estate, no ifs, buts, or maybes. Even if George died before Auntie, the money would still go to George's estate, and the loan could thus be paid off. And, no, there would be no problem in assigning George's inheritance to our bank as collateral for the loan. In short, the light was green. The chances of a woman in her eighties and in failing health having a child were too remote to measure.

We discussed the matter among all the officers of the bank. Everyone knew George, and no one liked him very much. But on the face of it, the loan was worth making. Liking someone is not a precondition to lending him money.

We declined; it was mostly a gut reaction. As expected, George blew his stack—in the middle of the main lobby, at lunchtime, with a few dozen other customers standing around. It was not a pretty sight. George threatened to take his *Sure Thing* deal to another bank. We encouraged him to do so.

Now we're getting to the weird part. Our decision to decline the loan was correct. George never did get the inheritance. Auntie, you see, didn't like George very much either. Whether out of malice or spite or some other motive, knowingly or unknowingly, she ruined George's *Sure Thing*.

This is what happened: Auntie had a gentleman friend (no fool, as the facts will demonstrate) who had a daughter, a woman in her fifties.

Auntie, in her eighties and in failing health, married the gentleman friend and then legally adopted his daughter as her own! The stipulation in the trust gave the money to George only if Auntie died without children. It didn't specify as between biological and adopted children. Thus the daughter of the gentleman friend became Auntie's sole beneficiary, and George didn't get a penny.

We weren't smart in declining the loan to George. We were just plain lucky.

*
**   *
**   *
**

Now, repeat after me:
There's no such thing as a *Sure Thing*.
There's no such thing as a *Sure Thing*.
There's no such thing as a *Sure Thing*.
If you ever doubt it, ask George.

Chapter Eight

Put Your Money Where
Your Knowledge Is

A frightful tale of what can go wrong when you sail into uncharted waters, and how to steer a safe course.

The other type of problem that often defies solution occurs when you send your money off to work and you don't know where it's going or what's going to happen to it. In short, if you invest or speculate (the critical difference between the two will be the subject of Chapter 23) in areas with which you're unfamiliar, you're more likely to lose it. You won't know where to go looking for it if it doesn't come back to you as expected.

The best way to avoid the problem is to put your money where your *knowledge* is. Put it to work in situations with which you're most familiar, most knowledgeable.

By the time I arrived to work for him, my father had had many years of successful experience in real estate investing. He did all types: buying property for the rental income; buying *shleppers,* as we called them—fixer-uppers—that would be refurbished, refinanced, and sold at a profit; developing commercial projects for long-term gains; mortgage lending; even speculating in vacant land. All of this went on during relatively prosperous times, in post–World War II upstate New York.

Some knowledge is learned, some is intuitive. Here's an example of a combination of the two that I gleaned from him. The lesson is self-evident.

My first entry-level task was to sell a *shlepper* that he had recently bought. It was a duplex on South Washington Street. Some may have called it a handyman's delight, but I called it an abomination. It was as close to derelict as a dwelling could get and still pass the local housing codes. Dad knew the neighborhood, and he knew he could turn a nice profit on it, of which I'd get a small piece in exchange for my selling it.

The first dozen or so prospects were either no-shows, "not interested," or "you've got to be kidding." I was not encouraged, particularly since everyone wanted to see the place during my dinnertime.

At long last I had a live one. A young couple looked it over at length and said they'd take it. "Wonderful," I enthused, telling them to come to my office at 2 P.M. the next day to give me the down payment check and sign the papers.

The next morning I went into my father's office gushing that I had sold the South Washington Street property. Without looking up at me he intoned, "Fine, son. Where's the check?"

"They're coming in at two to give it to me."

"Fine, son. Let me know when you have the check."

Two o'clock—nobody . . . 2:30—nobody . . . three . . . nobody . . . give it up.

A few days later another live one took the bait. Same routine: "Come to my office tomorrow at two," and so forth.

Same exuberance the next morning: "Fine, son, where's the check?" Another no-show . . . another disappointment . . . but I'm learning.

When the real thing came along a week later I knew how to handle it. I waited until they did come to my office, signed the papers, and gave me the check. Then, and only then, did I go into my father's office, probably looking like a kid who had just discovered a candy store.

"Dad, I sold the South Washington Street house."

"Fine, son. Where's the check?"

Ta-daa! "Right here," I announced proudly, showing him the elusive prize.

"Fine, son," he said solemnly, again without looking up at me or the check. "Now let me know when it clears the bank."

My heart made a thudding sound—lesson learned, and socked away in the memory banks for a lifetime. (The check did clear the bank, and I got my share of the profit.)

Now let's examine the specific tale that's the subject of this chapter: Putting your money where your *knowledge* is.

Dad had done very well in developing small office buildings for Metropolitan Life Insurance Company. Most of their branch offices in the smaller cities in our region were run-down tacky spaces in older office buildings. Met wanted to brighten their image, so they were contracting with developers to build freestanding new buildings, with plenty of parking, that they would occupy exclusively. Each building was about 5,000 square feet, and the buildings were built from a standard set of plans. With a fifteen-year lease from Metropolitan Life in hand, a developer could go to a bank and get a loan for 110 percent of the cost of the land and building. At least, my father had done so a number of times. He had the *knowledge,* and that's where he was putting his money to work.

Each Met deal followed a simple and easily workable pattern. The location would be on the fringes of downtown, in an area that had become zoned for office space. The property would be occupied by an old wood-frame house that the usually elderly owners were happy to sell for cash so that they could move into a retirement apartment. Demolition of the old house was simple, and construction of the new building was swift and easy. We had done the deal for Met in Corning, Elmira, Cortland, Endicott, and Oneonta, New York; Meriden, Connecticut, and, of course, in our hometown of Binghamton.

All of these cities, except for Meriden, were within an easy one-hour drive of home. (We were willing to go farther afield to Meriden because we were able to buy an ideal piece of land that was big enough for another commercial building, and we had a ready-made tenant to occupy that second building.) All of the projects proceeded smoothly and successfully. My father knew what he was doing, and he did it well.

Success breeds confidence, but confidence can often cloud common sense. Trouble was afoot: A lender had foreclosed on a building in Geneva, New York, and offered to sell it to us at a price too good to be true. We drove to Geneva to have a look. It was a monstrosity: a four-story concrete and brick behemoth in the heart of downtown, without a single square inch of parking space. It was vacant, windows were shattered, and it was filled with puddles and bats and pigeons and the poop that goes along with them. If the Addams Family had owned commercial real estate, this would have been called the Addams Building.

Downtown Geneva itself was becoming derelict. As was happening then in so many cities, a big modern shopping center had opened up in the suburbs, draining the downtown of both tenants and customers. The only possible saving grace for the Addams Building was that it was next-door to a department store, run by two antiquated cousins of the Addams family, and certain to fall into ruin itself as the suburban mall became more successful. But wait! Maybe, just maybe, if we bought the Addams Building, fixed it up and rented it out to the department store next door so they could expand dramatically, we could not only save the building and the department store, but we could be the saviors of all of downtown Geneva! That was my father's thinking, and I felt my blood chill as I heard him agree to buy the property.

He was clearly going *out* of a field where his *knowledge* excelled and into the Twilight Zone. We did not have a ready-made top quality tenant signed onto a fifteen-year lease. We did not have 110 percent financing available. We did not know the commercial patterns of Geneva as we had known the other cities. We did not have a building that could be cheaply demolished if the need arose. We did not have access to any parking that might be required to satisfy a tenant. And we did not have a one-hour drive to get there. Instead we had a drive that could average three hours each way, particularly in winter when the roads could be treacherous. The ease in getting to and from an out-of-town real estate project has a major bearing on how productively one's time, money, and energy will be spent.

I was assigned the task of leasing the Addams Building to the department store owners next door, and then overseeing the renovations to suit their needs. I was given a projected schedule of six months to accomplish that. I listened to the World Series on my first drive to Geneva to deal with what was now officially the Rosefsky Building. The next six months were hell. A wintry hell.

Here, in no particular order, were some of the problems we faced:

* The department store cousins wanted nothing whatsoever to do with the derelict building next to them. They could not be coaxed, cajoled, or sold on any part of it—not for expansion. Not for dead storage. Not for parking. Not even for advertising billboards on the outside walls. Nothing.

* Once it became known that we had bought the monster, everyone who owned any property in downtown Geneva called us to sell us *their* derelicts. I had to look into each and every possibility, if only to hopefully find a parcel close to ours that could provide us with some convenient parking space—a horrendous timewaster.

* As winter raged on, as it does regularly in that part of the world, the condition of the building worsened past the point of being able to cost-effectively rehabilitate it.

* As time wore on, with no hope of converting this folly into an income producer, our frames of mind grew ugly. That's counterproductive, and it began to tell.

We were in that dangerous territory of the unknown. We had sent our money off to work in a situation about which we were unknowledgeable, and it was haunting us. Oh, yes, the Geneva property had some similar aspects to all those other developments that had been successful. The similarities were paltry, and the differences—ignored, unexpected, or given short shrift—were overpowering.

If matters up to that point had been grim, they grew even more so: When all hope was lost about renting the hulk to the department store people, the decision was made to tear it down and keep it as a parking lot until a tenant for a new building to be built could be found. The cost of demolition was double what it had cost to buy the building in the first place.

Then we couldn't find anyone to operate the parking lot, so the empty parcel sat there for almost two years eating up tax dollars, insurance dollars, interest dollars, and even cleanup dollars—wind blew debris onto the lot, and the city ordered us to keep it tidy.

Finally a tenant was found, and we built a building to his specifications. Then, mercifully, it was sold. Span of the nightmare: six years; aggravation: eleven on a scale of ten; money lost: a whole lot—I've blotted the amount out of my mind.

*
**   **   **

We have plenty of company, not just in real estate but in the stock market, in personal and corporate business ventures, and in many aspects of personal financial planning.

Here are some common types of problems that have occurred when people send their money away outside the realm of their *knowledge.* If you work for, invest in, or are otherwise dependent on the well-being of any of these entities, you owe it to yourself to know how they are putting their (your?) money to work.

*   The problem is endemic in real estate. When you get out in unfamiliar territory, as the Addams Building debacle illustrates, you remain removed from the commercial history and rhythms and idiosyncracies of that other place. As a stranger you may see a neighborhood that looks like it's on the rise, but locals know that it's been in a steady decline. You may sense that a commercial migration to the suburbs has reached its peak, when in fact it's just gathering steam. You may have a notion that local government will protect its commercial center, when in fact the mayor and some choice city council people have been quietly buying up suburban parcels because they see (i.e., they can direct) the growth of the city in that direction.

You can't learn about these things the way you can learn about a company's earnings performance. It's not raw numbers; it's personalities and insider negotiations and matters of native intuition. Otherwise savvy foreigners—Japanese and Saudis in particular—have been stung badly by misguided investments in United States real estate. A Toronto family, the Reichmans, were the biggest landlords in the world through their vast Olympia and York holdings. They embarked on building the biggest office complex in Europe, in the Docklands of London, but needed Parliament to okay a government investment in a subway link to the property from central London. The project began in 1985, but Parliament balked, for years. The subway link, if it ever does get built, will not be operative until after the year 2000. The project, meanwhile, went bankrupt. Big doesn't always mean smart.

*   The stock market is a yawning pit of the unknown. It makes sense, doesn't it, to put your money into companies about which you have some *knowledge,* or at least into fields in which you have some *knowledge.* If you work in book publishing, you can better evaluate a stock purchase in a book publishing company than you can in an aerospace, computer, apparel, utility, or food processing company, because you have *knowledge.* So put it to good use.

By the same token, it makes sense to avoid the more exotic side bets that abound in the stock market, unless you gain *knowledge* about them. Side bets like put options and call options and derivatives and swaps and scores and primes and strips and convertibles and so on— you can get involved in these situations and not even remember if you've bet on the item to go up or down in value! Yes, you can rely on your broker's judgment. But you still need your own basic *knowledge* so you can evaluate your broker's *knowledge,* and to discern whether the broker really does have *knowledge* or is just pushing the goods that the company wants pushed that day.

You can also rely, at your own risk, on the boasts and conquests you hear from friends at cocktail parties about the killings they made in the market. Don't those guys ever make mistakes? Of course they do. But they keep their mouths shut about the mistakes. They don't want anyone to know how dumb they might have been.

* Business ventures offer their fair share of the unknown. Xerox makes copy machines—good ones. Some years ago they invested a lot of their money to buy insurance companies. Some of the big bosses must have thought, "If we know how to make and market copy machines, we certainly ought to know how to operate insurance companies," or some such insanity. My son-in-law worked for one of the Xerox insurance subsidiaries. When Xerox's inability to run insurance companies became evident, Paul told me, the chaos grew by the minute. Xerox finally sold off the insurance units, its tail between its legs.

If the big guys can goof, what hope is there for the little entrepreneurs? Those who venture into the unknown and succeed do so because of extraordinary hard work and an equal dose of luck. If they work hard enough to gain the needed *knowledge* before their capital runs out, they may stand a chance of succeeding. But the odds run high against them.

* Personal financial planning is a minefield for those lacking the requisite *knowledge.* The most important areas—insurance, investment, and retirement programs—are overrun with salespeople spouting jargon and statistics and performance ratings so fast that it makes your head spin. Many are honest and well-meaning. Many are out to make as much money as they can for themselves. Many boast credentials that may sound impressive to the naive. Many earn their living only through commissions on what they sell you, even though the sale may be more beneficial to them than to you. Many work on a fee-only basis, which at least gives you some hope that their advice will be objective, not slanted toward any particular product or company. Sorting all of this out takes *knowledge*. As with the stock brokers, you can't evaluate their knowledge unless you have your own *knowledge*. Some of the *knowledge* you'll need you can get from this book. But please, let's not pretend that that's all you need—far from it. Read more specific material diligently, take classes, and seek a second opinion whenever you have even slight doubts about where you're sending your money. Remember: All the answers in the world might not be worth spit if you haven't asked the right questions.

Chapter Nine

Lend Me Your Ears

A sampling of horror stories that a banker heard from customers, and lessons to learn from them.

✔ *The Big Print Giveth and the Small Print Taketh Away*
   . . . what those contracts *really* say
✔ *Who's Who?*
   . . . foulups in your credit history
✔ *Captive Borrowers*
   . . . the sinister lure of "E-Z" credit
✔ *The Insidious Advance Fee Loan Scam*
   . . . anyone can be a victim
✔ *Those Incredible Flying Squirrels*
   . . . don't laugh, it could happen in your family too
✔ *It Can't Hurt to Ask*
   . . . the value of getting a second opinion

Harken, friends, to some tales of travail that crossed my desk in my banking days. Lenders hear as many peculiar stories as do psychiatrists. There's something to be learned from all of these life experiences.

The Big Print Giveth
and the Small Print Taketh Away

Mr. and Mrs. H. had been valued customers of our bank for decades. They had both worked on the assembly line at the local shoe factory, making a good enough living between them to afford a modest home that was now all paid for. Theirs was a simple but pleasant life, and while they were uneducated and certainly unsophisticated, they were delightful folks. You'd call them "salt of the earth."

They had done all of their banking business with us: checking and savings accounts, car loans, and a variety of other personal loans. Their credit rating was excellent. Payments were never late; indeed, more often than not they were early. Mr. and Mrs. H. had also instilled their good financial habits in their children: They also had become good customers, and we were always happy to be able to meet their loan requests.

Mr. and Mrs. H. appeared at my desk one day in a state of extreme agitation. She was crying, and he was barely able to speak. "We need to borrow money to buy our house back," he finally blurted out.

This was a most incredible statement. I was shocked. When I calmed them down they told me this story.

A salesman had called at their house selling aluminum siding. The house was getting run-down looking, and his pitch was convincing— guaranteed this, money back that, and brand-name products here and lifetime warranties there. And what about the financing? "He said that they could arrange all of that," Mr. H. said. "The salesman told us that we didn't have to bother going to our bank. They could probably get a lower interest rate for us anyway."

The salesman produced a flurry of papers, and insisted that they be signed right then. The clincher was, "My special low price is good today only! If you don't sign right now I can't offer you the $1,000 discount." The salesman hustled them so much that they had time to read only the big print that highlighted the super deal they were getting, but not the small print.

A few days later workmen showed up to begin the job. The work went in fits and starts. The installers were rude, sloppy, and often drunk. When the work was done Mr. and Mrs. H. were not happy with it. They tried to locate the salesman, but found that he had moved to another city and left no forwarding address or number. They complained to the contractor, who all but told them to fly a kite. They threatened to withhold payments on the contract until the work was finished properly. The contractor told them that their IOU had been sold to an out-of-town finance company, and that if they missed any payments they'd have to deal with the finance company.

A letter of protest to the finance company brought no response. So Mr. and Mrs. H., without the benefit of legal counsel, refused to make the first payment on the home improvement loan; it was to have been $55.

Within a few days they received a notice from the finance company stating, in effect, that since they had defaulted in their payments, the finance company was availing itself of its legal rights. One of the documents that the H's had unwittingly signed was a deed to their house. The agreement stated that if they were in any way delinquent, the finance company had the right to record the deed, which meant that the finance company had become the legal owner of their house!

Mr. and Mrs. H. owed about $3,000 on the original contract. This notice from the finance company said that they could get back the ownership of the house, and pay off the improvement contract, by immediately sending $5,000 to the finance company. Otherwise, they'd be evicted and lose their home!

They sat in front of me wanting to borrow $5,000 to buy their house back from some thieves who had unconscionably swindled them. It was truly a pathetic scene.

Bob to the rescue: I telephoned the contractor and the finance company and told them that I represented the H.'s. I said that the matter would be reported to the State Attorney General's Office of Consumer Protection and the Contractor's Licensing Board as a flagrant fraud. Further, I would notify all of the media, Better Business Bureaus, and Chambers of Commerce in our city and all the cities in which the finance company had offices.

The matter was quickly rectified, although the siding work never really was properly fixed up. Mr. and Mrs. H. were grateful beyond words, and also embarrassed that they had let themselves fall into such a trap, and that they had not sought our counsel along the way.

*
**   *
**   *
**

The big print giveth, the small print taketh away. In the case of Mr. and Mrs. H. the small print tooketh away nothing less than their house! This kind of chicanery might not be as easy to pull off today as it was many years ago, for there are some laws now in place that protect consumers. Most important is the three-day cooling off period, which gives anyone who is pledging a security interest in their property as part of a transaction three days in which to back out of the deal. There is a federal law to that effect, and many states have their own version of it as well. Further, the rights of someone who has bought your IOU have been weakened in many respects by consumer protection laws. This does not mean you can let your guard down when faced with a contract filled with small print. The laws protect you only if you initiate action. If you don't do it yourself, no one else will do it for you.

The big print/small print gambit is not the sole province of the con man. Many legitimate businesses use it, often legitimately, sometimes, shall we say, cleverly. The big print can be used to attract you to a product or service, even to a point of getting you to make a phone call or visit a store where the salespeople can get a shot at you. Then the small print, which you may not have read, kicks in and you find yourself having to spend a lot more than you planned to get what you want.

It's like a typographical version of the old reliable scam, bait and switch. The bait is an ad from, say, a market: "Sirloin Steak only $.99 a pound!" Lured to the store you find the advertised steak covered with ugly green spots. "But as long as you're here," says the butcher, switching you to the high-priced goods, "let me show you some really fine cuts."

One kind of big print/small print ploy that's been used a lot is the television ad for an auto lease. The top half of the screen shows the car, and the bottom half shows what look like mouse tracks, but they really are words. The announcer's message, and the BIG print on the top of the screen are designed to grab your attention and yank you bodily into the showroom.

Reading experts estimate that the average adult can read and comprehend about 150 words per minute, presuming that they're legible words, which the ones on the TV commercial are not.

I taped, timed, and transcribed a number of these messages. The following is typical of them. Please note that I've put many of the words in CAPITAL LETTERS. I have done so because these words and phrases tend to be *restrictive,* or *misleading,* or *confusing,* and/or could result in *hidden extra costs* over and above what the big print said. I've deleted the name of the car and the manufacturer because all of them that advertise in this way are equally guilty.

LIMITED TIME RATE of $169 for a 36-month CLOSED-END LEASE of a new xxxxxxxxx 4-door, 5-speed with VALUE OPTION PACKAGE MODEL #43153 available at PARTICIPATING xxxxxx dealers to QUALIFIED lessees through xxxx. SUBJECT TO AVAILABILITY. Rate based on $12,690.00 M.S.R.P.

including destination charges, LESS $169.00 CUSTOMER CAP-
ITAL COST REDUCTION DOWN PAYMENT and LESS
$869.62 REQUIRED DEALER CAPITAL COST REDUC-
TION. DEALER PARTICIPATION MAY AFFECT ACTUAL
COST. ACTUAL CAPITALIZED COST of $12,001.83 includes
a $350 NON-REFUNDABLE ACQUISITION FEE. Taxes, regis-
tration, title, insurance, options, and locally required equipment
NOT INCLUDED IN LEASE RATE AND MAY BE PAYABLE
ON CONSUMMATION.

*That message, just under 100 words, was on the screen for 2.7
seconds!* Read it at your leisure.

The possible restrictions, confusions, and hints of potentially
higher costs comprise about 60 percent of the total message! But as
long as you're here in the showroom let me offer you a test drive in a
real beauty.

Advertisers claim that they are required by law to present appropriate disclaimers to the public. There are different ways that that can
be done. Some won't insult your intelligence, or improperly subject
you to the risks that are inherent in the big print/small print game.

Who's Who?

With a name like Rosefsky, I'm not likely to run into this problem. But
if you have a more common name, like Smith or Jones or Green or
Johnson or Weber or Thompson or Lee or O'Brien or Cohen or Garcia
or a thousand others, you could face a frustrating case of mistaken
identity with your local credit bureau.

This experience was simple enough: A couple new to town applied for a car loan. We had some guidelines about lending, as most
banks do, requiring a minimum time an applicant has lived in town (at
least two years) and how long they've been at their present job (at least
one year). But those guidelines can be bent, as in the present case,
where the breadwinner had an executive position with a major company that had offices in Binghamton. Their last name was McDonald,
and both of their first names were equally common. They had moved
from New York where, we learned, there was an abundance of Mc-
Donalds.

It seemed a simple matter to check their credit history in New York and quickly approve the loan. The credit report from New York came in looking horrible. There were defaulted loans and overdue collection accounts and canceled checking accounts (yes, maintaining a checking account in poor fashion—too many overdrafts, for example—can end up as a big demerit on your credit history).

The McDonalds protested that the report was wrong. We searched again, and lo and behold came up with a credit report that was a beauty to behold. It was a simple case of mistaken identity. Another McDonald, from the deadbeat side of the clan, had a lousy credit history and we had been sent that one erroneously, but understandably: in addition to having the same last name, the first names and addresses were similar.

*
**   *
**   *
**

Billions of bytes of credit data flow in and out of computers every day, and mistakes can happen. Computers aren't foolproof, and won't be until they stop needing humans to program, operate, and maintain them. So while the poor McDonalds tore out their hair for a day over an alleged "computer mistake," it really was a human mistake somewhere along the line that caused them their grief, and that can cause you equal grief.

Similar names are just one of the pitfalls. Just plain erroneous information can find its way into your credit files. Old information that should be deleted might remain long past the proper date. Any of these glitches can cause you delay, discomfort, and dismay if you don't find them and correct them. The federal Fair Credit Reporting Law gives you the right to know what's in your credit history, and the right to have improper information corrected or deleted. Check with your local credit bureau for details. As a general precaution, review your file at least once every few years, and particularly in advance of a major credit request, such as financing a home.

Captive Borrowers

These two odd situations illustrate the dangers of "E-Z" credit, the lure of which can be particularly appealing to younger people just starting to build a credit history, and to anyone who has already suffered through credit problems. You've heard the siren songs: "Past problems are no problem for us! . . . Easy approval! . . . No questions asked! . . ." Note well: If E-Z credit is that easy to get, it can be very H-A-R-D to repay: interest costs can be sky high, and collection procedures can be very harsh if you're not on time with your payments.

Jan and Chris were a young couple who got caught in a captive borrower situation. They needed furniture for their first apartment, and they had no credit record to allow them to finance the furniture through normal channels, such as banks or better furniture stores.

They were lured by one furniture store's ad that promised to arrange E-Z financing for them. They bought what they needed, and though the interest rate on the financing was very high, they were happy to have it rather than live in an empty apartment. Further, they thought, maintaining a good payment record at this store would be their first step in establishing a sound credit history.

They made their payments like clockwork for two years. Then, when the loan was paid off, they applied to borrow at another place for another reason, giving the furniture store as their primary credit reference.

"I'm sorry," said the credit officer at the new place. "Your credit file doesn't indicate that you ever had a loan at the furniture store." Outraged, Jan and Chris asked the credit officer to call the furniture store directly. "I'm sorry," someone at the store said, "but we don't have any information on those people."

When Jan and Chris confronted the owner of the store he told them that he's not required to report this confidential information. But if they'd like to finance something through him, he'd be happy to take care of them because they paid so promptly on the first loan. Unwittingly, they had become captive borrowers of this unscrupulous merchant.

Jan and Chris came to our bank to try to bail themselves out from this awful situation. We did some investigating and learned what we needed to know. Jan and Chris became good customers of ours, and carried an excellent credit rating with them when they moved away three years later.

Pat and Fran had an equally frustrating experience. They applied for a debt consolidation loan, which seemed to be a reasonable request, given their income and the amount of debt they were carrying. In the loan application interview I asked them about what other debts they had had in recent years so that we could get a complete picture of their repayment performance. They listed a typical number of debts: car loans, department store charge accounts, various other accounts with doctors, dentists, and the like. They also mentioned that they had had one loan with the XYZ Small Loan Company. They specified *one* loan; that stuck in my mind.

Lenders are careful to seek the truth in loan applications. Anything that's not divulged or not accurate can show up in a credit report, and such items can reflect unfavorably on the applicant. This is as true for small personal loans as it is for huge corporate loans. Keep it in mind.

When Pat and Fran's credit history was delivered I was perplexed to see that they had had not one, but *sixteen,* loans with the XYZ Small Loan Company. Naturally my suspicion was aroused: Had they been telling me the truth, the whole truth, and nothing but?

I asked them, and they were just as perplexed as I was. So I called XYZ to ask them directly just what was going on. If Pat and Fran had really had sixteen loans from XYZ, that could be a sign of addiction to borrowing. Perhaps they owed a lot more money than they had admitted to. Further, small loan companies usually accept higher-risk borrowers, and charge a higher interest rate accordingly, and maybe we should just leave well enough alone and leave Pat and Fran to XYZ.

I got a most interesting answer from XYZ. Pat and Fran had received a loan for $800 about five years ago. XYZ, as did all small loan companies, charged certain initiation fees for their loans, and the interest payments were structured so that a much higher amount of interest was charged to the borrower in the early months of the loan than in the later months. This is all perfectly legal, but often unknown to borrowers. The rationale for charging more in the early months is that the borrower has the use of more of the money in the early months. Then, as payments are made, the borrower has use of less and less money, thus respectively lesser amounts of interest are charged in the later months. The overall effect of this is that if a loan is refinanced in the early months, the costs to the borrower will be much higher. The interest calculation is known as the Rule of 78s.

Anyway, after a few months Pat and Fran came up a bit short on the loan payment that was due. They went to XYZ to explain and to work out some way of keeping their credit record clean. XYZ could have accepted a partial payment then, and the balance a week or so later, as Pat and Fran offered to do. The late charge would have been a few dollars, but that could have been waived in the interest of good public relations.

XYZ chose another course: They quickly prepared some new papers for Pat and Fran to sign, which they did, and then told them that they were up to date, and that there would be no late charges. Wonderful, right? Wrong!

A few months later Pat and Fran ran into another temporary bind, and they went again to XYZ to straighten matters out. Again the new batch of papers were signed—everything's up to date, and no late charges.

Over the course of the past five years they had done this sixteen times. They were honorable borrowers, taking great pains to keep their payments timely and their credit record exemplary. Each time, sixteen times, XYZ had written a new $800 loan from scratch, keeping the initiation fees and the heavy doses of interest charged in the early months.

After five years of making payments, Pat and Fran still owed $800, and they had spent well over $1,000 in interest! Indeed, they had had only one loan from XYZ. But XYZ kept rewriting the loan as a new one each time, thus showing that Pat and Fran had had sixteen loans, a credit history that other lenders would shy away from as dangerous.

Pat and Fran had become captive borrowers of XYZ. We gave them their debt consolidation loan, which enabled them to pay off XYZ once and for all.

Oh boy, did I catch hell from the owner of XYZ when he learned that our bank had paid them off. I was accused of "stealing" one of their best customers. Well, there you go. It's a dog-eat-dog world out there, isn't it? I hope that these tales will help you avoid getting caught by some of its more vicious dogs.

The Insidious Advance Fee Loan Scam

This was a situation I've regretted ever since it happened. Harry had been a good customer of our bank, but he had fallen on hard times. He ran a small bakery that employed ten people. But Harry had other dough problems. He liked to gamble just a little too much.

He had always paid his debts, but his well-known gambling activities put a cloud over his credit reputation. He came to our bank seeking a $40,000 loan to upgrade his business equipment. He said that he had sworn off betting, and that the new equipment was essential to his ability to continue running a successful bakery. In short, he needed the money in a bad way, and he vowed that he was going to end his gambling career so that his primary source of income could flourish.

We had to reject his request. After all, as all borrowers must recognize, banks are not lending their own money. They're lending their depositors' money, and they, the banks, must answer to the government regulators who scan every loan document to make sure the depositors are being protected.

Other local lenders also rejected Harry's request. He was in a tight spot, and he all but begged us to reconsider. But without a co-signer (and he had none) or good collateral (there's a very slim market for used bakery equipment) we couldn't help him.

Then Harry called me with his good news: He had found someone to lend him the money, quickly and on good terms. He didn't want to divulge any details, so I wished him well.

Two weeks later Harry came to see me. He was devastated. He had fallen victim to the Advance Fee Loan Scam, and he now faced ruin: The bakery would have to close, his employees let go, and he had no choice but to declare bankruptcy.

This is what had happened. In his zeal to borrow money, and having been turned down by all the local lenders, he responded to a classified ad that appeared under the "Money To Lend" category. A very friendly chap assured Harry that he could get the money he needed from an out-of-town investor. Having thus inflated Harry's expectations, the con artist cleverly extracted $4,000 from him as an "advance fee," which had to be paid before the loan could be processed.

Harry fell for it, and paid out his last $4,000. When the day came to receive the loan proceeds, Harry was crushed to find that his supposed benefactor had skipped town without a trace. Harry's $4,000 was gone, his hopes of getting the $40,000 loan were wiped out, and his spirit was in a state of decay.

The end of the story is not quite as disheartening. Harry did indeed have to close the bakery, let his workers go, and declare bankruptcy. Some of his employees also found themselves in financial straits, not being able to find new jobs. Harry got a decent job as a pastry chef at a large local restaurant, though at a much lower income than he'd been accustomed to, and little by little he rehabilitated himself. When I moved away from Binghamton he was already talking about having enough money saved to open his own bakery again.

*
**   *
**   *
**

I've not heard about Harry since then, but I have heard about the Advance Fee Loan Scam more times than I care to remember in the intervening years. In good times and bad times there are always an abundance of ready victims, and rarely are the perpetrators ever caught.

In one case that I knew about—and no doubt there are countless others like it—the victim was approached by a stranger who knew that he was in need of money. The nature of the approach was such that it made the victim that much more susceptible to the scam. How would a stranger know of someone's financial plight? Snake Oil Sam had an accomplice that worked in a local bank. The accomplice knew who had been refused loans, and fed that information—for a fee—to Sam. That's certainly immoral and unethical, if not illegal. Take note—it's the real world.

Those Incredible Flying Squirrels

This story was told to me by a good customer of ours, a local roofing contractor who referred many home improvement financing contracts to us. I'm glad that I never had to actually pass judgment on a loan application for this particular job. It could have jostled my sanity, for reasons that you'll soon understand.

I saw my friend, the roofing contractor, at a local restaurant one evening. He was sitting alone, and he was going in and out of fits of laughter. This seemed rather peculiar behavior, so I approached him to see if he was okay. Yes, he was, he assured me; he had just come from giving a job quote, and the circumstances were so bizarre that he couldn't help himself from breaking out in laughter.

He had been at the home of an elderly widow who called him for an estimate on repairs to her roof. She lived in an old home that was overhung by even older elm trees. In the elm trees resided a number of squirrels. The widow had been terribly concerned that the squirrels might leap from the trees onto her roof, and then find their way into her attic where she kept a lot of antique furniture. The furniture had more sentimental than real value, but the widow feared that once the squirrels found their way into her attic, they would gnaw on the furniture and ruin it.

Some weeks earlier she had been called on by a salesman who offered a variety of home improvement projects. The salesman had quickly won her confidence by admiring the pictures of her grandchildren on her mantle. That done, she was ripe for the plucking. She confided in the "nice young salesman" about her squirrel phobia. The clever salesman had just the thing to solve the problem.

"We will install squirrel deflectors on your roof," he told her. "These are shiny aluminum panels set scientifically to reflect the sunlight. If any squirrels attempt to jump from the trees onto your roof, the sunlight glinting off the deflectors will blind them, and they will fall to earth quite dead and out of harm's way!"

All of this would be done for only $1,500. That's mid-1960s dollars mind you, when a glass of draft beer was still fifteen cents.

What the salesman did not discuss with the widow was what would prevent the squirrels from jumping onto the roof when the sun was not out, or when clouds blocked the sun. (Binghamton has the distinction of having the most cloudy days per year of any American city.) Never mind all that. The widow was so pleased with having her problem resolved that she signed a contract on the spot, and gave the salesman a check for a down payment.

The work was done a few days later—I imagine it took the salesman a while to find some shiny aluminum panels and bend them into shape. The work was a horror: The installers simply nailed them onto and through the roof shingles. At the first rain—which was within a few days of the installation—the roof leaked like a sieve, damaging not only the furniture in the attic, but much of the rest of the house as well.

The widow then called my friend, whose reputation was impeccable, to repair the damage done by the installation of the deflectors. His price was another $1,500, for the roof had to be all but completely replaced.

My friend did not lack sympathy for the old woman. Indeed, he felt very sorry for her. His laughter—as was mine, and as may be yours—came part from incredulity, and part from relief that "there but for the grace of God could have been my mother or grandmother."

*   *   *

**   **   **

Was this an out-and-out swindle? Could the salesman honestly (but stupidly) have thought he really had a legitimate solution to the woman's problem? Whichever it was in this case, or in any of the myriad situations that can result in an unexpected hemorrhaging of money, the critical importance of *getting a second opinion* and *examining alternative solutions to problems* comes through loud and clear.

It Can't Hurt to Ask

Getting a second opinion is as important in financial matters as it is in medical matters. I often was approached by borrowers who were seeking debt consolidation loans. They wanted to eliminate "all those pesky little debts" the ads so often describe, and consolidate them into one great big pesky debt. I'm not a fan of debt consolidation loans, and thus I often confronted my applicants with a second opinion; which is to say I presented them with alternative solutions to their problem.

In almost every case, they'd be better off hanging in there with their current payment schedule rather than taking on one big new loan. Here's an oversimplified example: The Smiths have five debts they want to consolidate. They're paying $100 a month on each one. If they continue with their current plan, one debt will be paid off in three months, another in six months, another in twelve months, another in twenty-four months, and the last in thirty-six months. Total debts right now: $8,100. Total monthly payments: $500.

They want a new thirty-six-month loan to pay off all five debts. Based on prevailing interest rates, an installment loan that will do the job for them will mean signing a new IOU for about $10,000, of which about $2,500 will be for interest. They'll then have to make thirty-six monthly payments of $278. (These figures reflect the fact that if they pay off all five existing loans early, they'll get some interest rebates, thus dropping their actual payoff figure from $8,100 to about $7,500).

If they can squeeze through just three more months on their current payment plan, one loan will be all paid off, and their monthly outlay for debt will shrink to $400. After another three months another of the debts will be paid off, reducing the hit to $300 a month. In just one year from now the third debt will be wiped out, and their monthly payments will total only $200. So, at the end of one year their outlay will be $78 a month *less* than with the debt consolidation plan, and they will have avoided committing themselves to an additional $2,500 in interest expense. Another year down the road they'll be even better off, as the next-to-last loan is paid up and their debt service drops to just $100 a month.

Another framework in which the exploration of alternative solutions occurs is when time is pressuring you. There's a crisis and only one remedy seems possible. Take a deep breath and count to ten before you commit yourself—there may be a better way.

Case in point: I owned two small apartment buildings and in one of them the central water heater died on a Saturday afternoon. I was a conscientious landlord (if I fulfill my obligations on time, so will my tenants—an understanding we had that worked time and time again). My regular plumber was not available, so I had to call in an emergency service. (One of the rules of investing in residential real estate is that you must have a plumber that makes house calls.)

The emergency service told me that it would cost $1,200 to install a new water heater immediately. I had six tenants, and four of them were right there looking over my shoulder. The price seemed excessive; I knew that such units could be had for a much lower price. How much did I want to spend to be a hero to my tenants? Conscientious is one thing; heroism is another. I made them a proposition: Can you survive until Monday morning without hot water? (It was summertime, and an unheated shower would be tepid anyway.) If so, I promised to have a new heater installed Monday, and I would knock $25 off each of their rents for the following month. It was a deal too good to refuse; they accepted it unanimously. I paid the emergency plumber $85 for the service call. On Monday morning I called my regular plumber, who installed a comparable water heater within a few hours for just over $600. Savings to me, after the rent reduction: $365, and that's after paying the $85 for the Saturday service call. Not a bad piece of change for taking an alternate route. I recommend such deliberations for your frequent consideration.

The High Cost of High Anxiety

*Examples of the unhappy fate awaiting anxious sellers and anxious landlords.
Don't let it happen to you.*

In any financial transaction, the more anxious you are the more your
common sense will be clouded, and the more it will cost you. This may
seem like an overly simplistic rule of human nature. It's really a very
slippery proposition: Anxiety can creep up on you in subtle and insidious ways.

The following two cases of *High Anxiety* also serve to introduce
another seemingly simplistic yet constantly overlooked rule of human
behavior known as Rosefsky's Rule #738b: "You don't ask, you don't
get."

Our bank was in desperate need of a new location for the main
office. (We had only our main office and one very modest branch.) We
were tenants in a building owned by the YMCA, on a side street a
hundred yards from the main drag. It was a gloomy north/south–
running street, getting a touch of sun only for a short time around
midday. It was a one-way street heading away from the center of town.
Our space was far too small. We could hear basketballs bouncing on
the Y's court and often got wafts of chlorine from the Y's swimming
pool. We had no visibility from the street unless you were standing
right in front of us. And, most important, it looked like a dump. No—
make that, it *was* a dump.

We were anticipating rapid growth, and we needed not only more
space, but a premier location on a main corner with high visibility and
prestigious architecture. We had to have it at a price that was a frac-

tion of what downtown Binghamton real estate was going for—a *fraction*.

We were despairing of finding such an opportunity, when lo and behold along came Geneva, The Sequel (see Chapter 8). One of the three downtown department stores—Sisson's—that had begun to suffer from the competition from suburban shopping centers announced that it was closing down.

The Sisson's building was a perfect site for our bank: a premier location on one of downtown's main intersections, plenty of space, highly visible, and with a new cosmetic exterior it could be the landmark building in the central city. Ben Sisson wanted to sell and we wanted to buy. There were precious few other buyers, for Binghamton had seen its better days. The building was long past its "sell-by" date, and if it sat too long unoccupied, it would be a replica of the monstrosity in Geneva.

Our first brilliant idea was to buy the building ourselves—that is, our family would buy it—and then we'd lease it to the bank. Tax laws would give us very attractive depreciation deductions on the building, and we'd pass the tax savings on to the bank in the form of a low rent lease. We knew that we would have to disclose every iota of the deal, and we did so, but the New York State Department of Banking shot us down. Too much potential conflict of interest, they said, with a family owning a building that it leased to the bank, while the family held a substantial interest in the ownership of the bank.

Okay, back to the drawingboard—but not for long.

A local contractor, Ed N., was interested in the ownership side of real estate, and he knew that our bank was seeking a new location. He approached us: "I'll buy the building," he announced, "and I'll fix it up to your specifications and give the bank a long-term lease." Such an arm's-length transaction certainly couldn't be objected to by the Department of Banking. We expressed an interest in Ed's offer, but we took our time and explored other possibilities.

That's when *High Anxiety* began to creep up on Ed. It began as an ego trip: to become the owner of what could become *the* prestige building in the city, with a bank as the major long-term tenant. The lure began to seduce him, and he in turn tried to seduce us to sign a deal so that he could get on with buying and renovating the building.

We held steady, and his anxiety noticeably increased. It quickly reached the danger point (for him). He was so confident that we wanted that location for our bank, and he was so confident that we would not be able to find another suitable location, that he committed to buy the building from Sisson before we committed to a lease.

Now he came to us with a *fait accompli*. "If you want to move your bank here, you'll now have to deal with me," was his firm but friendly announcement.

"Fine," we replied, "if we want to move there, we'll deal with you. If we find another location, we won't have to deal with you. Let's keep in touch."

Round Two: "If you want to move your bank here, you'd better sign a lease, or we'll rent it to someone else."

"Fine," we replied, "go find someone else."

We knew, he knew, everyone in town knew that there was no other possible tenant who offered the potential that our bank did. We waited, and we waited some more. Winter, with its cruelty to empty buildings, was fast approaching. And Ed's *High Anxiety* index, as we expected, began to go off the chart. He couldn't even bluff that he had any possible other tenants.

Round Three: Rosefsky's Rule #738b takes effect. Ed's state of *High Anxiety* had put him into a terrible negotiating position, and us into an excellent one. You don't ask, you don't get. We asked, and we got. We signed a 15-year lease at an extremely attractive rate. In fact, it was so attractive that when, a few years later, we sold our interest in the bank to Bankers Trust of New York, our low rental cost at the new building was a major factor in getting a few extra dollars per share for our shares in the transaction.

Rosefsky's Rule #738b can be used in many other kinds of situations, not just when you're facing an anxious landlord or an anxious seller. We'll discuss the Rule more in later chapters. Meanwhile, here's another example of the high cost of *High Anxiety*.

My time had at last come to run away from home (see Chapter 1). We had been in the new bank building for barely a year when a long-developing restlessness in me began to surface. Despite the security of my position I didn't feel comfortable with the long-range prospects of furthering my career and raising a family in Binghamton. The economic foundations of the town were deteriorating (and have since crumbled), and I felt there were more fertile pastures elsewhere. Further, my eyes were open to the fact that we only get one trip along the road of life. I wanted to take mine on the sunny side.

To make a long story short, I invoked Rosefsky's Rule #738b again: I went to the 1966 annual convention of the American Banker's Association intent on seeking out job opportunities in the southwest. I met, I asked, and within a few months I got an offer to become a vice president and house counsel for Pioneer Bank of Arizona, headquartered in Phoenix. That was followed swiftly by a househunting expedition to Phoenix, where I met a most decidedly, if not fanatically, anxious seller.

Phoenix, for all of its sunshine, modernity, and delightful ambiance, was (and still remains) a city subject to horrendous growth surges and recessions. When it grows, it grows in incredible spurts, aided in part by rampant speculation in residential and commercial building. Overdevelopment is the normal result. Then it takes the city a few grim, high-unemployment years to absorb all the excess—empty houses, empty condos, empty stores, empty office buildings—and eventually another growth spurt begins.

I arrived in Phoenix to hunt for a house when, just by pure luck, the housing market was at the bottom of a cycle. Mel was a homebuilder who speculated in the higher end of the market. For almost a year he had been sitting on one brand new house he had built: 4,000 square feet on almost an acre of ground, with forty orange trees and a swimming pool and top-quality amenities throughout. He had not had a nibble at his original asking price—about $100,000 (it's okay to giggle; that was way back in 1967). He was bleeding interest through the nose every month on his original construction loan, and every time he dropped his price the housing market went further into the doldrums. Then along came Rosefsky and his Rule #738b.

Mel wasn't just anxious, he was frantic. He was obsessed. He was driven. His asking price, then in the 80s, was realistic, but beyond my reach.

I asked: "I want a one-year lease with an option to buy at $68,000." (Moving to a distant city with a young family I wanted an out if things didn't work out well.)

I held my breath (for about 10 seconds).

Mel held his breath (for about 20 seconds).

I got.

Then came the weird part. I was entering into a complex transaction (a lease with an option to buy) in a state whose laws regarding property were quite different from New York's (unlike New York,

Arizona is a community property state). So, as I would have advised anyone else to do, I hired a lawyer. He prepared an accurate memorandum of our agreement, and I then flew back to Binghamton to wait for the final paperwork to come through.

A few weeks later the contract arrived, and it was drawn as nicely and as tightly and as carefully as Mel's lawyer could manage. It had been reviewed by my lawyer, and it had been reviewed by the escrow company, which would finalize the deal once it received all of the documents from the seller and the money and IOUs from me.

All of the terms of the sale were spelled out precisely. There was just one tiny little item omitted: the one-year lease!

The single most important part of the deal had been excluded from the final contract. Mel's lawyer, who had drawn the contract, had inadvertently (intentionally?) left it out. The escrow company had accidentally (inexcusably?) overlooked the omission. And my lawyer, *my own lawyer*, had stupidly (stupidly) failed to catch the foulup.

I caught it, and I raised hell. The contract was corrected and we moved to Phoenix. We loved it. At the end of the first year we exercised our option to buy at the agreed price. I yet again learned about dealing with an anxious seller: Find one. Don't become one.

*   *   *
**   **   **

A few other lessons were derived from these experiences.

1. No one twisted Ed's or Mel's arm to sign the agreements. They may not have been happy with the deals, but they found some valid reason to sign. They held up their ends of the bargains as professionals and as gentlemen. More pressure might have produced lower prices for the tenant/buyers, but that could also have produced misery, complications, and endless counterproductive bickering, if not costly lawsuits. Both parties to a deal have to be content with it, or you really don't have a deal you can live with comfortably. In trying to dig for the last nickel you could rupture a sewer line.

2. When lawyers draft agreements on behalf of their clients, you must be aware that the agreements will favor their clients, not you. If you sign any such agreement without having your own lawyer review it, you risk being taken advantage of.

3. As my weird incident illustrates, even having your own law-
    yer review an agreement doesn't guarantee you're being
    properly protected. Most of the time you will be, but there's
    always that slim chance . . . .
        The remedy, at the risk of having your lawyer think
    you're a pain in the butt, is to review every single item in the
    initial understanding to be certain that it's been properly
    included in the final draft. You shouldn't worry if your lawyer
    thinks you're a pain in the butt. For what you're paying him
    or her, you're entitled to be regarded in any way you like.

Chapter Eleven

You'd Think They
Should Know Better

Bankers can make mistakes too, even whoppers, and you can learn from their folly.

No matter what your financial status, there will always be people you look up to as being smarter and richer than you are, or than you might ever be. You could call it a form of idol worship. But what are you to think if your idols are smashed? Maybe they weren't that much smarter than you after all.

My move to Phoenix was a very exciting event. Binghamton was provincial, arthritic, and stagnating. Our bank was small, conservative, and limited in potential by the city's own limitations.

Phoenix was dynamic, growing, rife with potential. Opportunities at Pioneer Bank seemed equally abundant, or so I thought. And so thought Arnold S., who owned a controlling interest in Pioneer Bank. And so thought Allan R., a former pharmacist and ex-president of the Phoenix Chamber of Commerce, whom Arnold had hired as president of Pioneer Bank. And so thought the Board of Directors of Pioneer Bank, a who's who of the Phoenix business community.

If Arnold and Allan and the Board all thought that Pioneer Bank was overflowing with potential, who was I to disagree with them?

We were all wrong.

These were my perceptions of what went on: Arnold and his family had owned a steel business in Phoenix, and they had recently sold it to a big national company. In order to shelter their profit on the sale from income taxes, they had to reinvest the proceeds of the sale in another business. A controlling interest in Pioneer Bank was for sale at that time, and Arnold felt that owning a banking charter, not to mention a seemingly successful up-and-running bank in dynamic Phoenix, was a can't-lose proposition. He bought the controlling stock without really getting his nose into the nitty-gritty of the bank's loan portfolio.

Allan, as noted, had been a career pharmacist. He was a highly respected and extremely well-liked person. Just a few years earlier he had left the pharmacy business to become president of a small bank in Scottsdale (in suburban Phoenix), a bank in which Arnold also had an investment interest. Pharmacists and steel people don't necessarily make good bankers.

When Arnold bought control of Pioneer he merged the Scottsdale bank into Pioneer and made Allan the president of the combined operation. I had met Allan at the 1966 banking convention and he had offered me the job with Pioneer. I was a vice president and unofficial house counsel, to become officially so after I had passed the Arizona bar exam. I was also unofficially being groomed as a candidate for top management in the bank. I was 32. Allan was just a few years shy of retirement. When we first met, Allan had been impressed with my combined law/banking background, and my conservative nature: Banking in Arizona, I was to learn, was still a shoot-from-the-hip approach. Allan had also dazzled me with all the incredible opportunities that could come my way as a result of the high-level contacts I could make through the bank.

Arnold and Allan were very nice people, and they were particularly friendly and hospitable to this young chap that they had brought into the fold from "back East." But hard-nosed bankers they weren't—not by a long shot.

Two things happened during my first week on the job at Pioneer that told me I was in a sort of Twilight Zone of banking—at least in comparison with the kind of banking I had known.

First, I was informed that I had been given authority to okay loans of up to $100,000 without getting the approval of any other officers. In Binghamton my authority was $5,000, and any loan in excess of $25,000 had to be approved by the full loan committee. $100,000 on my own? They had to be crazy. They had no idea of my track record as a lender, and they were just plain out of order in giving such high lending limits to an unproven new officer.

Second, I was given a stack of files almost two feet high and was told that this represented *some* of the most delinquent loans they were then carrying. I was given instructions to "clean them up." As I reviewed each of the dozens of files I saw a banker's worst nightmare being played on a screen in my head. This was the loan portfolio from hell. Virtually all of these bad loans represented "paper" that the bank had bought from land development companies. The hope of collecting the delinquent debts was all but nil.

A brief explanation is in order. At that time—the late 1960s—there was an epidemic of land sales going on in the country. Mr. and Mrs. Fox of Gooseliver, Rhode Island, would see an ad on the back of a matchbook or in *Wrestling World* magazine urging them to buy "their very own retirement ranchette in beautiful, sunny Arizona . . . only $50 down, and easy payments." If they responded to the ad, they would get a hard-sell pitch to sign a contract to buy not just one ranchette, but several: "If you buy ten ranchettes today for $2,000 each, what with the prices going up by about 30 percent per year you can sell off nine of them in just three years and double your money, and you'll still own your own at virtually no cost." Such a deal! (See the film *Glengarry Glen Ross* to learn how the pressure cooker worked.)

The Foxes, and thousands of people like them, signed many millions of dollars' worth of contracts to buy ranchettes, rancheros, and ranchinis all over Arizona. Many other people bought similar deals in Florida. The developers would then sell their contracts to banks like Pioneer. "Here we have the contract of Mr. and Mrs. Fox for ten rancholas, amounting to $20,000, plus high interest, to be paid over a five-year term. We'll sell it to you for $16,000, so you'll earn the interest, plus a $4,000 kicker." These contracts were called "paper," and Pioneer had bought a ton of it. And they were choking on it.

A number of bad things can happen with this kind of debt. (1) Since this is not a high-priority item on the Fox's agenda, they start to fall behind on their payments. Once they get 60 or 90 days delinquent the bank must report it as such, and it becomes a big demerit on the bank examiners' reports. That can restrict the bank's lending activities in general. (2) The Foxes simply stop making payments on the loan. They may have visited the property and seen that it was barren desert with no hope in hell of ever becoming habitable. They may have read the profusion of reports that so many of these land deals were blatant ripoffs. They may have just decided they wanted out of the deal, and they'd take their chances with the collection agencies who'd come after them. In any of these cases, the bank was in a position of having to initiate collection procedures against out-of-state individuals, and the cost-effectiveness of doing so was highly doubtful. (3) There were no Foxes in the first place. They were fictions, inventions of the land developer who was creating counterfeit contracts, selling them to banks, and pocketing the money. Oh, yes, they'd send in a few months' worth of payments from the "Foxes" to give the lender a false sense of security. Then maybe the "Foxes" would notify the bank that they had sold their deal to the "Wolfs," who would be making the payments henceforth. Maybe the developer had "guaranteed" the "Fox's" IOU, and after chasing the Foxes for months the bank would seek payment from the developer, only to find that the developer had gone bankrupt, or had been sold to another developer headquartered in Paraguay, or some equally devious scam.

Pioneer Bank's loan portfolio had an abundant sampling of all of the above bad loans; what they lacked was any equivalent sampling of good loans. In all fairness to Arnold and Allan, these loans had not been initiated under their watch. They had inherited them from the previous owners. But Arnold and Allan had not done their due diligence in inspecting the loan portfolio before they bought the bank, so they had to live with the consequences. Further, Arnold, in his zeal to generate a return on his investment in the shares of Pioneer stock, was directing the officers of the bank to maximize profits, which meant taking higher than prudent risks in making loans. In short, he was condoning, if not outrightly urging, a continuation of the lending policies that had resulted in the portfolio from hell.

In the ensuing months I had the opportunity to get to know some of the players and some of the games in greater detail. I observed the following:

* Many of the land development companies that had been selling, and continued to sell, paper to Pioneer had been created by and/or were silently controlled by an ex con who reputedly had ties to organized crime interests. My urgent plea that the bank stop buying this paper was met with a shrug.

* The loan officer who handled most of the paperwork involved in approving and buying these land contracts was accused of accepting kickbacks from the developers. He was tried, convicted, and jailed.

* One loan officer who handled more normal commercial loan requests was explaining to me (as the in-house cop) why he had approved a very large loan to a company that was losing money hand over fist. The loan had no collateral, and it looked like it would end up a total loss. He explained to me, with an astonishingly straight face, the "benefits of having a negative cash flow." I'm still not clear on the concept, but the loan did go into the dumper and the officer went on to become president of another bank.

* Another loan officer invited me to go with him to the Sedona area, a few hours' drive north, where the bank had foreclosed on some land that had been the collateral for a loan to a now-defunct developer. The bank had made the loan originally based on the fact that the land had frontage on Oak Creek, a popular resort area. Oak Creek itself was much more than a creek: Even during the dry summer months it was a rushing waterway from the runoff of the mountains in the Flagstaff area. Any property with frontage on Oak Creek was regarded as having premium value—well, almost any property. No one from the bank had ever seen this property. The loan had been made years earlier by the previous owners of the bank. The lots, we understood, were laid out for summer vacation homes; each was 50 feet wide and 150 feet deep, with the rear line running along the creek. Sounded like a great idea at the time.

What we saw made us laugh at first, and then all but cry. The lots were exactly what the official *survey* described: 50 feet wide and 150 feet deep, with the rear property line along Oak Creek. The survey was not *topographical*, it didn't show elevations. What we saw were lots that were 50 feet wide, and then 10 feet back the lots plunged down a cliff. Hundreds of feet below was the creek, running nice and cool. Roughly 120 feet of the lots' 150-foot depth was nearly vertical! Building on the lots would have been impossible, but tobogganing on them in the winter would have been great fun. We'd have been embarrassed trying to sell the property at a foreclosure sale. The entire project was a complete loss for the bank.

It didn't take me long to realize that for at least the next few years my work at Pioneer Bank would be as smelly as cleaning out septic tanks. As fond as I was of Arnold and Allan—though my affection fell well short of idolatry—I knew that this was not what I was cut out for. Deep down inside, and as part of my reason for leaving the tight constraints of Binghamton, I wanted to turn my career toward writing full time. Sooner than later, Phoenix would become my venue for that (more in Chapter 12).

Soon after the above episodes with Pioneer Bank I was called to New York City on urgent family business. We were selling our family holdings in the Binghamton bank to Bankers Trust, one of New York's, and the nation's, biggest and most prestigious banks. My father wanted me to be there with him to help out during the final stages of negotiation at a meeting in the Bankers Trust offices.

Even before I announced my plans to leave Binghamton we had talked about selling our interest in the bank. New York State's banking laws had been changing to allow statewide branching, and the big city banks were all eyeing purchases of small city banks as a way to expand quickly and relatively inexpensively. Our bank was an ideal target, and there was a nice profit to be made. My father, who was in his early sixties, could easily dictate a nice contract for himself to take him to retirement, and I could likewise have worked out a good long-term deal with a purchasing bank. My leaving Binghamton accelerated our thinking about selling out, and Bankers Trust had come forward with the most attractive proposal.

Thus I found myself seated with some gentlemen—the Bankers Trust moguls—who could easily be idolized by anyone in the banking industry. This bank was huge. It was powerful. It was enormously profitable. It was incredibly well respected. It was uncannily well managed.

At least until a few weeks earlier: In the months prior to my visit there one of the biggest names in American business—Penn Central Railroad—had been in the headlines frequently. It appeared to be going broke! This was shocking news to the business world. Not in over 40 years, since the Crash of '29, had such a revered company been in such a precarious condition.

Week by week the omens were worsening. From all reports it appeared that Penn Central was doomed. It was just a matter of time.

In one last dying gasp, hoping to fend off the inevitable, the railroad was able to borrow some $90 million from a group of major banks. This last infusion of cash might stave off, or at least delay, the ultimate disaster.

We in the banking business thought that this midnight-hour loan was foolhardy. There seemed no justification at all to make the loan. It was impossible for the railroad to repay it within the 90 days set forth as the term of the loan. There's one common syndrome with which all bankers are familiar: the borrower who is going down the drain, and pleads for one last loan. "All I need is this last $xx,xxx. With that I can get everything straightened out, get back on my feet, and pay you back the $xxx,xxx that I owe you. If you don't give me this last $xx,xxx that I need, I can never repay the original $xxx,xxx that I owe you."

This is also known as the "throwing good money after bad" dilemma. Sometimes it works, but usually it doesn't.

That was indeed the case with Penn Central. Sure enough it soon went into bankrupcty and the last-minute $90 million loan went into default. Ninety million dollars, shared by a number of banks, may seem like penny-ante today, but then it was the talk of the financial world. Why did they do it? How could they justify it? You'd think they should know better.

And now I sat face to face with one of the men who had committed his bank, Bankers Trust, to participating in this ill-fated loan to Penn Central. (His name mercifully escapes me.) It was brash of me, perhaps, to ask him, but I couldn't resist: "Why did you do it? How could you justify it?"

His answer—candid and forthcoming—amazed me. "We called around to the other banks . . . good old Charlie and Manny and Vic and Dave," he went on, rattling off the names and the major New York banks that had gone along with the loan, "we all thought it was a good thing to do, so we did it."

Simple as that: Like a bunch of guys in a touch football huddle, and one says, "you run as fast as you can toward the goal line and I'll throw the ball as far as I can in your direction." Hail Mary.

*
** 　 *
** 　 *
**

Some more questioning during unguarded moments convinced me that the $90 million loan was made by a good-old-boys network that commuted, golfed, played, partied, and loaned together. Why otherwise could Penn Central get $90 million of loans that it didn't deserve when at the same time 1,000 small businesses might be refused loans of $90,000 each that they did deserve, or 10,000 households might be refused home improvement loans or other personal loans of $9,000 each that they did deserve?

Thus are idols smashed.

The Penn Central debacle was not a terminal event. Rather, it's a sporadic phenomenon in lending and economic cycles. Fast-forward to the 1980s when hundreds of *billions* of dollars of highly questionable and ultimately bad loans were made to build a wretched excess of office buildings, shopping centers, condominium projects, and housing developments, all of which ended up having to be paid for by United States taxpayers. This plague, otherwise known as the Savings and Loan bailout, harmed millions of innocent people, particularly when Congress finally turned off the easy money spigot and lenders started to refuse to make otherwise good loans, lest the government regulators punish them.

You might safely idolize parents and clergy and teachers and sports heros and celebrities, but beware of idolizing lenders. They're frail humans just like all the rest of us. They can make mistakes; whoppers indeed, as these stories illustrate. And they can't be relied on to be there whenever you need them. They won't throw the Hail Mary pass to you (though they might to their good old buddies). And they can turn the spigot off when you least expect it.

Recall the old adage: "When you owe the bank $1,000 that you can't repay, *you* don't sleep nights. When you owe the bank $1,000,000 that you can't repay, the *banker* doesn't sleep nights." Know well which category you're in. Wherever you are on a lender's priority list, keep in touch with him or her regularly. Keep your financial statements up to date. Keep your credit history clean. Keep in touch with the bank's ever-changing lending requirements. Keep yourself familiar with more than one officer, since they all have ways of moving on and you don't want to be an orphan. Do all of this, and the *banker* may well end up idolizing *you*.

(P.S. We finalized the deal with Bankers Trust, and my father was sitting on a very fat profit. I urged him to sell the Bankers Trust shares he had received, put the money into tax exempt bonds, and go find a nice beach in Hawaii to sit on. He didn't sell, because he didn't want to have to pay the capital gains taxes. Months later Bankers Trust stock went into a tailspin, losing about 60 percent of its value. Oh, the pain. Such is fate. Thus again are idols smashed.)

Chapter Twelve

Behold the Turtle:
It Makes Progress Only when it
Sticks its Neck Out

Trials and errors in becoming an entrepreneur. Ordeals to be survived and lessons to be learned.

✔ *The Other Crash of 1929*
  . . . learning to take *nothing* for granted
✔ *With Friends Like That . . . or, Rod Serling, The Sequel*
  . . . learning who can help you, and what to do when they don't
✔ *Being in the Right Place at the Right Time*
  . . . forget what you know and who you know; just learn how to spot miracles and take advantage of them when they happen
✔ *Basic Turtle Rules*
  . . . how to stick your neck out safely and wisely, not too far and not too long

As the events in Chapter 11 indicate, all was not well at Pioneer Bank. I began to view its destiny, and mine along with it, with grave concern. You may have had similar concerns with your job from time to time, and you likely reacted the same way I did: How can I get out of here and become my own boss?

Becoming an entrepreneur is something that many people aspire to. With the possible exception of marriage, it's the one human endeavor that has the greatest potential for uncertainty, exhilaration, stress, pain, joy, anger, bewilderment, pride, disbelief, and, hopefully, financial reward.

Above all, taking steps to become an entrepreneur involves exposing oneself to risk. Entrepreneurial risk means, in plain talk, that you could lose money. You could lose time. You could lose self-esteem. You could lose friends who have invested in you. It can be a hefty price to pay. On the other hand, of course, comes the chance for gain: money, freedom, respect, and a sense of accomplishment.

You can't reap the benefits without taking the risks. You have to stick your neck out. But how far to stick your neck out—that's the tough question for which everyone must find their own right answers. The following tales of my own neck-sticking-out may help you formulate sensible guidelines for your own ventures.

I had been at Pioneer Bank barely eight months when I decided that the future there looked grim. If I was to stay in banking, I wanted the chance to be with a healthy company where creativity and innovation could pay off. The bank regulators were hovering around Pioneer's bad loan portfolio like buzzards, and it seemed likely that they would take action to severely constrict Pioneer's lending abilities until the junk had been gotten rid of. Spending the next few years cleaning up someone else's mess was a dismal prospect.

It was thus easy for me to make the decision to leave the bank and begin my lifelong but deeply supressed desire—to make my living as a freelance writer. I had enough resources to get me through a year or two of hard times. I had the confidence. I had the necessary skills. I had the support and encouragement of my wife and family. And I had the best motivation of all: If I didn't make the grade before my money ran out, I'd have to go back to law and banking, a fate I dreaded.

I gave my notice at the bank and officially began my new career the week my youngest child, Joshua, was born. That makes it easy for me to remember how long I've been involved in this entrepreneurial venture.

My first task was to find an office. Working at home was then totally impractical, but my budget for rent was about a dollar a day. With nothing to lose, I invoked Rosefsky's Rule #738b: "You don't ask, you don't get." I asked a friend who was a property manager if he had any small spaces that were for rent. I offered to move in literally on a day-to-day basis: If he found a proper tenant, I'd be gone the next day. Lo and behold, he had a little one-room office not far from my house. I offered, and he accepted most reluctantly, a rent that suited my meager budget: $25 a month. Fate must have smiled on me in that little space. I stayed there for over five years and finally moved out when I could afford bigger and better.

Over the years since then I've always been bemused by people who start out in business for themselves and spend so excessively on getting set up that they undermine their whole financial foundation. I even fell into the same trap myself many years later (see Chapter 20).

I then went to a second-hand office supply store, and for less than $100 I bought an army surplus desk and filing cabinet, took them to my $25 a month office, and I was in business. I knew that I had to watch my spending extremely carefully, but the next expense, under $5, seemed like the best possible investment I could ever make—and it could have been.

The Other Crash of 1929

The stock market wasn't the only problem related to that year. Something else happened that taught this novice entrepreneur some of the most valuable lessons of his career: Take nothing for granted, and be prepared for the fact that anything can happen, even the impossible.

I was browsing in an antiquarian bookstore near my office and I stumbled across a mint-condition copy of the *1929 World Almanac*. This was a most delightful find for me, because at that time the publishing industry was on a nostalgia kick. Someone had published a reprint of a turn-of-the-century Sears Roebuck catalog and it had been an overnight best-seller. Any publication that smacked of early Americana was fair game to be reprinted, and this *Almanac* seemed a natural. Not only did it have articles and statistics on such phenomema as Babe Ruth and prohibition, but flappers, Al Jolson, and talking movies. It was also, unlike present-day almanacs, chock full of quirky advertisements such as: "Artificial Eyes, $5, Largest Stock in America, We Fit By Mail" and "Correct Your Nose With The Marvelous Anita Nose Adjuster" and hundreds more of that amusing ilk.

I bought the *Almanac* for $5 and immediately began to envision that investment returning to me many thousandfold when the reprint hit the stores.

Through a mutual friend I was introduced to Peter Workman, who was almost as much a novice publisher as I was a novice writer. He was as thrilled with the *Almanac* project as I was. It was too big for him to tackle alone, he told me, but he promised he would pursue the matter in the New York sea of publishing.

I was speechless when he called me just a week later to tell me the good news—no, the Great News!

1. The original copyright on the *Almanac* had expired, and it was now public domain, which meant that we could have it reprinted without having to get permission or pay for any rights.

2. The first major publisher Peter contacted jumped at the chance to get involved, and they immediately offered us a contract. That publisher was McGraw-Hill, one of the nation's largest and most prestigious houses.

3. McGraw-Hill controlled the American Heritage archives, one of the best resources for all things Americana. They were going to tap into those sources and create a 32-page addendum to the *Almanac,* filled with photos and an essay by a prominent historian, at no cost to us.

4. McGraw-Hill would publish the book as one of their major Christmas gift items, in both hard and soft cover, accompanied by a national advertising campaign.

5. McGraw-Hill would absorb all production costs, and we would split the income 50 percent for McGraw-Hill and 50 percent for Peter and me (which he and I had already agreed we'd split down the middle).

The only catch was that if the book didn't generate enough income to cover production costs—fat chance—then Peter and I would have to ante up our share (50 percent) of any shortfall.

There I was, a novice author, having sold a deal to one of the country's biggest publishers, and *I didn't even have to write the book.* Did I begin to have inflated expectations? You'd better believe it. Did I start to spend the sorely needed money that I thought I'd earn from the book? Thankfully, no—my common sense remained firmly intact in that respect. Did I start setting aside a reserve to pay my share of the production costs if the book failed? No—that could not happen.

All the omens were good, not the least of which being that I was dealing with honorable people. Consider: McGraw-Hill, Peter, or anyone else for that matter, could have found a copy of the same *Almanac* and commenced to reprint it without cutting me in on the deal. I was soon to learn there was one person who was not so honorable.

The project moved forward rapidly toward its pre-Christmas publication. The American Heritage photos and essay were completed. The printing plates were prepared for the presses. The advertising campaign was created—indeed, we had a half-page ad announcing the publication in the *New York Times Book Review*—and the publicity people were churning up a storm of interest. Orders were coming in from bookstores around the country in very encouraging numbers. Success was just a few weeks away!—a fatal few weeks.

One of America's most eccentric folk heroes was the billionaire recluse, Howard Hughes. In his time he had been an inventor, aviator, industrialist, and squire to numerous Hollywood starlets. He was the original Rich and Famous whose lifestyle was the subject of speculation by every tabloid newspaper and gossip columnist in the country.

Rumor now had it that Hughes had gone dotty and was living the life of a hermit in a suite at the Desert Inn resort, which he owned, in Las Vegas. The rumors (no doubt fed by a clever press agent) suddenly came to a head: An otherwise unknown author, Clifford Irving, claimed to have written the *only authentic authorized biography* of Howard Hughes, and it was going to tell the *whole truth*.

The nation's press and talk shows went into a feeding frenzy. Who was this Clifford Irving, and how could he have gotten to Hughes, through his reputed army of bodyguards and keepers, where no other author or journalist had ever been able to penetrate? What garish tales did he have to tell about Hughes? Read all about it when the book is published . . . just before Christmas . . . by none other than McGraw-Hill, one of the nation's largest and most prestigious houses. If any house was going to publish a legitimate biography, surely McGraw-Hill was capable of doing so. Adding to the credibility of the whole venture was the fact that *Time* magazine had become a partner with McGraw-Hill, and between the two of them they had paid Irving $750,000 for his efforts.

When Howard Hughes' people began stating that there was no such authorized biography the vultures from the press began circling McGraw-Hill headquarters. Could a publisher as large and as prestigious as McGraw-Hill be defrauded by a lone and audacious author? "Certainly not," said McGraw-Hill. "Certainly not," said Clifford Irving.

I never met Mr. Irving. . . . Or Mr. Hughes. . . . Or Mr. McGraw . . . Or Mr. Hill. But I regret the day I heard any of their names. "HUGHES BIO A FRAUD" one of the newspapers trumpeted when Irving finally admitted to his chicanery. Swiftly, oh so swiftly, after that did McGraw-Hill's general book division fall into an abyss. The fraudulent manuscript had not yet been printed, but the shame, the embarrassment, the mortification of this fine publishing house was so great that their business all but ground to a halt—including the marketing of the *1929 World Almanac.*

It had been printed. Ads had run. Distribution had begun. But it died aborning . . . not a slow lingering death . . . a loud sudden crash. The editors, the marketing people, the promotions department—all of the extensive support staff that gets a book from the presses and into the hands of the buyers—all suddenly had more important things on their agendas. It was the other crash of 1929.

Here's one tiny example to show that bookstores need marketing help from publishers in displaying and promoting the books they've ordered. Without that help they can make innocent mistakes that can kill sales of a book. I visited one of Chicago's main bookstores looking for a copy of the *Almanac* just after it had been published. It was not, as it should obviously have been, in the Current Nonfiction section, or even in the Nostalgia section, which most stores had then. It was in the Reference section, where no one would likely ever look for it. "Well, after all, it *is* an almanac," said the perturbed clerk who was obviously not clear on the 1929 concept.

My initial investment of a few dollars in the original copy had turned into a loss of many thousands of dollars—dollars I could ill afford to lose at the time. McGraw-Hill was kind enough to give us a few years to pay it off, and the pain eventually eased. Peter went on to become a very successful publisher, and I get to tell stories about how Howard Hughes almost demolished my book-writing career before I had even written my first book.

What lessons can you, the entrepreneur, learn from this tale of woe? As I learned: (1) You can become a little paranoid about entering into business transactions with anyone and, moreover, a little paranoia is better for you than none at all. That twinge of paranoia can convince you to take very little for granted, and can motivate you to check and double-check all the "what-ifs" that can pop up to foul a deal. (2) You must evaluate the downside, the worst case, before you enter upon any kind of venture. Further, you must have a fallback position if that worst case does occur. True, the Irving/Hughes/McGraw-Hill scenario was utterly implausible (but not wholly unpredictable). I took a hit on that one, but I've been more cautious, and successfully so, ever since.

I was lucky to have had this experience early. Youthful enthusiasm got me into it, and helped me survive it. I could then learn to almost chuckle (through the tears) when other debacles occurred later on.

With Friends Like That . . . or, Rod Serling, The Sequel

Once you learn that you must stick your neck out in order to make progress, you then must learn how *far* you can stick it out, and for how long. During this learning process you may have friends, advisors, and investors who will offer some help. It's essential that you evaluate what kind of help they can give you. You know where good intentions can sometimes take you.

My new writing career, having survived Howard Hughes, was moving along in fits and starts. I was getting assignments from local magazines in Phoenix, but they wouldn't pay the mortgage. I needed bigger bucks, and everyone knew that the real big bucks for writers was in Hollywood.

I was about to learn the classical Catch 22 about the writing business—and similar Catches exist for almost every business venture. In my case it was: You can't get meaty writing assignments for movies or TV unless you have an agent. And you can't get an agent unless you've had some credits writing for movies or television. (By way of analogy for other entrepreneurs, say, retailers: You can't buy from the important suppliers until you have a good credit rating, and you can't get a good credit rating until you've done business with the major suppliers. Sound familiar?)

I learned about this Catch 22 quite simply by writing to the story editors at a number of production houses inquiring about how I could submit script ideas to them. "Get an agent," they all replied. Agents act as a screening device, separating the good material from the junk, and thus saving the producers the time in sorting through hundreds of submissions each week. Similar customs prevail in the book, magazine, acting, modeling, and popular music industries.

Then I proceeded to contact all the agents listed in the appropriate directory, and they all told me that they only took on writers who had credits.

So how do new writers break in? With great difficulty; with that realization, a major lesson of the past came roaring into my head: It's not *what* you know, it's *who* you know. The time had come to reestablish contact with my erstwhile mentor, Rod Serling.

Rod had been flying high with *The Twilight Zone* and *Night Gallery*. Even though we had had no contact for over ten years he was happy to hear from me and volunteered to help. "I'll get you an appointment with my agent at the William Morris Agency," he said, and my heart fluttered. The William Morris Agency was then the ultimate powerhouse agency in the entertainment industry. To have them represent me would be tantamount to instant, permanent, and immeasurable success. (Inflated expectations? Of the worst sort.)

I almost didn't need an airplane to fly me to Los Angeles. I approached the William Morris offices in Beverly Hills like Dorothy approached the Wizard of Oz at the Emerald Palace. I was greeted similarly by a small man sitting behind a desk that was carved from some exotic wood and was as large as a tennis court. There was nothing on the desk but a single telephone, and in the course of about one minute, before the small man acknowledged my presence, he spoke into the phone saying what sounded like the following: "See you Tuesday, Lucy . . . say hello to Desi for me." "Let's have lunch, Hume, and give my best to Jessica." "Hi Frank, I'll see you at the first tee at nine with Dean and Sammy."

If you could have done a scan of my brain at that moment the readings would have been off the chart.

Then the small man turned to me and, after looking at his watch, spoke to me much as the Wizard first spoke to Dorothy: "Rod tells me that you're a lawyer and now you want to be a writer. What shows do you want to write for?"

I blurted out the names of a few shows that were popular that season, including the lawyer show *Judd for the Defense.*

"You go home and write. Send it to me. I'll look at it." Then he looked at his watch again, signaling clearly to me that the meeting was at an end.

Those were twenty of the most memorable seconds in my life. Did I have an agent? I didn't know. I had someone with a tennis-court-sized desk who was on a first-name basis with Lucy and Desi, Hume and Jessica, and Frank, Dean, and Sammy who would "look at" what I wrote, whatever that meant.

I was elated, but my common sense held full sway and I again did not start spending the money I knew I'd earn as a result of this contact . . . good thinking.

I watched a number of episodes of *Judd for the Defense* until I got a sense of the characters, the type of plotting, and the pacing. Recalling some intriguing cases that had come to my attention in my lawyer days, I then proceeded to write a script for this one-hour show. When it was finished and polished a few weeks later I sent it, as instructed, to the small man with the big desk in Beverly Hills. And I began the waiting vigil.

It was one of the shortest vigils on record. Three days later the script was returned in the original envelope marked RETURNED UNOPENED. It was as if the Wizard himself had written those words.

Flabbergasted, I phoned my man at William Morris and asked why, after he had promised to "look at" my work, he had returned it unopened. As the Wizard roared at Dorothy, he roared, "You smartass lawyers are all alike. You send in scripts and then you sue us for plagiarism when something remotely like it shows up on TV a few years later! I don't read *anything* unless you've signed a full release!"

I almost asked him why he hadn't told me about this when I was there, but I was afraid I'd be greeted by a blast of fire from the monster's mouth. "Please send me a copy of the release form," was all I could meekly say.

The release form arrived and it was one of the most extraordinary legal documents I had ever seen. It said, in effect, that in exchange for their reading my material, I promised I would never bring any kind of legal action against them, in perpetuity, on the planet Earth, in the Solar System, or in any universes yet to be discovered. If I did bring suit, they could lay claim to all my assets, now or ever in my possession, not limited to personal property, spouse, and children now living or yet to be born.

If I wanted my script read by this questionable human being, I would have to sign the release. I made my pact with the devil, signed the release, and sent it along with the script back to Gulag Beverly Hills.

Three days later it was back again, this time at least in a new envelope. A tiny slip of paper was attached to the script. It contained the simple words, "Can't use this."

Devastated, I phoned him again, certain that I would never have gotten through to him if I hadn't been Rod Serling's friend. I didn't believe that he had even read the script, given the short turnaround time. He was brutally brusque. "We can't help you . . . get another agent."

With one final effort I asked him, "What if I just sent the script to the producer of *Judd*?" "You can't," the agent replied. "They don't read anything unless it comes from an agent."

"I can't?" I asked incredulously.

"That's right, you can't!" And he hung up.

Needless to say I was frustrated, enraged, and in a state of utter disbelief over this turn of events. But if I had stuck my neck out this far and lived to tell about it, I could stick it out a little farther, with Rod's help or not.

I calculated carefully: What's the *worst* thing that can happen if I send my script directly to the producer? Will they have me arrested? Will they bomb my house? Will they kidnap my children? No—they'll return it. That's the worst case, for which I was willing to risk another postage stamp.

Now I had a long vigil, and I grew more optimistic with each passing day. About three weeks later my script was returned, and there was a very nice personal letter from the producer attached to it. He told me that he liked the story line and the way I had treated the characters, and he thought I had a good touch for this kind of drama. But they weren't buying any more scripts at the moment since their renewal with the network was up in the air. However, he concluded, if I had any more script ideas I should feel free to contact him.

So much for your horse manure, mister small man with the big desk in Beverly Hills! So much for your "You can't." I can, I will, and I did! I learned a lot about assertiveness from that incident, and it came to my aid in the future as later chapters will illustrate. My entrepreneurial spirit, instead of being stifled, was actually stimulated. I moved forward.

Being in the Right Place at the Right Time

Forget *what* you know. Forget *who* you know. If you can just manage the simple miracle of being in the right place at the right time, you can hit a jackpot. Easier said than done? Of course it is. But sometimes you get lucky. When you do, it sure beats being in the *wrong* place at the right time, or being in the right place at the wrong time.

My suspicions about the kind of people one deals with in Hollywood were validated when I contacted an old schoolmate who was climbing the show business ladder as an assistant producer for various television shows. I sought his counsel as to whether or not I should take the plunge and devote myself to writing for film and television. We spent an entire weekend talking about it.

For old times' sake he wanted to lure me to La-La Land, but his own experience and honesty were more convincing. To most briefly summarize his very anatomical description of the life of a television/ screenwriter: "Between all the ass-kissing and the throat-cutting that's constantly going on, you might find that your writing has to be severely compromised."

That definitely swayed me. Hollywood, it appeared, was the wrong place for me, even if the time was right.

My last conversation with Rod Serling was the clincher. I had telephoned him to thank him for introducing me to the small man with the big desk, and I caught him in a very ugly mood. Rod was very caustic at times. This was the worst I'd heard. He was badmouthing the same industry I was thinking of entering, and I recall his words as follows:

"I helped create modern drama on television . . . I was one of the pioneers, and now I have to put up with a bunch of *&¢%#@* 25-year-old story editors who don't know *@#¢ about writing, and they're telling me that this character should be a man instead of a woman, and this setting should be inside instead of outside, and this dialogue should say such-and-such instead of what I wrote! Drives me @#*¢%$ crazy! Then there are the sponsors. I had one script that opened up with a panorama of the New York skyline. It was setting the scene for the dynamics of the story. They wanted me to change the opening scene to people going into an office building . . . but that wasn't the feeling I wanted. They insisted. Why? Because in the New York skyline you can see the top of the Chrysler Building prominently, though who in hell knows or cares that that's the Chrysler Building. Well, the sponsor of the program did. It was Ford! They're all full of @*$&#¢$*%((@*%&@. All of them!''

I needed no further convincing. The right place for me as a writer was in the print media, and I didn't have a whole lot of time to go exploring.

Peter Workman, my partner in the McGraw-Hill mess, put me in touch with a New York literary agent named Theron Raines, a very sweet man who told me he wasn't taking on any new clients, but he would do me a favor because I was a friend of Peter's. For many months I submitted material to Theron—children's books, short stories, poetry, even a miserable attempt at a novel. Theron kept telling me that he wasn't able to sell any of it. I was beginning to run out of time, and money.

Then the lesson that I'd heard from every writing teacher I had ever had came reverberating into my head: WRITE WHAT YOU KNOW. What I knew was personal finance—I had spent the better part of a decade as a lawyer and banker helping people deal with their financial concerns. I knew that I had a knack of making complex financial concerns understandable. If I could explain things to people in person, I could certainly explain it in writing.

Though the Age of Consumerism was in its earliest dawning moments, I sensed that there was a growing need for the kind of information and advice I could impart. I developed a concept for a newspaper column. I titled it "Speaking Dollar-Wise," wrote a bunch of samples, and sent it all to Theron with instructions that he sell the idea to a newspaper syndicate.

Theron laughed. "You don't *sell* a syndicated newspaper column. You either labor in journalism for a few decades until your work reaches a point that many newspapers want to share it, or you apprentice for an existing columnist until he or she dies, and then you inherit the column. But you don't sell it. That doesn't happen."

This, of course, smacked of the Beverly Hills midget telling me that you can't send scripts directly to a producer. I told Theron that I would not accept his reluctance to sell the idea. Perhaps I intimidated him. He grudgingly told me he'd give it a try, but that it was futile to hope for any success.

Right Time, Right Place: Two weeks later Theron called, almost giggling, to tell me that he had sold my idea to a small newspaper syndicate on Long Island, and that the contract would be in the mail shortly.

I was delirious. Was Theron a genius? No—Theron admitted to me that he knew nothing about newspaper syndicates. His specialty was novels. He had simply looked in the New York City Yellow Pages under Newspaper Syndicates, and for starters picked one he had never heard of: Newsday Specials, a tiny syndicate by industry standards that was affiliated with *Newsday* newspaper, then a small suburban daily. He had sent them my package. For this you need an agent to take 10 percent of your earnings?

So, then, it was *me* that was the genius, right? Wrong—*on the very day* that my package arrived at the chief editor's desk at Newsday Specials, they had just canceled another financial column they had been offering, and were just beginning to look for a replacement. My bundle, by a simple miracle, landed in the Right Place at the Right Time. They called Theron to make a deal, and my career began its upward ascent.

Given this stroke of luck, I then had to perform in accordance with my contract: three columns per week, fifty-two weeks per year, all on timely subjects and professionally written—all for the sake of earning how much money? My first *monthly* check from the syndicate was for $167, of which Theron Raines was entitled to $16.70. It didn't pay the mortgage, but it was a start.

Basic Turtle Rules

Sticking your neck out—taking a chance, exposing yourself to risk— occurs not just with entrepreneurial activities. Like it or not, you're sticking your neck out when you speculate with your money, such as in the stock market or mutual funds. You're sticking your neck out when you sign on for a long-term financial plan, such as with a retirement program or an estate planning program. You're sticking your neck out if you change jobs or careers. You're sticking your neck out when you sign on the dotted line to buy and finance a home.

There are some basic rules to observe in any neck-sticking-out situation:

* Beware of Inflated Expectations. Your common sense can get clouded, and your ability to act intelligently is thus impaired, when you allow yourself to see only the positive side of a situation.

* Keep Your Eye on the Downside. Evaluate the worst-case scenario realistically and continually. It can change as circumstances change, so you must always know what actions, if any, you can take to avert trouble.

* Know Who Can Help You. Friends, family, and assorted well-wishers can indeed help, or they might hinder your efforts. You must know what *their agendas* are. And you must know what their qualifications are to be able to give you the proper kind of expert assistance.

* Avoid Selective Listening. Selective listening is a subconscious activity that causes you to hear only what you want to hear. When the tipster tells you, "This stock can triple in two months if the company can get the Justice Department off its back on those money-laundering charges," your selective listening antenna allows you to hear only, "This stock can triple in two months. . . ." When left unattended, selective listening can lead to terminal cases of inflated expectations.

There's a flipside to all these rules:

* Are you the cause of someone else's inflated expectations? Are you unwittingly fanning the wishful thinking of a friend or family member who's sticking his or her neck out?

* Are you the cause of someone else's failure to keep their eye on the downside? Have you said to someone who trusts you, even with the best of intentions, "Don't worry about that . . . that can never happen?"

* Are you letting your own personal agenda intrude into the counsel you're offering someone? Have you ever said (and meant) "Invest in this stock (because by doing so you'll validate my decision to have done so)," or, "Certainly you should open your own restaurant (because then you can rent the empty space I've been trying to get off my hands for eight

months/buy all your equipment from me/buy all your insurance from me)," or, "I think $365,000 is a very good price to pay for that house (because that will help boost the value of my house, which is just two blocks away)"?

* Are you exacerbating someone's case of selective listening? When called upon to evaluate both sides of an issue do you pooh-pooh the bad-news side, thereby reinforcing the selective listener's bias toward the good-news side?

If any of these situations exist, you could be causing that someone else serious harm, financially and personally. Evaluate, analyze, reflect, and, if you're guilty, stop the dangerous behavior *and* go to the other person and explain what you've done. That can help undo some of the problems that already may exist.

There are three additional concerns that relate more directly to the stuck-out-neck of the entrepreneur:

1. Do you pay yourself first or last? I have seen many new ventures fail because the entrepreneurs wrote themselves excessive salaries as part of their overall financial plan. In other words, they paid themselves first. The capital they raised to start the business—whether saved, borrowed, or attracted from investors—went in part to pay a regular income to the entrepreneur. This is not a bad thing. Indeed, for many, it's necessary if they want to eat. It can be a dangerous thing if the capital is tapped too much for your own personal spending purposes. That capital might be better spent on supplies, advertising, rent, help, research—any of a number of things that can keep the business afloat in the rough early months. By paying yourself first, you risk cutting off the oxygen supply to other vital organs that are essential to the fledgling business's well being.

It might be preferable to pay yourself last—that is, you just take what's left after all the proper business expenses have been met. This might take some sacrifice on your part. It might be a tough choice: Do you make the personal sacrifice of living on a very restricted income until the business can support you? Or do you sacrifice the possible success of the business by overindulging yourself with respect to the money you personally take out of the enterprise?

For everyone there is, of course, a happy medium that should be sought: a modest salary to start, matched by a modest life-style until the business can afford you better.

2.   Can you be your own boss as well as your own employee? That's one of the toughest challenges, and you don't know how you'll react to it until you're actually on the firing line. Do you have what it takes, as a self-employed individual, to wear both hats at once? As the boss, can you provide the motivational force and the hustle that will be needed to generate income-producing opportunities? Will you be able to follow through as a manager, seeing to it that all the necessary tasks are being carried out properly? As the employee, will you be able to follow through on the detail work, the leg work, and whatever else is involved to execute the orders that the boss has put on your desk? As a boss you can't decline to do a necessary task because "bosses don't do that." And as an employee you can't say, "I won't do that because it's not in my job description." Entrepreneurs *must* wear two hats (sometimes more) on the head at the end of that stuck-out neck.

3.   Know what you're giving up before you give it up. One of the sorriest tales ever to cross my desk was that of a young man who quit his job to go into business for himself. He had been on the job for nine years and eleven months. In his fervent desire to quit he failed to pay attention to his employer's pension rules. Had he paid attention he would have known that after ten years on the job he'd have certain pension rights vested, locked in solid. If he had stayed on the job just one more month, thirty little days, he'd have had more than $10,000 worth of pension rights that he could claim some day. He learned of this too late, after he had quit. That's a steep price to pay for any new venture. That's sticking your neck out and into a noose. Any other job benefits that you'll be giving up should also be evaluated: health insurance, life insurance, expense accounts and other perks, tax-sheltered retirement plans (401ks and the like), educational grants, day

care facilities, accrued paid-vacation time, and so on. Losing these benefits should not deter you from sticking your neck out in a new venture, but if you have to replace them out of your own pocket, you must factor those costs into your overall planning.

From the time I first stuck my neck out to start my writing career, until the syndicated column took hold and began to show the promise of comfortable income, was about two years. I was doing better than average: The rule of thumb is that it take about thirty months for new business ventures to *break even*. Plan accordingly; your neck can get awfully cold and stiff if it's sticking out that long.

Chapter Thirteen

Success, the Bitch Goddess? Bitch Back!

Who, and what, determines your success? And the benefits of bitching back at those who attempt to control your fate.

Just when you thought you had reached a certain level of success, along comes someone saying, or insinuating:

* "More!"
* "I did better than that, and so can you!"
* "If you didn't show a gain of at least 10 percent, you just weren't doing your best."
* "So much for yesterday . . . what are you going to do for me today?"
* "Good . . . but not good enough!"
* "You think that's good money? You don't know good money!"
* "I don't care what *you* think. *I'll* tell you what constitutes success."

Bitch, bitch, bitch.

It could come from a parent, a spouse, a co-worker, a competitor, a boss, a lender, an investor, a partner. From whatever the source, the pain is real and the frustration searing.

Who determines your success? Someone else? Or yourself? Money is the common denominator of success in the minds of most people most of the time. Money is tangible and easy to measure. But money can also be a false indicator. There are many other criteria that can measure success: job satisfaction; the ability to have your desired allotment of free time; the creativity you're able to put forth; the pleasures you derive from the people you're working with; the development of new skills and interests; the being part of a successful team; the enjoyment you can bring to other people; the attainment of self-respect and the respect of others.

If you have only one criterion for success, such as money, and you don't achieve your specific goal in that regard, you suffer accordingly. If you set for yourself many indicia of success, shortfalls in some can be more than offset by gains in others.

If you allow *others* to *define or control* your criteria for success, you will forever be at their mercy. The more you define and control your own destiny, the more success will be within your reach.

So when you hear the bitching over what you deemed a success, bitch back. I did, and it worked.

*
**   *
    **   *
          **

My syndicated newspaper column had been circulating for almost a year, and the number of newspapers subscribing to it grew steadily, and so did my income. But the income was still far from the fully self-supporting level. I still had to scramble for other assignments while the syndication income inched upward month by month.

The steady growth of the column lulled me into a false sense of security. Every month there were a few new subscribers, and none of the papers had yet dropped my column. It came as quite a shock, then, when the *Dayton* (Ohio) *Journal Herald* canceled out on me. (For relatively unimportant columns such as mine, newspapers can usually cancel on one month's notice.)

I phoned the sales manager at the syndicate and asked if he knew the reason for the cancelation. "These things happen," was all he could tell me. He had to put up with such events on a daily basis, and had long since grown calloused to this harsh (to me) fact of life. Had I done something wrong? Had I offended some reader? Had my advice or information been incorrect? The syndicate hadn't a clue.

This was extremely important to me. If I was going to have a successful—by any standard—column, I simply had to know what could go wrong that would cause an editor to cancel me.

I took matters into my own hands, just as I had when I sent my television script directly to the producer. I phoned the editor of the canceling newspaper and asked him forthrightly, "Why did you drop my column?"

He was as cordial as a mosquito. "We did a reader survey and the results indicated that we should drop the column, sorry."

I couldn't (or didn't want to) believe that readers would have been so negative about the column. The feedback I'd been getting, albeit minimal, was that readers liked my advice and the style in which it was being delivered. So I pressed on with the editor.

"May I ask how you surveyed your readers?"

"Like we always do." More prickly now. "We stop running a feature, and if not many readers complain, we drop the feature."

This primitive, but obviously inexpensive, form of market research astonished me. I gulped before proceeding. "So you never actually got any negative feedback from readers?" I asked.

"Right," said the editor, "but if a column doesn't generate a lot of reader response, the only way we know if it's being read is by stopping it and seeing how many complaints we get."

This editor was not a man to be argued with. Further, I sensed that he likely represented the mindset of editors of hundreds of other medium and small newspapers around the country, for whom market research often consisted of flipping a coin. Was my success to depend on these whims, inklings, and notions of journalism's decision makers?

It was time to bitch back. My column ran only three times a week, which meant that it did not have the regularity and familiarity that attaches to columns that run every day. So, as the Dayton editor had indicated, I would have to find a way to generate reader mail.

This was Survival 101: How do you get newspaper readers to send you mail? You either insult them, or you offer to give them something for nothing. The latter course seemed more prudent. So I stuck my neck out yet again, in order that I might better control my success.

Since my columns were short—about 600 words—I could cover most of my subjects only superficially. And most of the subjects I covered were indeed deserving of more in-depth treatment: investments, insurance, estate planning, consumer fraud, credit and borrowing, and so on. Thus I decided to create lengthier discussions of certain important subjects and offer these longer essays to my readers.

Newspapers call them "shirt-tails": They're paragraphs at the end of a feature that say, "If you'd like more information on this subject, send a self-addressed stamped envelope to. . . ." These, I hoped, would be the means by which I would attract enough reader mail to convince editors that my column was a success.

I wrote a few extended pieces—about 2,500 words each—on some of the more important subjects and offered them *free*, in shirt-tails, to readers who sent in for them. I crossed my fingers and awaited the results.

BOOM! I had struck a mother lode. Most of the newspapers ran the shirt-tail offerings, and scores of requests came in from smaller papers, hundreds from the bigger city papers. Once a lot of readers had taken pen in hand to address the envelopes, they also took an extra moment to write a few kind words about the column. I forwarded these letters to the syndicate to show to other newspapers, and my list of subscribers began to grow at a handsome rate. That, in turn, further increased the amount of mail I was receiving.

Sooner than later, BUST! I was now spending about 90 percent of my time opening and stuffing envelopes. The cost of printing, even cheaply, the copies of the essays was exceeding my income from the column.

I had created a monster. I had wanted to be a writer, a syndicated columnist, not an envelope stuffer. If I kept things up at the current pace, my success would show: satisfied readers—millions, bank account—zero. There had to be a happy medium.

I had reached a critical juncture. If I stopped the offerings, I'd lose my proven reader pull. If I kept up the offerings, I'd soon have to be talking to a bankruptcy lawyer.

One last possibility: What if I charged, say, 25 cents for each essay? Easier said than done. The newspapers would likely refuse to continue running the shirt-tails, since that amounted to giving me free advertising. If I offered to cut the newspapers in on any revenues, they would likely resent muddying their editorial content with crass commercialism. If readers had been accustomed to getting these essays from me at no cost, I couldn't imagine that they'd now be willing to pay for them.

I had two choices: sink or swim. If I was going to go down, I'd at least go down trying. So in the next shirt-tail I asked for 25 cents plus a self-addressed stamped envelope for the newest essay. Then I crossed my fingers, and waited for the mailman.

My incoming mail *tripled* immediately. And there was a shiny quarter in each envelope. Go figure—virtually all of the newspapers ran the shirt-tail and were happy to forward the bulky parcels of quarter-laden reader letters to me. The readers who responded multiplied because "something for nothing" can't be worth much, but if you have to pay for it, it must be worth something.

The cash flow quickly reversed to the positive side. I used the first influx of money to have the booklets properly designed, illustrated, typeset, and printed, to replace the tacky photocopies of typewritten material I had been sending out. Then I created more titles, finally totaling sixteen of them. I sent out catalogs of all the titles with each order, and that generated still more income. Soon a lot of orders were coming in with dollars in them instead of quarters. And envelope stuffing became a worthwhile after-school endeavor for my two teenage daughters.

Within less than a year my income from the shirt-tails was well in excess of my income from the syndication itself. Then I learned about recycling: Once you've created something, sell it every which way you can. Each of my newspaper columns was ideal in length for a radio commentary. I was able to sell the idea to a major bank as a sponsor. My recycled columns became radio scripts, and at the end of each script I invited listeners to come into the branch offices of the bank to pick up free copies of the booklets, which I had sold to the bank in bulk quantities with their logo on the covers.

I had defined and, up to this point, controlled the criteria of my success. The income was important—mouths to feed and all that. But also important were the creation of a product (the series of booklets) in which I could take great pride, and the creation of free time to pursue other projects, which was afforded me by the income that the booklets generated.

But there was a glitch. I had known about it early on but was unable to correct it. Had I been able to correct it this radio/booklet program might have become the only project I'd ever need in order to live comfortably. The glitch was this: The offering of the free booklets was designed to bring people into the bank's 100-plus branches. Once I had accomplished that—the credible radio commentary coupled with the offer of something for nothing—it was up to the bank to turn those people into customers. To do so, each branch would have to have a controlled distribution of the booklets so that the public would have to ask for them, and give their name and address in return for the gift. That, at least, was how I thought it should work.

The bank saw it otherwise. They simply spread all the booklets out on the counters and let the public pick them up by the handful. No names, no addresses, no thank you's, no follow-up. I pleaded with the bank to organize a better system so that they could reap the benefits, but that would have involved a lot of personnel in controlling the distribution, gathering names, and so on. They were happy just to give away the booklets willy-nilly.

A key element of control had slipped out of my grasp.

Finally the end came. As inevitably happens in big corporations, committees are formed to probe the success of other committees. After a very healthy three-year run for this particular advertising campaign, the overseeing committee determined that the campaign was not generating enough new accounts. I could have done an "I-told-you-so." I would regret the sudden loss of cash flow when the project ended, but I had more intriguing things awaiting me.

*   *   *
**   **   **

Bitching back at someone who questions or controls your success can be a daunting challenge. You must meet their assertiveness with an assertiveness of your own. This can take different shapes:

* You can go head-to-head, in diplomatic fashion of course, and say, in effect, "I'm pleased to know what your criteria for success are. I have criteria of my own, thank you very much."

* You can do an end-run around their criteria, much as I did with the editor from Dayton, and prove yourself in an alternate way.

* You can simply ignore their implications. Silence can be a very powerful form of assertion if accompanied by the right demeanor: upright, forthright, and perhaps just a hint of a knowing smirk.

Your best weapon, overall, is to have realistic success criteria of your own, beyond simple dollars and cents. If you strive to define those criteria, and indeed set them, that alone might be the most valuable wisdom you'll have gained from this book.

A Most Disabling Problem

A terrifying insurance experience that can happen to anyone, and how to protect yourself.

This is a very big lesson in a very small chapter. It's important enough to stand on its own. Most simply put: If what almost happened to me ever happens to you, you might never be able to obtain any kind of life insurance, health insurance, or disability insurance. If you can obtain them, you might have to pay an exceedingly high price for them.

My writing career was proceeding quite nicely, but every penny that came in was spent quickly on the mortgage, food, car payments, braces, clothing—you know the dilemma. I was earning good money, but wasn't yet able to put anything aside. With four school-age kids, Linda Sue was totally involved with the Five Cs of full-time motherhood: Cooking, Chauffeuring, Cleaning, Counseling, and Caretaking. So all of the family income was dependent on my being able to work steadily. Without my income we had nothing to fall back on. Not yet, at least.

It was time to consider disability insurance, which would provide us with money if I became unable to work due to illness or accident. I contacted a friend who was an insurance agent to get the application process underway.

Just a few months earlier I had had a complete physical, so I knew that my health condition was excellent and there should be no reason why I'd be denied the disability coverage. As a matter of fact, I was so careful with regard to my health that at the physical I asked the doctor to do a stress EKG: That's when they strap the electrodes to your chest and have you go rapidly up and down some steps. This measures your heart function under stress. I had absolutely no heart problem, not even a hint of a hint of one. I merely wanted to create a baseline against which we could measure future EKGs, if and when the need ever arose. This had been recommended for people my age, late thirties.

My doctor was reluctant to do the stress EKG if there was no apparent physical need to. He thought it was foolish to spend the money. (That was some doctor!) I explained that I wanted it just for a baseline, for future reference, and so he went along with my whim and gave me the test. As I suspected, the results showed that I was as strong as a bull.

My insurance agent had told me that the insurance company might not require a physical exam for the policy; if anything, they might want a simple paramedic exam: vital signs, a few blood tests, and the like. Thus the agent and I were both surprised when the company asked me to undergo a stress EKG test.

Why, I wondered? The agent asked and learned that since I had had a stress EKG lately, they had reason to suspect that I might have some heart problems. (They knew of the recent EKG because I had given them my doctor's name on the application, and he had reported the facts as he knew them.)

I protested that I had the stress EKG just to get a baseline, and that I had absolutely no heart problems. The insurance company was skeptical: "No one gets a stress EKG done unless they have some problem. If you have no problem, you have nothing to hide. So take the test; we're paying for it."

Thus I agreed to take the test, which was administered by a doctor of their choice. When I went to their doctor's office I was flabbergasted at what I saw: The doctor looked like a ranch hand, except that he was wearing a white doctor coat, smudged here and there, and a lit cigarette was dangling from his mouth. He told me that he only did insurance physicals; he had no regular practice, which made me all the more suspicious of who he was, and what I was doing there.

The test was completed quickly, and I awaited the issuance of the disability policy. My agent called me a few weeks later and there was doom and gloom in his voice: "Bob," he said, "I've got bad news and worse news."

"What's the problem?" I asked, my heart all but skipping a beat awaiting his response.

"First, the bad news. The insurance company has rejected your disability policy. Now the worse news: According to the EKG that their doctor did, you have a very serious heart problem. I'm really sorry. I think you should see a heart specialist right away."

News like that could give a healthy person a heart attack. I was incredulous. This was beyond belief. I immediately called my doctor and discussed the matter with him. He got out my EKG results and reviewed them as we spoke: "My machine functions properly, and so does your heart," he reassured me. "There's something wrong with the insurance company's test. Have them send me the tracings." Since I had absolutely no symptoms of any heart problem, my doctor was certain that I would not have developed such a serious problem in the few months since he had tested me.

My insurance agent carried the ball, getting the tracings from his company's office to my doctor's office in record time. I nervously awaited the results, which came in the following week, most apologetically, from my agent.

"You're perfectly healthy. There's no problem whatsoever, except with our company doctor's EKG machine. We had it tested and found it to be defective. The tracing device was tamped down too hard on the paper, so it jerked up and down erratically instead of properly measuring your heart functions. Sorry about that. The policy will be issued without delay."

That was the easy part.

Now came the real challenge. Because I was actively writing about consumer and financial matters, I had become aware of a phenomenon that very few people knew about unless they had read the few columns I had written on the subject. Even today, twenty-plus years later, very few people outside the insurance industry are aware of it.

"It" is a big computer in Boston, Massachusetts, that is run by an organization called MIB, or Medical Information Bureau. MIB is like a credit bureau, except that it deals in medical information instead of credit information. Virtually every person who has applied for a health, life, or disability insurance policy has signed a form with some small print on it giving the insurance company the right to check out all possible sources that might reveal anything about your health condition. All the information gathered on you is reported to the MIB computer. If you have ever been granted or refused coverage, or given a high-risk rating on any health-related policy, the computer knows about it, and the reasons why.

Because my disability insurance company was quick to report its initial findings on me, the MIB computer *already* had a record that said, in effect, "Bob Rosefsky, rejected for disability policy because of serious heart condition." With that information in my file, I would never again be able to get any kind of life, health, or disability insurance. That could have been ruination for me, as it could be for you.

I got into high gear on this issue instantly, telling my insurance agent that I wanted that information expunged from my MIB file immediately, and I wanted a letter from the insurance company confirming that it had been done. I was not just being assertive. I was *demanding in no uncertain terms!* Again the agent carried the ball, and the requested letter was in my hands within two weeks.

That was the end of the story as far as I was concerned. But the story may just be beginning for many other people whose MIB files may contain damaging or outdated or erroneous information that can and should be expunged or modified. More than a few times in the intervening years I've spoken to people who've told me about their difficulty in getting health, life, or disability insurance, or in having to pay excessive premiums for same. In each case they traced their problems back to the MIB computer. For some, the problem was real and couldn't be changed. For others, like mine, the problems were correctable.

We've previously discussed errors that can appear on your credit record, and the importance of checking that record periodically. The same holds true for your MIB records. The results of having errors in that file can be more devastating than being turned down for a loan. Even if there is a governmental plan to guarantee health insurance for everyone, the problem can still exist with regard to life and disability insurance. Don't take any chances; ask an insurance agent to help you obtain information on what's in your MIB file.

By now I'm sure you've noticed two continuing threads in this narrative. One is that a lot more things can go wrong than you might ever imagine. The other is that a lot of people tell you what you can't do, when in fact you *can* do those very things if you put your mind to them. These things have happened to me, and I know they can happen to you. Being able to anticipate them and deal with them is essential to both sanity and progress. Read on. There's more.

Chapter Fifteen

Rosefsky's Rule #738b:
You Don't Ask, You Don't Get

A positive attitude to see you through the financial glitches and denials of life.

Given a world overflowing with gremlins that can make even the most carefully planned events go wrong, and given a world overpopulated with people who purport to tell you what you can't do, it makes sense to formulate a positive attitude to see you through the glitches and the denials that you'll ultimately confront.

Mine is Rosefsky's Rule #738b: "You don't ask, you don't get." Simple as that! If foul-ups and naysayers are messing up your life and your financial affairs, and you just sit back and let them get the better of you, you'll be a victim all your life. No one is going to come and make nice or say "there-there." If you want a wrong to be righted, or a naysayer to be proven wrong, you must take action. You must be assertive. You must ask for what you think is right. Even if it just means asking *yourself,* "What must I do to resolve this problem?" that's an important start. Having asked that question, answer it productively, and then go about setting the matter right. If you don't ask the right questions, you'll never get the right answers.

If things are going along fairly well and you want them to go better, you must take action. If you are content to relax with the status quo, that's your choice. If you want more, you must ask for it if you want to get it. Recall the words I quoted from George Bernard Shaw in the Introduction: "People are always blaming their circumstances for what they are. I don't believe in circumstances. The people who get on in this world are the people who get up and look for the circumstances they want, and, if they can't find them, make them." Rosefsky's Rule #738b is my version of that quote. You want to know why the rule number is 738b? Don't ask.

There's an important corollary to 738b: If you do ask, and you do get, grab whatever it is and run with it. The opportunity may never present itself again. (Needless to say, the same applies if an opportunity falls into your lap without your having asked for it: Grab it and run with it.)

Following is the tale of how I put 738b, and its corollary, to its most important use. You can do the same when the right circumstances present themselves to you.

The Ins and Outs of Writing Books

I wrote a column for my syndication on the problems people have when they move. It dealt briefly with such matters as packing, hiring a moving company versus a do-it-yourself move, and avoiding the rip-offs that can occur. Shortly after the piece had run I received a nice letter from a man who said he was a book publisher . . . sort of. He had read that particular column and suggested that it could be expanded into a full-length book. He was willing to pay me a $500 advance for a complete manuscript, plus future royalties that would be generated by sales of the book.

My sort-of publisher explained that he was really a "packager." That is, he didn't actually publish books. He contracted with authors for the writing and he developed a marketing plan and a cover design. That done, he would attempt to sell the completed package to a real publisher. This seemed to me to be on the outer fringe of legitimate publishing, but no one else had asked me to write a book, let alone pay me something to do so. I was intrigued, but skeptical.

A brief explanation of how publishing contracts work might be helpful at this point. A typical deal sets forth that the publisher will pay the author an "advance against royalties of 10 percent of the retail price of the book." Let's say that the advance amount is $10,000 and that the book will sell for $20 in the stores. The author will likely receive half the advance, $5,000, on the signing of the contract, and the other half on delivery of a satisfactory manuscript. The book is then produced at the publisher's expense. As each copy is sold to a retail buyer, $2—10 percent of the retail price—is credited against the advance. In other words, the author doesn't receive another penny until the book has sold 5,000 copies—$2 per copy times 5,000 copies equals $10,000, which is the amount of the advance. For each copy sold after the 5,000th the author will receive $2. If the book sells fewer than 5,000 copies the author generally does not have to reimburse the publisher for the difference. Through this common arrangement the author risks the time in writing the book, and the publisher risks the money in producing and marketing the finished product. And the risk is abundant for both parties.

With the foregoing in mind, I evaluated the prospect of writing a book about moving. About 10 to 15 million families move each year, and there were no other books on the subject other than little pamphlets that the moving companies hand out to prospects, so the market seemed ripe. On the other hand, the marketing prospects were not as promising. At that time American publishers were producing about 30,000 new book titles each year (not including technical books or textbooks). Today the number is closer to 50,000 titles per year. Roughly, only about one in twenty new titles turns a nice profit for the publishers. In a given year only a few hundred books will make the best-seller lists, which is where the big money is. Interestingly, it takes upward of 10 million ticket sales for a movie to attain "hit" status, but a book can make the best-seller lists with sales of 100,000 copies, sometimes even less.

On top of these foreboding odds are the facts that a typical bookstore can stock only a few thousand titles at a time, and many of those are so-called "backlist" books, steady long-term sellers such as dictionaries, cookbooks, travel books, and bibles. In a given week even the largest newspapers can review only a few dozen books, and television talk shows can interview but a handful of authors who are touring the country promoting their work.

In short, the chances are minimal of an author earning anything more than the advance. And to write a book for a $500 advance (that's about a buck for each typewritten page) one must be either certifiably insane, or willing to take a giant leap of faith that the first modest effort will eventually lead to bigger and better things. I was a bit of both.

So, here was the minefield I was preparing to cross:

1. I had to write a book that was worthy of publication.
2. My sort-of publisher then had to find a real publisher who would take it on.
3. The real publisher would have to actually publish the book. (A completed manuscript, even a brilliant one, is not assured of actual publication. A publisher can always pay off the author and decline to actually publish it if it feels that it would not be cost-effective to do so.)
4. Once published, the publisher's sales force must convince bookstores to stock it, noting that they are competing with hundreds of other publishers and tens of thousands of other titles for a few inches of space on the bookstore's shelves.
5. Facing the same competitive factors, the public must be made aware of the book, and be motivated to go to the store and actually buy it.

Not having any better offers in hand, I decided to take my chances and write the book. First I had to sign a contract, and that was an occasion for Rosefsky's Rule #738b to be invoked. I must now point out an extremely important bit of preventive medicine that you *must* put to use *any* time you're thinking of signing *any* kind of contract with *anyone*—buying or selling a house or car, performing work or having work performed for you, borrowing or lending money, or *anything* that will create *any* kind of rights or obligations that can affect you. It's this: *Any* contract that you're given to sign that has been prepared by other persons (or their lawyers) *will favor the other persons.*

If you ever sign *any* contract without having it properly evaluated, you could be like a lamb going to the sacrificial altar. Contracts are not drawn to be fair. They are drawn to favor the parties who are drawing them. You can avoid untold financial woe if you protect yourself accordingly *before you sign anything.*

With this caveat in mind I put on my lawyer's cap and invoked 738b before I signed the contract that the sort-of publisher offered me. I insisted that the following clause be inserted: "If packager should fail to obtain an acceptable deal from a legitimate publisher within six months of delivery of manuscript, then *all rights* shall revert to Rosefsky." Without that clause I'd be up the creek if he failed to perform. Of all the millions of words I've written since, those 27 may have been the most important.

This is what happened. I wrote the book. It was a good little manual that told moving families all they needed to know about the financial turmoil and trauma of moving from one place to another. I drew a blank on the title, but the packager came up with a clever one: *The Ins and Outs of Moving.* He then had a good cover design prepared.

The months began to tick by. After about three months he told me he had found a real publisher. I was elated at first, but concerned when he told me that the publisher was based in Israel. It's tough enough for United States-based publishers to get along here; I was fearful that a Tel Aviv publisher might be underqualified to sell an American-oriented consumer book in the United States. Lacking anything better I was willing to take the chance. But my concerns were shortlived: Just before the six-month reversion limit was reached the Israeli publisher went bankrupt.

My packager wanted more time to try to market the project, but I said no. I had used Rule #738b to good effect to be able to reclaim the rights to my work, and there was a lot of fuel left in 738b to take the project further.

There I sat with a completed manuscript, a good cover design, and the recollections of the $500, which had long since been spent. Timing was important: It was now late spring. Since the bulk of family moving is done in the summer months when school is out, a book on moving had to be published in the spring. If it comes out in the fall or winter, it will die on the vine. Given a normal production time of about nine months from finished manuscript to bound books, my window in time was wide open. If I could interest a publisher within the next month or two, my book could be ready in time for publication the following spring. Otherwise a whole extra year would have to pass before the timing would be right again. I didn't know how much stamina I'd have to keep after this project. Rule 738b's corollary echoed in my mind: I had asked for it, I had gotten it. Now was the time to run with it.

I next came face-to-face with another dilemma that confronts would-be authors. There is an unwritten rule in the publishing trade that states, "If you want a publisher to read your work and give it a fair chance of being considered for publication, you must submit that work to only *one publisher at a time.* That's fair enough if you're a publisher: If they like a manuscript they know they have first dibs on it. If it's a multiple submission—that is, many publishers have been shown the manuscript at the same time—then they may have to get in a bidding war for the rights, and publishers don't like that. So, exclusive submissions are proper; multiple submissions are not.

This system is not so fair if you're an author because it can take many months for each publisher to read, analyze, and decide to accept or reject a manuscript. (This is partly due to the fact that most major publishers are offered hundreds of manuscripts for each one they publish.) If you submit your manuscript exclusively to one publisher at a time, it could take *years* before it finds its way to a publisher that wants to buy it. That may not be a problem if you don't have any mouths to feed, but I did.

Shades of the little man with the big desk at the Beverly Hills talent agency who told me what I couldn't do with my television script; I counseled with myself and invoked 738b. "What's the worst thing that could happen if I made a multiple submission of *The Ins and Outs of Moving?* Would they have my citizenship revoked? No. Would they have my credit cards canceled? No. Would they read my manuscript? Maybe, maybe not."

I decided to send off a teaser—the table of contents and a few sample chapters—plus the cover design and my ideas for marketing, such as offering the book through one of the major moving companies. In the interest of honesty and integrity, the covering letter would disclose that this was a multiple submission. If they liked what they saw, wouldn't they want to move forward? What's the worst that could happen?

I submitted the package to 55—count 'em, 55—publishers at the same time. That's what you call a serious multiple submission. Within two weeks eleven had responded asking to see the full manuscript. (One out of five is not bad, I figured.) Of those eleven, six were form letters and the other five were personal letters. Targeting those five as the best prospects (and also to keep down the photocopying costs) I sent the full manuscripts to those publishers who had been considerate enough to send me personal letters.

Within another two weeks I had receieved three offers to publish the book. One contained a firm dollar amount: an advance of $3,000 from a Chicago house, Follett Publishing. The other two were sketchy as to how much they'd pay, but I didn't perceive a sense of generosity in the offers. ("We like to spend our money on advertising and promoting your book, which is why we have to keep the advance low, but it all works to your benefit in the long run." That's the language they use to convince an author to accept a piddling advance. But I'm a short-run kind of guy.)

I harkened to 738b's corollary: Take the Follett money and run. I immediately accepted their offer. Not only was my bank account tidily enhanced by a simple exchange of documents in the mail, I also was given a rare opportunity that authors seldom get: I could now send rejection letters to the other two publishers, telling them that the book had already been sold. One of those publishers, lo and behold, was McGraw-Hill—shades of Howard Hughes.

The next spring Follett did indeed publish *The Ins and Outs of Moving*. As I had expected, I didn't see another penny over the advance. The people at Follett had faith in me, which they evidenced by giving me a contract for another book, and then three more after that, each one at a higher advance than the last. But it was the one right after the moving book that made the biggest impact on my career, as you'll see in the next chapter.

Meantime, consider for your own purposes how you can put Rosefsky's Rule #738b, and its corollary, to good use for yourself. Also muse over the facts, which are no doubt true in your own life, that one thing can lead to another in an increasingly productive way, if you keep your head screwed on straight and create and/or seize opportunities as they come along. In my own case: The chance purchase of an old copy of the *1929 World Almanac* led me to meet Peter Workman. Peter introduced me to the agent, Theron Raines, who was instrumental (lucky?) in selling my syndicated column. The article on moving in the column led to a book contract, which in turn was the spark for a new dimension in my career, television.

Chapter Sixteen

I Owe, I Owe, So Off to Work I Go

When work becomes a drudgery you may want to make a change. You need the right skills and the right attitudes to see you through. Lessons from life:

✔ *A Sobering Experience*
   . . . a worst-case scenario that could have had a happier ending
✔ *And Now, Heeeeeere's Bobby*
   . . . learning that change doesn't hurt . . . it can feel good, even exhilarating, particularly with help from Johnny Carson
✔ *Skills and Attitudes, Analyzing and Evaluating*

Until you reach a point when you've stashed away enough money so that you don't have to work, you do have to work. You may have to do work that doesn't please you, for a boss who annoys you, with co-workers who spook you, and at a wage that doesn't satisfy you. Those bills have to be paid.

Perhaps you'll be more fortunate and enjoy most, if not all, of the elements of your work. Then along comes a glitch in the economy and the job you've been enjoying ceases to be. That can happen all too often in this rapidly changing world of ours.

Whatever your work situation today, it could change tomorrow, either through your own actions or the actions of others. The more flexible you are with your job skills and your attitude, the better you'll be able to change directions productively and cost-effectively.

Regarding skills: The more of them you have, and the more you know about how to put them to productive use, the easier it will be to generate income from them.

Regarding attitude: The more willing you are to explore change, the easier it will be for you to accomplish it if and when circumstances dictate the wisdom of a change.

Two stories illustrate this concept. Before I tell you of my own decidedly upbeat adventures, I first must relate a sadly downbeat tale.

A Sobering Experience

For many years Don was my best friend. We had met during high school, had caroused during college, had galavanted through Europe together for a summer, and had remained in close contact once we had settled down into our careers.

Don was a very talented writer but unfortunately had a very low rejection threshold. His first effort in the real world was to write a screenplay. That's one of the toughest sells a writer can face, particularly a novice. A mutual friend of ours who was in film production read the script and told Don he didn't think it could sell. Don was devastated. He never again tried to create anything to sell as a freelance. Instead he went into advertising as a copywriter so that he could get a regular paycheck.

Perhaps Don was overly sensitive to criticism. Though I wished that he could have allowed his talent to flourish, I certainly couldn't deny him the right to crave a regular paycheck. There was one other compelling influence: His father was a doctor, and had always wanted Don to become a doctor. When Don made it clear to his father that a career in medicine was not in the cards, his father became openly derisive of Don's occupation in advertising. "When are you going to get a real job?" was either expressed or implied in virtually every conversation Don had with his father. A job with an advertising agency may not have seemed like a real job to Don's father, but at least Don could tell his father that this was a lot more secure than freelancing.

Don's early years in advertising were quite successful. In his early thirties he had achieved a high status as copy chief for the Shell Oil account at Ogilvy and Mather, one of Madison Avenue's foremost agencies. It was through Don that I learned first-hand what the three-martini lunch was all about. Many in the advertising crowd drank heavily; it was all but part of their job description to provide liquid entertainment for clients at lunch, and often until well into the afternoon. I lunched with Don whenever I was in New York, and I was both amazed and concerned at how much alcohol he consumed. There was no way I could come close to keeping up with him and remain vertical.

I recall one particularly bizarre afternoon: We were having lunch at a nearby watering hole where many other Ogilvy and Mather people dined and drank. It was nearing three o'clock when Don urgently called for the check. He had a three o'clock meeting with the creative staff on the Shell account. One of Shell's consumer products was the No-Pest Strip: a chemical formulation that you hang in your home to repel insects. A cartoonist had drawn the ultimate bug/pest that was to be used in all the No-Pest Strip advertising, and the artwork was to be unveiled in the conference room that afternoon. Don invited me along so that I could see how decisions are made on multi-million-dollar advertising accounts for major national clients.

Five or six people from the creative staff sat in the room awaiting the cartoonist. From the conversation, and from the aroma, it was readily apparent that if the No-Pest Strip didn't incapacitate the bugs, the alcohol content of the air in the conference room would. I think I was the only one remotely near sobriety. The cartoonist arrived and, with a flourish, revealed his bug, and a mean-looking critter it was. In unison the half-dozen boozy thirty-somethings started *oohing* and *aahing:* "Wow, that's really some bug. . . . I never saw a bug like that one. . . . That's the buggiest-looking bug I ever saw. . . . Are there really bugs that look like that?" This babble went on for a minute or two, at the end of which time it appeared that the bug was unanimously approved by the assemblage, and it went on to be the poster bug for all No-Pest Strip advertising for years thereafter. What the outcome might have been if the creative staff had been sober that day one can only speculate.

Don married. Security then became a higher priority for him in a business that, he was learning, was notoriously insecure. He was tied to a major account, and if that account should leave the agency, his job could be in serious jeopardy.

The following sequence of events may come as no surprise to you: To alleviate his worrying over job security Don drank. His drinking began to affect his job performance, which in turn gave him greater cause for worry. That prompted him to drink still more—the consummate vicious circle.

I was hoping that there was still time to break the downward spiral when Don came to me urgently. He expressed fear that his days at the advertising agency might be numbered, and he thought he should begin to look for a job with another agency. I suggested that the insecurity of the advertising agency business was at the very core of his problem. If he could find a more secure situation, he might be able to give up the booze and get back on a steady track. Even if it meant taking a cut in pay, it could be worth making such a change.

"But I'm an advertising agency person. That's what I know," Don protested.

"You know advertising. And that knowledge, and those skills, can be put to use in places other than advertising agencies," I suggested.

"Such as?" he asked.

"Such as working on the in-house side of the advertising process . . . working for the advertiser instead of the agency . . . working, for example, for Shell Oil instead of Ogilvy and Mather. The advertiser may change agencies, but they will keep on advertising. If you're in-house, helping to develop the advertising ideas that the agency then brings to fruition, you'll still be working even if your company changes agencies."

Don couldn't grasp the concept. To him, the in-house people were the ones he had to lock horns with. They questioned his ideas. They asked for changes in the work that Don and his creative team had done. They had to be pleased, and sometimes pleasing those people meant kissing butt. They were, in a sense, the enemy, and Don couldn't bring himself to even give serious thought to making such a change.

Time ran out. Don's drinking reached a critical level. He was told to shape up or get out. His family life deteriorated. He switched to another agency that was willing to take a chance on him. He stayed with them long enough for his group life insurance policy to become incontestible, no matter what the cause of death. Then Don took his life.

Later, when the grief and the anger had subsided, I realized that my counsel to change jobs was probably far too late to matter. Other friends had offered similar counsel, and we all had to admit that we didn't realize how seriously the drinking had impaired Don. But the underlying lesson that I was trying to impart was valid: Don certainly could have put his skills to use in a productive and less stressful situation. And the course of his life could have been altered drastically.

Don's lesson is a severe one. You may never find yourself in such a worst-case scenario, particularly if you let Don's case serve as a subconscious reminder.

Analyze your own skills, those well in hand and those that you can acquire using the existing ones as a foundation. Analyze all the ways in which those skills can be put to use. Analyze your attitude with respect to your willingness to *explore* change, and your capacity to *make* change. It costs nothing to ask these questions of yourself. And remember: you don't ask, you don't get.

And Now . . . Heeeeere's Bobby!

I had already made one major career change. I gave up law and banking, and used the skills and knowledge I had obtained in those endeavors as the foundation for my writing activities. I had thus already learned one of the most important lessons about change: it doesn't hurt. As matter of fact, it can make you feel good, even exhilarated. I was programmed now to accept more change, and it came about in a way I never would have expected.

After the *Ins and Outs of Moving* was published Follett asked me to do another book for them on a subject of my choosing. I was delighted with the opportunity and quickly outlined a book on the exploits of my con man creation, Snake Oil Sam. As earlier chapters in this book will attest, I had long been fascinated with the curious flaws in human nature that let us be swindled so easily and so often. In the few years that I'd been writing the newspaper column I had focused frequently on swindlers and their methods, as well as on swindlees and their vulnerability.

The title of the book came easily: *Frauds, Swindles, and Rackets.* That was it, plain and simple. Perhaps the most intriguing part of my research—and the most fun to write about—was becoming an intentional victim of a number of scams, particularly in the mail-order category. I sent away a lot of good money to dozens of questionable mail-order offerings so that I could learn first-hand just what kind of games were played on the minds of the victims. It was money well spent. You can tell a story so much better when the events have actually happened to you.

Here's just a quick smattering to give you an idea of the ripoffs I encountered:

* Earn money at home in your spare time addressing envelopes. For my ten dollars I received a packet of envelopes with instructions on how to address them. I was then to approach local businesses and offer to address their envelopes, which, I was told, I could do more cost-effectively than their mass-mail addressing machines could.

* Earn money at home in your spare time making baby booties. For another ten dollars I received a kit that consisted of a few pieces of felt, some yarn, and instructions on how to assemble them as baby booties. I was promised that the company would buy the finished booties back from me for fifteen dollars. They told me there was no limit on how much profit I could earn as long as I kept turning out baby booties. When I sent them my finished pair they responded that my work was not up to their standards. They were very sorry, but if I wanted to send them another ten dollars, they would send me another kit, and I could try again.

* Earn big money from your baby's photograph. This purported to be a magazine consisting of pictures of beautiful infants, from which Hollywood directors and major advertising agencies chose baby models for their films and commercials. The babies' parents could thus reap a fortune on the fees their toddlers would earn. I sent them a picture of my cousin Herb, who was then about thirty, tipped the scales at well over 200 pounds, and in the photo looked like he was in the middle of an indigestion attack. APPROVED FOR PUBLICATION was stamped in big red letters on the form they sent back to me. All I had to do to assure publication was to send them $12.95. Hollywood directors and advertising people I checked with had never heard of such a publication. The fact that they would approve a picture of Herb for publication was proof enough of their scam.

* Songwriters wanted . . . earn big money by having your song published. I wrote an intentionally atrocious song to see if it could be published, and I sent it to three of these outfits. If they would publish this song, I figured, they're certainly not legitimate music publishers. Decide for yourself. Here are the lyrics, exactly as I submitted them:

Ethel Is My Only Love

(Sing Slowly)
Oh oh oh oh Ethel
Ethel Ethel will you be my blessing
Cuz when I look at you and sigh,
It makes me feel high. Oh me oh my.
It seems like only yesterday that we were in high
    school together.
I can't believe how old we are now, forever.
Oh oh oh oh Ethel
I feel just lousy without you.
You are my only love—not Rita anymore.
Seriously, I mean it.
Oh oh Ethel. Yeah, yeah, yeah.

This drivel was accepted not once, not twice, but by all three of the "publishers" to whom I sent it. Here's one of the responses I received:

Dear Mr. Rosefsky:
    We have good news for you! Your song has been rated #5 on our top 30 evaluation chart. We sincerely believe that your song poem, with the proper servicing, has the potential for a hit song. We have already contacted nearby publishers, and the response to it was positive. Publishers' acceptance seems assured. If you have as much faith in your song as we have, you'll want to take advantage of our offer.

Their offer was to provide "servicing" for my lyrics if I sent them $80 to $90. The next step after that would be to pay them $200 to $300 for complete scoring and orchestration. From then on there was no limit as to how much money I could send them for making, distributing, and promoting my hit.

That's not how hit songs are made. Do not try this yourself at home.

All of these gambits, and more, were set forth in the book. Next came the long wait until publication, during which time we discussed ways of promoting the book. Follett was a smallish publisher based in Chicago, so they were not high in the consciousness of the New York and Los Angeles major media outlets—the television talk shows, the popular magazines, and the like. I was a Phoenix-based writer, little known except in those cities where my newspaper column appeared. The promotional budget was pretty skimpy, so Follett had to proceed with great caution to get any mileage out of their marketing money.

This was the plan they worked out: Since I was close to the West Coast they would concentrate their efforts with a media blitz in San Francisco and Los Angeles. If this effort seemed to generate sales of the book in those cities, they'd proceed eastward. They hired a Los Angeles–based publicist whose job was to get me maximum media exposure.

No sooner was the book off the presses than I was on my way to San Francisco, where I had three busy days of radio, television, and newspaper interviews. It quickly became apparent that the aspects of the book the interviewers liked most were the Bob-as-intentional-victim segments. By the time I left San Francisco I had recited *Ethel Is My Only Love* so many times that I was beginning to think maybe it *was* a good song.

In Los Angeles the publicist showed me my schedule, and one chunk of time stood out above all the others: a preshow interview for Johnny Carson's *Tonight Show*. The publicist made it clear to me that this was nothing more than an initial screening process that dozens of potential guests went through, and from which only one or two might be chosen to actually appear on the show. It was quite a coup just to get to this preshow interview stage, but no one would ever see it, and so it couldn't sell even a single copy of the book.

On the last day of my three-day Los Angeles tour—and I remember distinctly that it was a Wednesday—I went to my *Tonight Show* "tryout." Paul Block, one of the talent coordinators for the show, was to interview me. He was quite pleasant, very show-biz in his blue jeans and open-neck shirt, contrasting with me in my guest-interview blue blazer and necktie. For the first few minutes we chatted jovially about my promotional trip to date, about my work, my family, and the writing of the book. He was clearly putting me at ease . . . quietly, gently, soothingly relaxing me.

Then the interrogation began. In rapid fire, Paul asked me about some of the most subtle aspects of the book. He had clearly done his homework, a rare treat compared with the all-too-common interviewers who don't open the book until you're there on the set with them. Paul had me recite *Ethel*, he examined the sample baby booties and the picture of Herb that I had brought along. He probed and poked looking for holes, for inconsistencies. This was no longer an interview; it was becoming a cross-examination, an inquisition.

Fortunately the publicist had not scheduled anything after this interview, for it went on for three hours! I had been on debating teams; I had been on mock court teams in law school; I had been a lawyer in court and a negotiator in some tough business deals involving very large sums of money. But I had never gone through a grilling like Paul Block gave me that day.

When it finally ended Paul smiled warmly and said that he liked what he had seen. He apologized for putting me through the paces, but he had to determine if I'd fold under pressure—the pressure that comes from being on national television, on the most popular late-night show in the history of television. I thanked him for the opportunity to prove myself, and he responded, almost as an afterthought, that maybe there was a chance, a slim chance, that in six months or so he might be able to get me on the show. Don't call us, we'll call you.

There were no inflated expectations this time. I was too exhausted, plus it seemed like such a remote possibility that I wouldn't let myself get tempted by it. That was Wednesday. Copies of *Frauds* . . . were in a scattering of stores on the West Coast; the bulk of the print run was still in the warehouse awaiting shipping orders. It can take two weeks and longer for books to get from the shipping dock of the warehouse to individual stores. Then it can take another week or two before the stores unwrap the cartons and put the books on the shelves for the public to see. Wednesday . . . my quick West Coast media blitz was done, and I awaited further instructions.

On Friday afternoon my telephone rang. It was Paul Block. He asked me if I could return to Los Angeles on Monday to tape the *Tonight Show*, which would air on Tuesday. (This was in 1973. A few years later they changed their scheduling so that shows aired on the same day they were taped.)

Could I be in L.A. again on Monday to tape the *Tonight Show?* Just a minute . . . let me check my schedule. Yes, it looks like I can make it. Thanks for the call. Have a nice weekend.

After I had scooped my brains back into my skull I called the publisher in Chicago, catching them just minutes before closing time.

"I'M GOING TO BE ON THE *TONIGHT SHOW* NEXT TUESDAY!!! HOW SOON CAN YOU SHIP BOOKS ALL ACROSS THE COUNTRY???"

The sad bad news was that there was no way they could get the books even moving before Monday morning. Worse, they hadn't really solicited orders yet from most eastern stores. They were waiting for the results of the West Coast promotion before they started hustling in the East. You can't send books to a store until they've ordered them. But that wasn't going to stop me from being on the *Tonight Show.*

What had caused this sudden interest in having me on the show? As Paul Block—who to this day is a dear friend—told me later, he had been responsible for booking a certain guest on Thursday night, and that guest had bombed. It was Uri Geller, the magician/psychic who supposedly could bend spoons with his mind. Only the spoon didn't bend while they were taping his segment, and everyone came off looking foolish. At the production meeting on Friday morning Carson told Paul, in words to this effect: "If you ever bring me another act like that, you're history!"

Paul knew that Carson had a soft spot for tomfoolery, and he felt that I could tell my scam stories in such a way as to make up for the Geller goof. Paul told Johnny, "I've got a guy who's written a book that you're really going to like. It's titled *Frauds, Swindles and Rackets.*" Johnny said, "Let's go for it."

There I was, on national television, promoting a book that Johnny Carson raved about, and there was not a single copy of it in any store in the United States outside of California.

We had a rollicking good time. I showed the picture of my chubby cousin Herb. And I showed the baby booties. And Johnny, the man himself, recited *Ethel Is My Only Love* to the delight of his legions of viewers.

And deep down inside I cried, and the people at Follett cried, because this publicity of incalculable value would not generate even one penny's worth of revenue for our efforts.

When my segment with Johnny was ending he said, "Come back *again* real soon."

Three days later Paul Block called me *again* to have me on the show once more the following week. Two whiz-bang appearances on the *Tonight Show* in the space of nine days.

And there still were no books in the stores. Grown men called out for their mommies in the executive offices of Follett Publishing Company in Chicago.

Skills and Attitudes, Analyzing and Evaluating

I obviously was doing something right. Though I had had no meaningful broadcasting experience, I seemed to have a knack for it that offered promise. Yes, I had done the radio commentaries for the bank, but in my mind that wasn't really broadcasting. It was just another way to market my writing, the booklets. I began to think about making a major shift from the print media to the broadcast media.

My exposure on the *Tonight Show* paid off, but not in book sales. I went on to do a total of about ten appearances for them over the next two years, and that led to numerous invitations to appear on other shows. I became a semiregular on Dinah Shore's national talk show and Kathy Crosby's San Francisco–based show. (I met Bing one day after a taping, during which I had discussed IRA plans. He was very sweet: In his inimitable croony voice, this man with a gazillion dollars told me that he liked my ideas, and he said "Some day I'm going to get myself one of those IRAs.") I also had a number of appearances on the *Merv Griffen Show*.

Doing these guest spots involved my flying out of Phoenix. All of the talent coordinators I worked with told me that if I lived in Los Angeles they could use me a lot more. That was promising, very promising.

I found myself ready to do what I've suggested to you. I was ready to analyze my skills and the ways they could be put to use. I was ready to analyze my attitude with respect to my willingness to explore change and my capacity to make change.

The simplest underlying facts I had to consider were the following. You might find my analytical format helpful to you should you ever deliberate over similar issues. Note well also that all of these areas interweave. None of them exists in a vacuum.

*   As to financial matters, my two oldest children, Debbie and Michelle, were at or near their mid-teen years. College was not far off. College costs a lot of money. No sooner would the girls be nearing the end of their college years when the boys, Adam and Josh, would be ready to start. Income possibilities from broadcasting were vastly greater than they were from print. In order to tap into the big bucks I would have to be in a major market, such as Los Angeles, New York, or Chicago. Phoenix was strictly minor league by comparison.

*   As to personal matters, I wasn't ready to uproot my family. Living in Los Angeles, New York, or Chicago was not appealing. Commuting from Phoenix to do the guest spots was getting wearying, and I knew that I couldn't generate the income by commuting from Phoenix that I could if I lived in one of those major markets.

*   As to creative matters, I puzzled over making the switch from print to broadcasting. In a sense I initially thought along the same lines that Don had: I'm a print person. That's what I do. Writers write. They don't blather to a camera. Besides, the broadcast people are our competitors. How could I jump ship and go over to the other side? Silly thinking . . . I quickly resolved my puzzlement by recognizing that whether I was putting ink onto paper or magnetic impulses onto a tape, I was still essentially involved in the same creative process. The medium was different, but the use of my brain was the same.

*   As to working conditions, I knew that I had to remain a freelance. I was never meant to be a clock puncher. I shrivel in a corporate environment. I needed to retain the personal freedoms that freelancing offers (and I was able to deal with the uncertainties that it imposes). I knew that I could maintain that pattern if I stuck with print. I suspected that I'd have to give it up somewhat if I switched to broadcasting, if for no other reason than that you can't broadcast when you feel like it; you do so on their schedule, at their studio, on their terms.

These were the issues I wrestled with as I analyzed how best to put my skills to work, and how receptive I and the family could be to change. There was no rush to decide. Time was on our side, and I knew that alot of time was needed to properly evaluate all of these matters. We're talking about major life changes for a family of six people.

After months of analyzing and evaluating, the final impetus for change came suddenly and unexpectedly as a result of one peculiar human trait that we all have but don't always trust: intuition. I had decided that I wanted to try to make the change, but the sticking point was where I would do it—stay in Phoenix or move? I knew that I had to give it a try for at least a year, but L.A., New York, and Chicago still failed to beckon.

I was literally soaking in a hot shower when the intuition struck: London! They speak English over there. They have all the major media. Linda Sue and I had long been Anglophiles and we adored the city itself. What an adventure it would be for the kids to spend a year living abroad! (Note an important bit of vocabulary here: Intuition should not be confused with impulse. Intuition, as I use the term, arises from a reasoned evaluation of appropriate factors, while impulse arises from an unreasoned response to often inappropriate factors.)

It took Linda Sue between two and three seconds to agree with my proposal. Once we had decided, it then took a full year to get our affairs in order before we embarked on what was to be the most glorious single year our family ever experienced.

The skills were there. The attitudes were receptive. We were ready for an experiment in change. I know the results of having taken this giant step. I can't fathom how I might have felt if I had declined to take the step. I would have hated to dwell for the rest of my life on "what might have been." Think about that if you ever find yourself at the same crossroads.

Chapter Seventeen

The Bigger They Are, the Harder You Fall

Is bigger better? Pros and cons of big versus small companies for you as an investor, an employee, a customer, a lender, a supplier. And when all is said and done, who really can take the best care of you?

There's a parade going down the street and a crowd has gathered to watch it. You stand on a little footstool to get a better view. If you should stumble off it you might get some bumps or bruises. It's worth taking the chance.

If instead you bring a six-foot ladder you're well above the crowd and the view is exhilarating. You've got the best vantage point in town. But if you fall off the big ladder amidst the jostling crowd you could break a limb. Is it worth taking the chance?

Is bigger better?

Whether you're a customer, an investor, an employee, or a supplier, are your financial concerns better looked after by a bigger company than they would be by a smaller company? Does the big company offer you better potential because it has the assets:

* To do the best research?
* To allow it to take solid defensive positions if threatened?
* To protect and enhance its status in the competitive market-place?
* To do whatever it can to safeguard your interests?

Or does bigness mean:

* That you're dealing with a bloated dim-witted slow-moving dinosaur that can't keep up the competitive pace?
* That you're constantly getting lost in their giant computer, along with their thousands of other customers, investors, employees, and suppliers?
* That instead of being able to talk to a human being you're always being directed through a telephone labyrinth until you end up on someone's voicemail, if you haven't been cut off or marooned on hold in the meantime?
* That your potential is stifled because there are too many executives and too many committees in gridlock with each other resulting in nothing new ever getting done?

We all must make decisions about dealing with other entities. There is a predisposition to think that bigger equates with wiser, safer, stronger, and richer. That leads people to want to associate with bigness. But as history shows, that can be a mistake. Many mighty giants have been humbled, and as they are humbled so are their customers, investors, employees, and suppliers.

General Motors, the world's largest industrial corporation, saw its share of the market slip from about 45 percent to near 30 percent. Hundreds of thousands lost their jobs.

IBM, at one time the world's most profitable corporation, got clobbered by swifter, smarter, smaller competitors. Its stock plunged from over 100 dollars to 40 dollars per share in less than one year.

Once-mighty banks, thinking that they could not make mistakes, indeed made hundreds of millions of dollars' worth of bad loans, and then got gobbled up by healthier competitors. Thus was the fate of Manufacturers Hanover in New York and Security Pacific in California, both previously among the nation's most powerful financial institutions.

Olympia and York, mentioned in Chapter 8, was once the world's biggest landlord until it bit off more than it could chew in London and ended up in bankruptcy.

Macy's Department Stores, in good company with many of the nation's other largest retailers, overexpanded and couldn't pay the price—bankrupt.

The list goes on and on. Of course, many other big companies are healthy and dynamic. The point is that bigness does not offer immunity from bad times. If you're involved with a biggie when it falls—as a customer, investor, employee, or supplier—you can end up not with bumps or bruises, but with some serious fractures.

In *any* involvement, whether with a big or small entity, you must always be prepared for trouble. You must always ask the questions, "What's the downside? . . . What will be my backup position if this flounders or fails? . . . How will I get along if the income I'm expecting from this venture is cut off or sharply reduced?" Because *Big* often instills a false sense of security, that's all the more reason to ask these questions when you deal with *Big*.

Having asked the questions, develop plausible answers upon which you can take action. Despite these negative aspects I'm asking you to explore, you should, nevertheless, think and act positively about the venture. Just cover your butt.

*   *   *
**   **   **

The following story illustrates how a lot of people relied on *Big* and got hurt. The list of casualties ranged from beginners to well-established front-runners in their professions.

In the early 1970s the ABC television network (*Big*) had very little to offer viewers in the early part of weekday mornings, 7 A.M. to 9 A.M. NBC's *Today* show, which had been a success almost since the invention of television, had the lion's share of that audience. CBS's news-oriented programming grabbed most of what was left. All of the networks coveted that audience because it was mostly housewives whose spending habits made advertisers salivate.

ABC decided to have a run at the *Today* show. They figured they could put on a better program and snatch a large audience away from the competition. If they were to do this, they would have to do it right, right from the start. To do it right they would have to have the best market research that *Big Money* can buy; market research that would be so exacting, so insightful, so accurate that when the program finally went on the air it could not help but be a winner.

From the uppermost corporate levels ABC committed itself to spend a reported $8 million (*Big*) to research and launch the *definitive* breakfast-time TV program. The press was filled with reports about this daunting challenge that ABC was throwing out to its rivals.

ABC's research would reveal exactly what Mr. and Mrs. (mainly

Mrs.) America wanted to watch during those hours, and the end result would be spoon-fed along with the cereal to the audience. The research would tell them how many anchors there should be, and what sex, color, size, vocal qualities, background skills, and Q factor they should have. (The Q factor is television's way of measuring the personality quotient of on-air people. The higher your Q factor, so it's said, the bigger your paycheck.)

What about specialists? The research would reveal whether or not the show should have a weather person, a cooking person, a pet care person, a film reviewer, a financial advisor, a political commentator, a sports announcer, and so on. Again, what sex, color, size, hairstyle, and Q factor should these people have?

Then, what about the set? Homey or businesslike? Primary colors or pastel shades? Sofas or chairs? Desks or tables? Flowers or books on the desks or tables?

The research would also help them reach decisions on the myriad graphic elements of a television show. What should the show's logo look like? What should be the motif for the "bumpers," which are the visuals that pop onto the screen for a few seconds between segments, such as when they cut from live action to a commercial. And on and on . . . all of this was researched down to the most minute elements.

Once the research was done and the perfect show created, the network committed itself to keeping it on the air for *at least a couple of years*. That kind of commitment was felt to be necessary in order to build long-term momentum, and in order to attract all the needed talent who would have to change existing careers to take a chance on a new show—even if the show was being ballyhooed as a sure-thing slam-dunk. This was *Big* at its best.

The show was called *A.M. America* and it debuted in early 1975. It was, according to $8 million worth of market research, the perfect answer to what all of America wanted to watch on television at that time of day. The anchors were Bill Beutel, a handsome and respected newsman from New York, and Stephanie Edwards, a bright, vivacious, and attractive TV personality from Los Angeles. John Lindsay, erstwhile mayor of New York and a most articulate and telegenic spokesman, did political commentary. Frank Gifford, hunk and former football hero, did sports. Dr. Tim Johnson was the medical specialist. The names of the cooking, weather, pet, and movie persons escape my memory. I was the financial commentator.

This opportunity came my way during the earliest phase of our going-to-London planning. Since I knew that the London adventure was at least a year or more away, I felt that I could take a stab at this TV venture. If *A.M. America* was a raging success, I could always (though reluctantly) put the London plans on hold. If I wasn't happy doing the show, I could bow out in order to make the move to London. As it turned out, the decision was made for me.

Doing the show was not a day at the beach for me. I commuted from Phoenix to New York once each month for three days. I'd fly in on Sunday and, due to the time change, I'd have to awaken in the middle of the night—by my body time—to be at the studio by 6 A.M. New York time on Monday. This was cause for terminal jet lag. I would do live broadcasts for the first three days of the week, then tape a number of others to be broadcast later in the month. It was a grueling commute, but the money was excellent and I didn't have to give up anything else I was working on. But I digress. This is not my story. It's ABC's.

The morning of the debut was indeed tense and exciting. The entire cast plus numerous well-wishers crowded the studio to watch us take our stab at making television history. Optimism filled the air. This was, in its time and place, the biggest launch of a new daily program ever to be done by one of the big networks.

The morning of the second day was even more tense because the "overnights" (a relatively unscientific sampling of the viewership of the previous day) had come in and were being anxiously studied by all. Horrors! Would you believe that in the very first broadcast of *A.M. America* we did *not* beat the *Today* show in the ratings?

Indeed, our audience was so far *below* everyone's inflated expectations that doom and gloom began to pervade the set. By the third day, still lagging far behind our seasoned and well-entrenched competition, rumors began to circulate that the show might be canceled.

"Come on," said the optimists, "the network has sunk $8 million into this project and they've committed to run it for *at least a couple of years*. You can't expect to be Number One overnight! It takes time to build an audience. All the right research has been done. We're doing everything right. Be patient!"

In the weeks and months that followed some ominous signs appeared that everything wasn't being done right. One small but telling point had to do with our news updates, which took place every half-hour. The bumpers that came on before and after these updates showed newspaper stands and close-ups of newspaper headlines. Wait a minute. Newspapers are our competitors. Why should we introduce *our* product—the news updates—by showing our audience our *competitor's* products? Aren't we thereby saying that the *real* news is what you read in the papers, and we're just sort of being copycats? Isn't that self-defeating? Doesn't that, subtly but steadily, undermine our credibility?

Another telling flaw developed from the policy of prescreening guests or, better put, failing to prescreen guests. As the *Tonight Show* people had learned long before, and as I had learned from them, a proper prescreening is a prerequisite to successful guest interviews. And if a guest interview isn't flowing smoothly, you risk losing viewers.

If my own case was any indication, a proper prescreening could take hours. At that early stage of *A.M. America*'s existence, it did not have the clout to convince desired guests to take a few hours out of their busy days to be prescreened. And, it appeared, there was not enough staff on the show to conduct proper prescreenings.

One particularly painful example of this prescreening dilemma was the case of Dr. Alex Comfort. He was the author of a best-selling book called *The Joy of Sex*. The written words in the book were not particularly titillating, but the publisher had included many drawings of people in very candid sexual poses, and that was presumably what had helped to sell so many copies of the book.

Dr. Comfort was on the grueling mission known as an author's tour, and guesting on TV shows was one of the necessary evils of helping to sell books. Having done so myself, I knew that the grind was indeed wearying, often involving late-night talk shows followed by all too few hours of sleep to waken in time for early-morning shows such as ours.

A.M. America's dilemma on this particular morning was that they could not show drawings from the book on TV, so they had to interview the author. Dr. Comfort, in addition to obvious fatigue, was simply not a good TV talk show guest. He was nervous. He muttered and mumbled. He chewed on the end of a pipe. For those of us in the studio, watching the segment was painful. We could hear television sets all across the land switching to another channel.

Why did this happen? The producer told me that Dr. Comfort's book was so popular, and the show was so happy to get him on the air, that he had *not* been prescreened.

Mistakes and bad judgment calls and glitches and boring segments began to add up, and viewers began to lose interest as the initial hype wore off. Advertisers got antsy because the show wasn't delivering the numbers of viewers that had been promised. Executives at the network got restless waiting for the ratings numbers that would justify the $8 million that had been spent (or wasted, as some were no doubt beginning to think). Down on the set, producers and anchors and specialists and camera operators and stagehands and makeup artists and writers and production assistants got nervous and moody and irritable as it began to appear that their venture with *Big* may be collapsing.

This was *Big's* reaction: Barely six months after the show had debuted (not "a couple of years") Bill Beutel went into his office at the show's production facilities one Monday morning. As I was told, he immediately noticed that his secretary's desk was missing . . . so was his secretary. When he inquired as to the missing person and her furniture he was told, "You won't be needing them any longer."

All the other personnel were told in comparably abrupt fashion that the show was henceforth canceled. What about the network's commitment to run the show for *at least a couple of years?* They had changed their mind. *A.M. America* was an $8 million roll of the dice that crapped out.

Almost immediately ABC mounted a new morning show called *Good Morning America.* All of the costly research was thrown out, along with most of the staff, and new decisions were based, as I heard, on gut instinct and ego power. David Hartman was the new host; he was not the product of the market research, but it turned out that he had the right chemistry. All of the specialists were replaced except for Dr. Tim Johnson, who was still in residence last I looked. *Good Morning America* has been a long-term success, and it became that when, it appears, the Big bosses threw our their formula for surefire success.

Scores of people had been involved in *A.M. America,* and for many of them the swift cancelation caused severe disruptions in their careers, not to mention in their moods. People who work in television know that this is an occupational hazard, but that doesn't take away the pain, loss of income, and depression that can so often occur.

This type of treatment is not the sole province of *Big* companies. Smaller ones can be just as abrupt and uncaring, but *Big* can get away with it more easily. And certainly this doesn't necessarily mean that ABC or its peers behave in this way all the time.

There is one powerful underlying lesson to all of this that I implore you to remember: Whether big or small, old or new, there is no company, there is no union, there is no government that will take better care of you than you can yourself. This lesson will echo throughout other tales in this book, and throughout many incidents in your own life.

Chapter Eighteen

Quid Pro Quo

Who's scratching whose back? Legal lessons on contractual fundamentals that affect your money.

✔ *The PC and Me*
    . . . where carefully laid paper trails can lead you
✔ *Eviction Time*
    . . . asserting your rights

Quid pro quo is Latin. It means, in essence, one thing in return for another. I'll scratch your back if you scratch mine. *Quid pro quo* is the heart and soul of contractual relationships. It's what one party will do in exchange for what the other party will do: paying money, doing work, deeding property, allowing someone to use (rent) something that belongs to you, and so on. Lawyers call it "consideration."

With few exceptions, all the money you will ever acquire comes to you as a result of contracts, either expressly written and signed, or implied by mutual consent. Your paycheck, interest or dividends you earn on investments, profits you generate in your business or in speculating, your pension plans—all these kinds of income are generated as a result of one form of contract or another.

Most people pay very little attention to most of the details in most of the contracts they enter into. By blind luck, good faith, trustworthy human nature, and an array of consumer protection laws, most people don't run into too many problems with most of these dealings.

And most people cringe at the thought of paying a lawyer a few hundred dollars an hour to make sure they don't run into too many problems with their dealings.

There are two major areas in which you can take steps to protect and enhance your financial interests that arise from contracts. You don't necessarily need a lawyer, though if there's enough at stake it can pay to use a lawyer. These two areas are:

* creating a paper trail to validate your position when you enter into a transaction; and
* moving assertively to protect your rights when they are threatened.

I experienced both of these situations during my year in London. Perhaps you'll be able to adopt my strategies to suit your own needs.

The PC and Me

The age of the personal computer was dawning in 1976. IBM had developed their 5500 machine, which, though primitive by today's standards, could be lifted by one person and could occupy a space no larger than the top of a card table. As part of a national promotion, IBM invited a number of journalists, myself among them, to a two-day seminar in Denver where the concept of computing was explained by a man who had a genius for making the complexities understandable. It was a most enlightening conference, and though I had no particular knack for computing, I did feel that it was a subject that deserved the public's attention. In not many years, it was clear, the computer would become a popular and competitive consumer product.

That initial contact with the IBM public relations people led me to do some further homework. IBM let me try a 5500 machine so that I could get the feel of it, and very quickly I found myself asking alot of questions as to how this machine worked. What was the art or the science that let it do what it could do? I know, you don't have to know how to make a watch in order to find out what time it is. But my curiosity impelled me to want to know the inner workings of computers. I felt that if I could understand what made them tick, I'd be better equipped to put one to productive use.

If I could learn about and understand the workings of computers, I could write a book explaining them to other people who were as computer-illiterate as I was. Voila! Wouldn't it be in the interests of IBM to help generate a book that could educate the millions of potential buyers of personal computers? Of course it would. And so I approached IBM's public relations people with the idea.

I knew that it would be a tough sell for me. Though I had a track record writing financial books, I was an unknown in the field of computer books, and no publisher would risk any kind of advance money on a novice in a highly specialized field. IBM wouldn't be interested in helping fund the writing of a book unless there was a publisher willing to actually publish and market it once it was written. Further, publishers shy away from books when there is any kind of commercial backing from an outside source. Finally, I knew that I couldn't undertake the research and writing of such a book unless I had at least $10,000 to $15,000 guaranteed up front from whatever sources I could find.

I was able to get the following *informal* agreement from IBM: If I could get a firm contract with a reputable publisher, they would give me a grant of $10,000 as their contribution toward the project. When it came to putting this into writing, however, they balked. "Trust us," was their response. IBM? What's not to trust?

I recalled the words of a friend: "Trust everyone . . . but always cut the cards just in case." With that in mind I put on my lawyer's hat and wrote a letter to IBM that set forth the terms of what we had agreed upon informally. This, in a sense, is like the sound of one hand clapping: You can't create a two-party contract of this sort simply by unilaterally setting forth the terms of a spoken agreement. But it's the start of a paper trail that, given the right circumstances, can legally enhance one's position.

This happened shortly before we moved to London. I had plenty of other work on my plate, so the computer project was not compelling. Shortly after our arrival in London I went to a computer trade show where a new product from a quaintly named small new company, Apple, was being exhibited. Here, indeed, was the prototype for the personal computer that would soon dazzle the world. If upstart Apple had such a product, how long could it be before the Great Leader, IBM, would enter the market and intimidate all other pretenders to the throne? (It would be years, we'd later learn, much to the detriment and shame of IBM.)

This spurred me on to find a publisher for my book, and I did so quickly. An American publisher had recently taken over a British firm, Paddington Press, and they were flush with money from a hit book,

The White Lions of Timbavati. They were eager to sign a contract with me, realizing that IBM was interested in the project and that I could thus get by with a small advance—$2,000—from them.

I then sent letter #2 to IBM, telling them that in accordance with our agreement I had found a publisher, and that, *acting in reliance on their offer* to provide a $10,000 grant, I was going to forego other work to concentrate on writing the book. I suggested that they notify me directly if my plans were not in accord with their thinking.

I waited a few weeks and, having received no response from them, I signed the contract with the publisher. Then I sent letter #3 to Big Blue, stating that *acting in reliance on their offer,* and *having received no indications from them to the contrary,* I had signed the publishing contract to proceed with the book, and was giving up other work accordingly.

Why was I doing this? On a hunch that IBM might balk about paying me the grant, I wanted to lay a paper trail that, if not an actual contract, could constitute enough of a contractual environment to give me at least a sound arguing point. If IBM had responded to my letters by killing the deal, I wouldn't have had a leg to stand on.

My hunch was correct. IBM said that they would not pay the grant money. Taking IBM and its deep pockets to court was out of the question. I couldn't have even afforded the opening round of lawyer letters. Plus, I was in London, and that's a long way from the American courts that would have jurisdiction over such a matter.

I had to rely on my paper trail, which I had laid down knowing that there is a principle in contractual law that gives you some firm legal footing if you are:

A.   *acting in reliance* on the promises of another party,

and

B.   *the other party knows that you are doing so.*

In such a case, it becomes difficult for the other party to escape doing what they've promised you. This is particularly so if the other party, knowing what you're doing in reliance on their promises, has not attempted to stop you from doing so.

Having the law on your side, which I did, is one thing. Convincing a multi-billion-dollar international corporation of that fact is something else again.

This was a time when, as The Gambler said, you've got to know when to hold, and know when to fold 'em. I had a strong hand but a weak bankroll. IBM had the reverse. Thus far I had not spent the advance money I had gotten from the publisher, but I had begun to invest a great amount of time in the book, time that I could have spent more profitably elsewhere.

I was determined to play my hand. I had contact with some upper-echelon IBM people from my former days in the Binghamton area, where IBM had had some of its executive offices. I told my story, backed up by the documentation. My story fell on ears that were cognizant of the legal implications, compassionate, and aware that this could be a petty but annoying embarrassment for the company. Speaking of petty, the money was certainly petty cash for them. I got my check in short order and proceeded to write the book. But the book was never published. The publisher and I had creative differences, and before we could resolve them they went out of business.

Lessons: No matter how trivial a dealing, if there are dollars or rights involved, put *something* in writing to the other party to express your understanding of it. Naturally, it's best to have both parties agree in writing to the terms of any agreement. But if the other party doesn't sign it, at least you've established some of the boundaries of the relationship, and you can put the other party on notice to reject those boundaries; failure to do so can have some legally binding effect on the other party. You can use words to this effect: "Unless I hear from you to the contrary by return mail, I'm going to do such-and-such." Then, if you don't hear, you at least have some semblance of an argument that well could prevail in small claims court, if not in courts of higher jurisdiction.

Please don't misunderstand. There's certainly no assurance that even the best-laid paper trail will provide you with victory in a legal bout. But without one you're much more certain to go down to defeat. What have you got to lose?

Eviction Time

The other area in which you can take steps to protect yourself involves moving assertively when your rights are jeopardized. I mean *assertively.* That's what I had to do, and even though I'm a softie at heart, it was amazing how tough I became when there was a lot of money at stake.

We had rented out our house in Phoenix so that we could afford to rent a house in London. Unfortunately, we didn't find a tenant until the final days before we were scheduled to leave Phoenix, so I didn't have the opportunity to meet the prospective tenants. In all the years I have been involved in real estate, particularly as a landlord, one of the prime rules of life has been: Meet your prospective tenants personally. While their credit history is more telling of their actual financial performance, there's something about an eyeball-to-eyeball meeting that gives you an incomparable sense (intuition?) about whether these people will be good tenants or bad tenants.

These people had only a fair credit history. I might have turned them down if time was not so much of the essence. We had our plane reservations set (for six people) and my rent started on the London house whether we were living there or not. So it was with reluctance, combined with the need for the money, that I agreed to the rental.

There were no problems for the first few months. The rent checks arrived on time. Then they started to slow down. By the fifth month I had to call our realtor to shake out the rent. The tenants told the realtor that they'd been having some problems, and asked if I would bear with them if they were late in the coming months. I said I would not. I felt that with our distance from Phoenix, and my need for their rental check to pay my own rent, I had no leeway. I simply insisted that they pay the rent on time or get out. I told them that I would not accept any lateness.

No rent check came in the sixth month. The realtor suggested that I be lenient and give them a few extra weeks. It would be tough, the realtor said, to find new tenants if I kicked these out. The realtor also told me that the wife loved the house so dearly that she'd hate to have to leave, and that she, the wife, had some money of her own stashed away. That was good information.

I didn't budge. I called my lawyer in Phoenix and told him to draft and serve eviction papers by the next day.

"Gee, Bob, you're being awfully tough," he said to me.

"No, Joe, I'm just asserting my rights." I confess to you now that it hurt to say that; it hurt to do that. I didn't want to act that way, but I'd have been in a pickle if I played the patsy. Plus, I reasoned, what if the tenants are just calling my bluff? Debtors—and maybe you've done this yourself at times—will pick and choose which creditors to favor when they're in a bind. Well, despite the guilt I felt about being so harsh, I just couldn't afford to be the Stiffed-Creditor-of-the-Month.

Within a day after serving the eviction papers the rent check was in my attorney's hands. The wife had dipped into her own funds, rather than lose the house. And for the rest of the year the checks came in on time.

I've seen, and been involved in, countless cases of people chasing ineffectively after their rights and their money. Certainly there's room for compassion and understanding and mercy and forgiveness when some people can't deliver what they're obliged to deliver. Only you can gauge how much of those human virtues to display when you're put to the test, given each set of circumstances.

As with the laying of a paper trail, so it is with being assertive about pursuing your rights: There's no guarantee that being assertive will bring about the desired results. But by not being assertive you certainly increase the chances of not achieving your desired results.

Chapter Nineteen

Decisions, Decisions

Guidelines to help you make some of the tough financial choices, and how they worked for me.

✔ *Reviving a Dead Horse.* It may be worth the effort to try

✔ *Changing Horses in Midstream.* This too can pay off (with luck and good timing)

It was Harry's ninety-fifth birthday. The doorbell rang at his apartment in the retirement home. Harry's eyes bulged as he opened the door: There stood a beautiful young woman, seductively dressed.

"Hello Harry," she cooed. "Happy Birthday. Your friends all chipped in and paid me to help you celebrate the day with some supersex."

"For me?" Harry asked incredulously. "Supersex? For me?"

"Yes, Harry. Your wish is my command. Supersex, just for you."

"That's wonderful," Harry replied instantly. "But listen, it's only 11:30. That's a little early for me. Come back at noon . . . I'll take the soup."

*
**   *
**   *
**

Sometimes our decisions are made for us by nature. Sometimes finances force us to make up our minds. We must always be careful to recognize those forces over which we have no control. It can be counterproductive to battle against some of the hard realities of life.

As our year in London was nearing an end, I had to face the hard reality that the flow of income from my American sources was about to dry up. The whole family would have loved to remain in London for another year, maybe even longer. I had definitely made up my mind, based on our experiences there, that I was ready to make the move into broadcasting.

I had two choices. First, we could stay in London and I could scramble for work in the British media. But that was very chancy. The British economy was rotten, and the pay for any writing or broadcasting work was so low that we'd have trouble surviving. (Little did I know then that in another year Margaret Thatcher would become Prime Minister, and that she would start a revival of free enterprise that featured, among many things, a sharp increase in income for writers and broadcasters. If I had only known. . . .)

Second, we could return to Phoenix temporarily and prepare for a move at the earliest possible time to Los Angeles, which, I had decided, was the best choice of the major American markets in which to peddle my wares.

Unlike Harry, I agonized for weeks over the decision. I—we— really did want to stay in London. It was exciting, stimulating, adventuresome. But college expenses were looming just around the corner, and if I stayed away from my United States media contacts much longer, I'd soon become another forgotten face. This was not a time to take uncalculated risks, seductive as the prospects might have been. Like Harry, I took the soup. In late August of 1978 we arrived back in Phoenix. By December we had contracted to buy a house in Los Angeles, and in June of 1979 we moved there.

I had played my cards well, and the timing also helped. This was the tag end of the Carter years. The United States' economy was being buffeted by gasoline shortages and seemingly uncontrollable inflation, and the media were anxious to find people who could explain all of this to the public, and help them deal with it. Once again I found myself in the right place at the right time, and with the right skills. I was able to land a position on the evening news on CBS's local Los Angeles TV station. I went into the studio twice a week to do live commentaries, and while there I would tape two additional ones to be used on other days. For this I was paid $35,000 per year. That was more than double what I had been making from my column when I gave it up before we moved to London.

I also was hired by ABC's Los Angeles radio station, which had an all-talk format, to do a three-hour phone-in show every Sunday evening. This paid another $20,000 per year. This gave me a comfortable base income and a couple of spare days each week to do with as I pleased. My career as a broadcast "money advisor" was underway, and

I was on a roll. In Chapter 23 I'll review the most common financial concerns of the thousands of people who phoned me during the ensuing years, and what I advised them.

* * *
** ** **

Financial health or illness usually hinges on decision-making moments. Those moments can often be critical, with life-altering potential. The most major decisions can include investing (which ones to choose, as well as when to get in and out); employment (taking or leaving a position, or making a career change); housing (what to buy or rent, when, and at what cost); insurance (how much, and from whom); retirement and estate planning (what type, and with what kind of advisor or institution).

Herewith is a simple checklist of important things to consider when you are faced with momentous financial (and related) decisions. Some of these items also applied in the sticking-your-neck-out guidelines in Chapter 12. There's no guarantee, of course, that these tips will set you on the exactly *right* course. But if you *don't* exercise the judgments called for, you're more likely to make the *wrong* decisions.

1.   Evaluate your expectations. Are they realistic and attainable? Have you arrived at them through the dangerous processes of selective listening or selective reading, wherein you take in only the information that you want to take in?

2.   Project the best and worst scenarios, the ultimate upside and the ultimate downside. These are, in a sense, extensions of your expectations, but viewed in the harsh light of reality, not wishful thinking. Could you get along if the worst case came to pass? What would be your escape route if that did happen? Are the risks of the worst case worth the rewards of the best case? Another slant on this is to consider the *cost/benefit ratio:* Will the cost of taking this action generate enough benefits to make the action worthwhile?

3.   Set limits, whenever feasible, as part of the making of the decision. This can work especially well in the investment arena. Set limits as to what type of investments you will and will not consider. Set limits as to when you can alter the above ground rules. Example: Limit A—I will not invest in stocks/bonds/mutual funds unless they generate a range of such-and-such income. Limit B—I will not amend Limit A unless and until my total investment portfolio reaches a level of XXX

dollars, at which time I will allow ZZZ dollars to be put into more speculative ventures, defined as follows . . .

Set limits as to when you will bail out of a given investment. One of the questions I've been asked most frequently over the years is, "I bought XYZ stock at $70 per share. It's now $50 (or $90) per share, should I sell?" My answer: "Knowing what you know about the stock, would you, at today's price, *buy* more shares? If you wouldn't be willing to buy more shares, why keep the ones you have? Sell them. If, though, you *would* buy more shares at today's price, why sell the ones you now own? Maybe you should buy more." (See Rosefsky's Law of Investment Dynamics in Chapter 23.)

4.   Evaluate the advice you're getting, and evaluate the agenda of the people who are giving you the advice. What, if anything, do they stand to gain as a result of the decision they're suggesting you make? It needn't be just monetary gain that skews their advice—see the discussion in Chapter 6 on this subject.

5.   Evaluate all of the alternatives that may be available, some of which might not be obvious unless you do some negotiating. For example: Could you buy the property for less if you had a bigger down payment, or agreed to an earlier closing date, or eliminated some of the contingencies that you might have wanted? Could you get the loan on better terms if you provided a co-signer or collateral? Could you get the job at higher pay if you agreed to take fewer leave days, or could you get the more important title (if that's what you wanted) if you agreed to accept a lower pay, or fewer perks? Would this anticipated investment or venture turn out better for you if you waited a bit before you took the plunge? What's to be gained or lost if you delayed signing the final papers? Quite obviously, Rosefsky's Rule #738b kicks in here frequently.

6.   Evaluate how much you're acting on intuition and how much on impulse. As noted in Chapter 16, I define intuition as a result of a reasoned evaluation of appropriate factors, and impulse as an action arising from an unreasoned response to often inappropriate factors. Oh, what a difference that can make in reaching a sound decision.

*   *   *
** ** **

In the course of the next two years I was faced with two momentous decisions. I took my own advice, and the decisions came out right.

Reviving a Dead Horse

Yes, it can be done. A few years before we moved to London I was approached by an editor of a company that published college textbooks. His name was Gary DeWalt and the publisher was John Wiley & Sons, the same company that published this book. Gary offered me a most intriguing opportunity. Would I be interested in writing a college textbook on personal finance? And once the book was done, would I be interested in creating and hosting an educational television series based on the textbook? Gary had been a reader of my newspaper column and had seen me numerous times on television, and he felt I had all the necessary skills to develop both products successfully.

I was looking at a mountain of work and an anthill of money, but the appeal of long-term royalties—as they were described—was irresistible. Successful textbooks, revised every few years, can go on for decades. This is a far cry from the typical "trade" book, the kind you buy in regular bookstores, which, unless they hit the best-seller list, are gone and forgotten in a matter of months. I agreed to do both projects. The textbook was published and the telecourse began airing while I was living in London, so I didn't get any feedback on either until I returned to Phoenix.

The textbook was a disaster. It was poorly written and poorly marketed. It was clear that it would not survive even into a second year, let alone a second edition. The telecourse was weak, but it had a chance of surviving as a second-rate offering for a few years. It had been produced on a shoestring budget, and it looked that way.

I kissed them both goodbye. Why, you may ask, as I asked myself, was the textbook so off the mark? In the development of a textbook there are a number of quality control inspections that are supposed to catch and eliminate any shortcomings. A panel of five professors in the field of personal finance were well paid to scrutinize my work every step of the way. Wiley's own editorial people had hands on the project, and conferred with me on anything they thought might be a problem. I myself, with four other books already under my belt, should have known better how to structure the material in the proper way. But we were all wrong.

Thus it is with so many business ventures: The developers are too close to their project to see the flaws. Pat and Fran have a fantastic idea for a new restaurant. Bankers and family and friends are willing to lend them money, or in many cases *give* them money, to back the project. The landlord is willing to rent them space—space that he otherwise might have rented to a more proven venture. Suppliers are willing to extend credit so that Pat and Fran can buy equipment and furniture and food and booze. The local newspaper proudly announces the grand opening, with photos and a glowing article from their restaurant reviewer. Then, six months later, the place folds. With so much support, how could such a venture fail?

Look back over the list of supporters and you'll quickly realize that everyone expected to get something out of the deal. The banker would earn interest. The investors would make profits. The landlord would get his rent. The suppliers would generate future business. The newspaper would get advertising dollars. And all of them would be on the priority list for the best tables whenever they asked. Everyone hoped to gain. No one was *objective*. Pat and Fran got swept up in the enthusiasm, mistaking that enthusiasm as approval.

The caveat is worth noting yet again: When people are supporting your interests, you must discern what their agendas are if you want to know the true value of their support.

But I digress. The textbook was dead. And without the textbook the telecourse would languish. Then, in 1981, along came Len Kruk. Len replaced Gary at the publishing company, and he set about reviewing all of the books that had been published under Gary's tenure. Len telephoned me out of the blue and said, "I know your textbook was a failure, but there's a good book in there if you're willing to do a complete rewrite."

If I did rewrite the book, the entire telecourse would also have to be restructured if it was to remain compatible with the new text. Would the television people be willing to spend a ton of money to reshoot the entire course if I was willing to rewrite all the scripts and host all of the programs? Yes, they were.

Now I was looking at a mammoth decision: Did I want to climb that same mountain of work again for a similar anthill of money? I examined the criteria I set forth earlier in this chapter.

1. My expectations were now much more realistic. I had been clobbered once, and the pain had been particularly sharp because I had envisioned luscious rewards. If I made this new effort, I knew that the rewards would be modest, but more attainable.

2. The worst-case scenario was another total flop. I had survived one, and I could survive another. The best-case scenario, realistically,

would be a moderately successful book and telecourse that would survive many years, throwing off pleasant royalties, but nothing to retire on.

3.   I set strict limits as to my writing and production television schedules. I could do the bulk of the work during those extra days in the week when I wasn't doing my local radio and television appearances. If all the work could be done within the tight constraints I required of the publisher and television producer, I could live with it. They both agreed to do so.

4.   I evaluated the advice I was getting, which was primarily from Len. I knew that he was aiming for a winner, as Gary had been. But Gary had been caught up in the television side of the project; he was a visionary who foresaw the day when much of our education would come via the relatively inexpensive means of television instead of the much more costly live classroom format. As such, Gary's involvement in the book, the linchpin of the whole project, was diluted. Len had more of a financial background than Gary and promised that he would ride herd on me during the writing of the book. He was content to leave the television to the television people. All of this told me that we were on the right track.

5.   I evaluated the alternative, which, simply, was to not do the project at all. The first failed effort had given me a taste of how good it can feel to provide education to people who seek it. Money was not an issue in this specific deliberation. I wanted more of that good feeling.

6.   Finally, I examined the intuition and impulse aspects. Impulse had prompted me to pursue the first effort. This time I gave my intuition free rein, and it showed me a green light.

As I write this, almost eighteen years since I first was contacted by Gary DeWalt, I'm gearing up for the sixth edition of the textbook. It's now one of the best-selling texts in the field, and the royalties are more than just pleasant. The new version of the telecourse won an Emmy as Best Instructional Series, and it is distributed nationally by PBS. I had made a sound decision.

Changing Horses in Midstream

Yes, you can do that too. The other major decision during this period didn't require as much keen analysis. I was, as noted, working for the

CBS television station and the ABC radio station in Los Angeles. This was a very weird situation. The rivalry among all the broadcast outlets was fierce, and to be working for competing entities was an extremely unusual arrangement. Station management liked to have all of their "talent" within their grasp, and managers would do wild and crazy things to keep their rivals from stealing their on-air people.

I would have been happy to consider doing my radio work on the CBS station, but they didn't have the all-talk format. The other option was to switch from the CBS televison news to the ABC side. Or, I could just stay put; I had no particular urge to make a change.

Then one day the general manager at the ABC radio station, George Green, told me, "The fellows over at our TV station would like to talk to you when your contract is over at CBS."

When that day arrived in late 1982 I paid a visit to Dennis Swanson, then station manager at KABC-TV, and he asked me how much I was making with CBS. I told him. Then he did a very wild and crazy thing. "We'll double it," he said. When I could get my jaw back into its socket I asked where I should sign.

That decision swiftly reached, I went on to enjoy close to six years with ABC TV, continuing with their radio station as well, until the time came to move on to other things. More on that later.

By the way, keep this little incident in the back of your mind if you're ever perplexed about whether you can progress more by staying with one company, or by jumping ship and moving to another.

Chapter Twenty

A Chemistry Lesson

What can make a business relationship work, or fail?
Of entrepreneurs and corporate folks.

I don't know which is more challenging to the participants: a marriage relationship or a business relationship. In both cases the partners will have disputes about their money, about their location and the decor thereof, about how they present themselves to the public, about which social friends/clientele they should be seeking, about how to deal with their children/employees, about maintaining ties with their in-laws/investors, about their plans for the future, and more.

On the more positive side, marriage partners share a bed; business partners share a bank account. Everyone has their own priorities on those matters.

At the core foundation of both relationships is something called "chemistry." If there's a certain magical combination of attitudes and personalities and abilities, you've got a winner. But with bad chemistry, both types of partnerships can be hell. And both can be equally difficult—in terms of cost, aggravation, and energy—to terminate.

The Wisdom of the Ages dictates to us that the real chemistry in a budding marital relationship is all too often obscured by glandular considerations. Once the hormones have done their work and the picture clears, the couple finds to their horror that the chemistry is not right.

Similarly, the real chemistry in a budding business relationship is all too often obscured by greed. Once the partners find that the money is not rolling in, the real chemistry between them appears, and toxic reactions become commonplace.

In both situations you could identify inflated expectations as underlying causes of the eventual troubles.

The manual has yet to be written on how to guarantee successful couplings in either matrimony or business. Sometimes, it's thought, similarities between the partners—educational, religious, financial backgrounds, and so on—help assure success. But there are abundant cases in which happy partners are very diverse in all relevant aspects.

During my early period in Los Angeles I had one ill-fated business partnership that defied the odds. Steve A. and I had enough similarities and enough differences between us to satisfy any challenges. But neither destiny nor chemistry was on our side.

Steve and I had gone to high school and college together. We had not been close buddies, but there was always a fine and cordial friendship between us. Steve was very involved in athletics; indeed, he was a football, basketball, and baseball star in high school, and his repute stayed with him through college. I was more the bookish type: school magazine editor, literary club, that sort of thing. Steve had been president of our class in high school: This was a function of popularity, not politics. I had been the class jester.

Steve and I had been out of touch for twenty years, building our careers and families in Honolulu and Binghamton/Phoenix, respectively. Then fate, and a common friend from our school days, brought us together again in Los Angeles in 1980. Steve had been a top financial officer in a couple of large corporations and was looking for a new challenge. He seemed to have corporate burnout. I, as you've read, was about to dip my feet into the corporate world of the broadcast media, but still had chunks of time during each week that I could devote to other ventures.

Steve and I talked at length about our common interests in finance. Though his was at the corporate level and mine was at the individual level, there were many laws and concepts that applied similarly to both levels. One thing led to another and we soon found ourselves talking about forming a consulting partnership to give people and small companies financial advice.

I had done some private consulting over the years but I never really liked it very much. People sought me out because of my media exposure, and they were willing to pay for my counsel. I enjoyed the "diagnosis" stage: evaluating the problems and proposing general solutions. But I didn't like the number-crunching side: figuring yields and spreadsheet projections and future-value-of-money calculations. And, even though it could have meant substantial income, I didn't like the prospect of doing all the follow-through work (or even farming it out) that clients invariably asked for with regard to tax returns, estate planning and other legal documentation, and management of investments.

Steve, on the other hand, seemed to have a knack for all of that. He could schmooze with lawyers and accountants and stock brokers and property managers about all the odds and ends that need to be schmoozed over. He was comfortable with the number-crunching, or delegating it to someone else.

In short, it seemed to be a fine pairing: I would be Mr. Outside, with my media exposure bringing in clientele and my diagnostic knack setting the agenda for action. Steve would be Mr. Inside, doing the number-crunching and having the needed liaisons with the other professionals.

Thus our partnership was born. Alas, it was to be short lived. In hindsight, here are the factors that I think caused our failure. First, we went overboard on our location. We discussed this all-important element most thoroughly, and made our decision jointly. No arms were twisted. Our basic choice was to go for posh or to set up with a modest overhead. We chose posh. We found an office in the fancy business area of Los Angeles known as Century City, home to countless lawyers, accountants, insurance people, and all those other professionals with whom we'd presumably be doing business. The office was elegant, and would certainly impress our clients and colleagues. It was more than we realistically could afford, but we felt it was necessary to make the statement that the office would make for us. Further, Steve would be spending almost all of his time there, whereas I'd be out and about more. So he had to feel comfortable.

We started to feel the pinch of the office expense when we began to discuss how we would advertise ourselves. To our detriment, we had been so anxious to get into the new office that we didn't give adequate consideration to the other single biggest expense item: self-promotion. Not until after we had made our commitment to our landlord did we get to work evaluating advertising costs. We found that we didn't have enough in our kitty to do the necessary promotion.

Yes, you're right, we should have hired some good financial advisors to give us the guidance we needed to become good financial advisors.

Despite our similarities in education and skills, and despite our valuable differences in attitude (the Mr. Inside/Mr. Outside mix) there was one deep-seated divergence that we didn't become aware of until it was too late. That was, you could say, a cultural difference. I was a lone-wolf entrepreneurial creature and Steve was a corporate creature. We had each been in these respective modes for many years. The ruts ran deep. The habits were ingrained. This does not mean to suggest that corporate people aren't entrepreneurial, or vice versa. We were just of the more incorrigible sort of each type, and we didn't realize it until after the honeymoon.

Certainly those two types can blend harmoniously, and perhaps have done so more often than not. But that wasn't going to be the case with Steve and me. I sensed it early on and, with regret, couldn't shake the nagging doubts about our potential for longevity.

Our judgments regarding the office could be considered strategic. With hard work we could have overcome the financial jam that our expensive office had caused. But our failure to blend cultures was chemical: Nothing that I could foresee at the time could have corrected the chemical imbalance between our styles of doing business. This was a basic flaw in the structure.

Thus within a few months of its birth our partnership was disbanded. Financial obligations were met. Friendships were strained. Lessons were learned.

It's impossible to distill hard-and-fast rules about human relationships from these experiences. Perhaps all that can be said with assurance is that all people who enter into a relationship (business or any other kind) bring their own baggage along with them. The more you can explore what's in each other's baggage—including the dirty laundry—the better you'll be able to predict the potential for success. And if the other person doesn't want his or her baggage examined, maybe you ought to think about seeking another partner.

Chapter Twenty-one

Got You Covered?

Will your employer stand behind you through thick? Or only through thin?

The question is simple, yet rarely asked, and even more rarely answered:

* If you were performing some aspect of your work, and an action of yours caused harm or loss to another person, who would be responsible for such damages? Would your employer stand behind you? Or would you be left alone flapping in the breeze to fend for yourself? And further, how would such an event affect the future of your employment?

* On the flip side, someone else could cause you harm or loss in a workplace situation. Who can/should you look to for redress? An employee, who might be ill-equipped to put the matter right? Or the employer, whose deep pockets and/or insurance can easily reimburse you?

Technically, legally, there's no easy answer. It all depends on circumstances. There can be situations in which you're performing your work properly, as instructed, and something freaky goes wrong causing harm or loss to another. It's probable, in such a case, that your employer bears the brunt of liability. But if he denies it and pushes it off onto you, can you fight his deep pockets? There are other situations in which a worker's neglect causes harm or loss to another. That can mean that the liability for the damages falls on the worker's shoulders; it could also be grounds for termination.

We live in a very litigious age. There are attorneys out there who will start lawsuits if someone blinks wrong. Even groundless suits can cost thousands of dollars just to get rid of the nuisance. And some employers will leap at the chance to get rid of an employee (and further be able to cut off their pension, medical, and other benefits) even if the cause is an otherwise excusable oversight.

The more you know about your employer's policies and predilections the more you can protect yourself, either through a personal service contract that defines the issues, or through an agreement between your union and your employer.

I sweated out an incident that was indeed tragic. While I was with the CBS television station in Los Angeles I did a week-long series on the evening news titled "Mail-Order Madness." It was a follow-up to the book I had written on frauds some years earlier. In the series I sent money away in response to various mail-order offerings to test what consumers might confront if they were lured in by the ads.

I scheduled an interview with a man who had some notoriety in the field. His name was Joe Karbo, and his fame had come about as a result of a number of full-page ads he had placed in newspapers and magazines all across the nation. The banner headline across the ads read, "The Lazy Man's Way to Riches," below which was a photo of a man laying lazily in a hammock enjoying a tall cold drink.

The ad went on at great length to explain how its author, Karbo, had gotten rich, and how you could do the same if you bought the book he had written. The book had the same title as the ad, and it instructed you, in a nutshell, to put full-page ads in newspapers offering buyers a book that would tell them how to get rich by putting full-page ads in newspapers offering buyers a book . . . and so on.

It was ludicrous. It was almost silly. But it worked incredibly well, and the money came rolling in. To keep the whole matter squeaky clean Karbo offered a full refund—which he honored—to anyone who was not 100 percent satisfied. But, he said, the number of people requesting refunds was very tiny.

I visited his operation in nearby Orange County, and I saw a booming mail-order business in books and pamphlets, all originating from the initial come-on of "The Lazy Man's Way to Riches."

We adjourned to his sumptuous house near the beach and, sitting on his patio, we began the interview. Karbo and I sat just a few feet apart, facing each other, with the TV camera over my back facing him. He was a most friendly guy, willing to answer my questions frankly. I had always considered myself a gentle interviewer—having been interviewed myself so many times I avoided the confrontational approach that can be so mean-spirited and, ultimately, unproductive.

I was probing the quirk in human nature that prompts so many people to respond to a clever but empty ad, and then, when finding the product of little value, failing to request the no-strings-attached refund that was offered.

I never got an answer. Karbo looked at me strangely and raised his hand suddenly to his chest. His eyes bugged out, he gasped for breath and pitched forward onto the ground. It all happened so fast that the cameraman didn't react by stopping the tape. It was all recorded.

When the cameraman realized what had happened he ran to the fallen Karbo and attempted to give him CPR. But it was too late. He had had a massive heart attack, and when the paramedics arrived minutes later they said that he had probably been dead before he hit the ground.

I sat speechless for minutes. All of this had seemingly occured in response to a question I had asked him. That, at least, is how it registered in my mind.

Later, as I tremulously drove back to the television studio in Los Angeles, the lawyer segment of my brain kicked into gear: Wrongful Death! Despite the fact that I was utterly blameless—the man had simply had a fatal heart attack coincidentally as I was chatting with him—I became paranoid over the possibility that the family would sue me for causing his death, and CBS would tell me to go fly a kite! Even though I was acting properly within the guidelines of my profession, thus deflecting personal liability, it would cost me all I was worth to force CBS to defend me, and it would cost me more than I was worth to defend myself against such a claim. Was I ruined in my new career just months after it had begun?

Needless to say I, and the staff at CBS, were terribly distraught over the poor fellow's sudden passing. There was nothing we could do other than express our condolences.

I broached the subject to the station manager of a possible wrongful death action against the station and its employees. I was told not to worry. That was easier said than done.

Days and weeks and months went by, and the incident finally drifted off into deep background. My contract with CBS was silent on the subject, as were my subsequent contracts with ABC. It's a very delicate subject to broach with a contracting party, but these facts must be looked at squarely:

* If your work involves any physical interaction with another party, there is a risk of harm to both parties.
* If your work involves any financial interaction with another party, there is a risk of loss to both parties.

Personal liability arising out of nonwork situations can be easily covered by insurance, such as the public liability provisions of your auto and homeowner's policies. And you can obtain "umbrella liability" protection that will greatly increase the limits of your liability coverage in nonwork situations. For hundreds of dollars per year you can obtain millions of dollars' worth of such protection.

But liability claims—either by you or against you—arising out of employment situations are another matter entirely. Evaluate the risks you face; discuss them with your employer or union, and seek the best assurances of protection that the other parties are able to give. Yet again, Rosefsky's Rule #738b: You Don't Ask, You Don't Get.

Talk-Radio

Behind the scenes of radio call-in shows, and how I got there myself.
✔ Would you invest in a BOB CD?

This chapter will set the stage for our review of the most common financial plights that came to my attention from the public during my years as an on-air money advisor. But first I must tell you of a plight that I myself faced.

I vividly recall an incident involving Johnny Carson that convinced me that I never wanted to become famous. I was flying from Phoenix to Los Angeles on a Sunday evening in the mid-1970s. Having plenty of time to spare at the airport I went into the airline's private club lounge, of which I was a member. There sat Carson and his wife. Having recently been a guest on his show a number of times, I had no qualms about greeting him and having a brief chat. He was most cordial, as he always had been with me.

When the flight was called he waited in the lounge until the last possible moment, obviously not wanting to be mobbed by fans. Then he boarded and took his seat in the first-class section.

On arrival in Los Angeles he was the first one off the plane, and he must have had some secret way of getting to the terminal exit, for I didn't see him again until I found myself standing next to him at the curb. I was hailing a taxi; he was waiting for his limo.

It took only a few seconds for the public to recognize him, and just as his limo was pulling up a crowd began to swarm around him. People were shouting "Hi Johnny" and shoving notepads in his face for autographs. Some fans were tugging on his jacket and putting their hands on his back and shoulders to get him to recognize them.

Somehow he maintained his composure and even managed a smile, but it was quite evident that he didn't appreciate being mobbed and manhandled. He had to push his way through the throng to get into the limo. Then, once he was seated, people began slapping on the window and yelling even louder for recognition. This went on for about 15 to 20 seconds until the limo could pull out of the loading lane and into the moving traffic.

It was sickening. Well-intended though the people were their behavior was uncivil if not downright rude. I felt guilty that I had intruded on his privacy at the Phoenix airport, even though I knew him. I pitied him. To not be able to go out in public peaceably is a high price to pay for celebrity. I would never want that for myself.

The price I *did* pay was of a different sort. I was never mobbed or manhandled or asked for an autograph. People simply asked me for financial advice, whenever and wherever they happened to see me. Once I had become a regular on the evening television news in Los Angeles there was no escaping what I call the "Recognition Bug-eyes." It's unmistakable: People see someone who looks familiar, and at first glance they're not sure who it is. Then they suddenly realize it's someone they see *on television.* Their eyes sort of bug out and their mouth curls up in a peculiar little smile, and they stare with a sort of "gotcha" look for what seems an interminable amount of time.

Many will speak.

"You're Bob Rosphzowfski, right?"

"Right."

"Channel seven, right?"

"Right."

"Financial stuff, right?"

"Right."

"I thought so." Then, turning to a nearby companion or stranger, "That's Bob Rezfrejski, channel seven news. . . ."

Many leave it at that. Some will be more bold, no matter what the circumstances, approaching earnestly and saying, "Say, I've got a question for you. There's this mutual fund I've been reading about. . . ."

While I always tried to be as cordial as possible, and while I sincerely appreciated the good wishes and kind words most folks extended to me, I really did have a tough time handling intrusions when I was in a captive situation, such as when seated in a restaurant. I needed a defense—some bit of banter that would be goodhearted but could imply to questioners that they were being a bit pesty.

Most of the questions were of the "What should I do with my money?" variety. The defense that I devised worked like a charm. It went like this:

"You want to know what you should do with your money? You should give it to me. I'll give you a BOB CD (certificate of deposit), and that's the best investment you can make. Here's why. With a BOB CD *you* decide what interest rate you want to earn. And *you* decide whether you want the interest you earn to be taxable or tax-free. Not only that, I'll give you a personally signed guarantee. When you put your money in a bank CD all you get is federal insurance. They don't give you a personally signed guarantee. But with a BOB CD you get my personally signed guarantee, which says 'If you are ever unsatisfied with what I'm doing with your money, just let me know and I'll immediately return the unused portion to you.' All you have to do is telephone me at a toll-free 24-hour-a-day number: Just dial 1–800–BOB. . . ."

With rare exception the message came through loud and clear, and my questioners departed with smiles on their faces.

The BOB CD also illustrated how gullible some people can be. One night on my phone-in radio show I decided to tell my listeners about how the BOB CD helped me deal with people who interrupted my meals with their questions. I prefaced my story by saying that what I was about tell them was a joke and that there was no such thing as a BOB CD.

When I finished the tale there were callers waiting on the switchboard wanting to find out how they could get a BOB CD, and in the following week I received a number of letters at the radio station seeking the same information. No wonder Snake Oil Sam is so successful at conning folks.

*
**   *
**   *
**

The radio phone-in show on KABC was my main source of rapport with the public. My other radio and television exposure helped immensely in building the audience.

I averaged twenty to twenty-five calls during each three-hour weekly program. That calculates out to about 10,000 questions and answers over the nine years that I did the program.

I was curious as to how much money people were seeking my advice about. Over a period of many weeks I kept a tally, noting the amount inquired about in each call: "I have so much to invest. . . . I'm thinking about getting an insurance policy for so much. . . . I'm trying to collect so much that my deadbeat brother-in-law owes me. . . . I'm trying to get a home loan for so much. . . ." The average total per week was $1.6 million! I did periodic follow-up tallies over the subsequent years and the average remained in the same range: between $1.5 and $2 million per week.

Why would people telephone a complete stranger and divulge to him—and to the average 110,000 other listeners who were tuned in—financial information that they wouldn't dare mention to their closest friends or family? There were a number of reasons:

1.   Callers were completely anonymous. Only first names were used, and if the callers chose to use a false first name, that was their privilege.

2.   The station itself lent enormous credibility to all of its on-air people. For most of the nine years I worked there KABC was the top-rated station in greater Los Angeles (out of eighty-four stations). That meant that it had the biggest audience in virtually all adult age groups and at all times of the day and night. It was the pioneer station in all-talk radio; it had earned its laurels by maintaining the highest-quality broadcasting service for many years. Listenership covered a radius of roughly sixty miles, with a population of upward of 14 million.

3.   My exposure on television—both the news and the educational series—added to my credentials and credibiity.

4.   Perhaps the single most tangible factor that instilled trust in my listeners was a simple remark that I repeated frequently during the broadcasts: "I'm not selling anything." Listeners knew that I had no axes to grind, no products or services to tout, no gains to be reaped from any advice I gave or comment I made. The station was paying me enough; I didn't have to pander my position to generate more income, which in turn would have compromised my objectivity. I never diverged from these standards. (That included never reading commercials for financial products or services; I felt that doing so might have implied to listeners that I was indirectly endorsing the sponsor.)

Some details about the workings of a phone-in radio show will help you see the whole picture. As was typical at KABC during those years, I worked with an engineer and a screener, each of whom occupied a booth adjoining the broadcast studio. We could all see each other through glass partitions, and we could talk to each other through an intercom system. The engineer would push all the right buttons to air the commercials, public service announcements, and the five-minute ABC network news that came on at the top of each hour. He or she would also make certain that the quality and volume of the sound was proper at all times.

It was the screener's job to answer all incoming calls, establish what the callers wanted to discuss, and then slot the call onto a waiting board until I could get to it. We had ten incoming lines, and they were all full for almost the entire three hours. The average wait that a caller had to endure before getting on the air was almost forty-five minutes. I regretted this long delay they had to suffer, but there was nothing we could do about it. The screener would regularly come back onto each waiting line to keep callers up to date: "Are you still there Mrs. Jones? We're sorry about the delay . . . please stay on the line . . . there are still three calls in front of yours . . . we appreciate your interest. . . ."

I never envied the screeners their jobs. It was tough. They were not experts in personal finance, yet they had to understand the nature of each call, discern its importance, and decide whether or not the question was of broad enough interest to put on the air. They often had to coach callers into wording their questions most efficiently, and had a mammoth public relations job to do to keep callers in a good mood while they endured the long wait. This was particularly difficult at the end of the show when we had to go off the air and leave some long-waiting calls unanswered. (This was usually the caller's choice: Callers that phoned in late in the show were told that the switchboard was full and that they might not be able to get on the air, but they could wait on hold if they chose to.)

The screeners would summarize each question into a brief phrase and would type it onto a computer, which then flashed it on a screen in front of me. On this screen I could see about six incoming calls summarized and sequenced. I knew each caller's first name, age, area of residence, and the subject of the question: "Jane . . . thirty-six . . . Santa Monica . . . what to do with CD money that matures next week?" I always wanted to maintain a good mix of age, location, and subject matter, so it was sometimes necessary to ask the screener to change the order of the calls. Now and then a waiting caller would hang up. That would mess up the established sequence, and we'd have to move things around again. We normally did this fine tuning during the commercial breaks. Since calls would come in constantly during the three hours, the screeners often couldn't take a break for the entire program.

The screeners often told me that they didn't envy my job either. I had to be up to the minute on all laws, trends, court decisions, and news items that could impact on any part of the broad spectrum of personal financial concerns. I had to be cordial yet authoritative, sympathetic yet forthright, humble yet knowledgeable. I always did my best to maintain a sense of humor and to avoid the financial jargon that so easily muddies up a conversation.

I wasn't given any strict limits as to how much time I spent with each caller, but I knew that after four or five minutes things could get draggy. This was, after all, commercial radio, not a therapy or consulting session. If you get draggy, you lose listeners. If you lose listeners, you lose sponsors. If you lose sponsors, you lose your job. So I had to analyze the problem and respond with a plausible and realistic answer within those four to five minutes. And all my answers had to be geared to the widest possible audience, not just the specific caller.

I had to keep one lawyer-ear open for the random rascal who might later threaten to sue me or the station for advice I gave that they said caused them to lose money. (See Chapter 21.) And I had to keep a censor's-ear open for the possible foul-mouth or loony who might escape the screener's scrutiny and get on the air. Both ears worked well. The former never happened, and the latter occurred only twice in nine years. (To protect ourselves against such contingencies we broadcast with a four-second delay. I had a cutoff switch close at hand that I could use to delete any expletives.)

A major element of my program each week was to review the events of the real world and comment on the impact they'd have on the economics of everyday life. I did this as a four- to six-minute monologue at the start of each program, and I repeated it at the start of the third hour. We covered a lot of fascinating modern history in the years of my tenure: the recession and double-digit inflation of 1980–81; the Reagan tax cuts and budget deficits; more changes in the tax laws than I care to remember; the "trickle down" theory; the international balance of payments deficits; the booming stock market of the 1980s and the crash of 1987; interest rates that skyrocketed and plummeted; the savings and loan debacle; the junk bond crazies; the beginning of the end of the Soviet Union and all that that implied; and an unending series of frauds and scandals—too numerous to mention—on a national, state, and local level. It was quite a whirlwind.

I rarely had guests on the program; there were legions of stockbrokers, insurance agents, mutual fund salespersons, financial planners, and the like who would have delighted in the exposure, but I was concerned that their appearance would diminish my objectivity in the minds of listeners. When I did have guests they were, for the most part, people from government agencies who could explain specific consumer rights and how the government could help them.

In particular, I had representatives from the Internal Revenue Service on during tax filing season, and again for a year-end tax planning session. Since tax filing season peaks, as we all know, in early April, I took the liberty one year of playing an April Fool's joke on my esteemed visitors. It was perhaps the highlight of my nine-year stint on KABC. More of that in Chapter 24. Now on to the meat: The financial dilemmas most frequently faced by my 10,000 callers and, by extension, millions of other nice people who face the same aggravations in their daily lives.

Chapter Twenty-three

"You're on the Air . . . How Can I Help You?"

Of the 10,000 times I asked that question during the years of my call-in show on KABC Talk-Radio in Los Angeles, these represent the twelve most frequent and troubling areas of financial concern of the public.

✔ *Investing versus Speculating*
. . . the single most critical distinction in managing your money

✔ *Rosefsky's Age + 40 Rule*
. . . a safe and conservative guideline for putting your money to work

✔ *Rosefsky's Law of Investment Dynamics*
. . . what your stockbroker doesn't want to tell you (and this is not a figment, Newton)

✔ *Shopping for Mutual Funds*
. . . filet mignon or puppy chow?

✔ *Why So Negative?*
. . . someone (who isn't selling anything) has to shine some light on the dark side

✔ *Forget about the Stock Market?*
. . . no-can-do, but there are other options open to you
. . . a brief and simple introduction to bonds, tax-exempts, compounding, and yield curves

✔ *Ups and Downs*
. . . preparing yourself to ride the bond market roller coaster

✔ *The Tax-Exempt Catch*
. . . they're not for everyone; how to tell if they're right for you

✔ *"I've Never Had to Do This Before . . ."*
. . . the sad and frequent plight of the recent widow, and how to avoid it

✔ *"Financial Planners"*
. . . how to sort out the pros and cons

✔ *Don't Retire . . . Regenerate!*
. . . looking at the bright side of an often gloomy issue

✔ *How Are Debtors Like Ostriches?*
 . . . the absolutely worst thing you can do if you're in debt trouble, and the easy ways to stay out of trouble in the first place
 . . . people and laws that can help you
 . . . overcoming the worst debt threat: the budget-destroying credit card

✔ *Complications*
 . . . jargon: Trauma, Rosefsky's Rule of Thumb, and the Greater Fool Theory

"You're on the Air . . . How Can I Help You?"

I asked that question on KABC Talk-Radio roughly 10,000 times during the nine years I hosted a phone-in show, which I called "Money Talks." Callers ranged from kids asking questions about their allowances to seniors concerned about their pensions, and all ages and wealth levels in between.

The following montages represent a cross section of the issues people asked me about most often. The common thread among them was *a lack of understanding of some basic concepts that left the folks exposed to financial peril.* I did my best to pull them back from the brink and give them a grasp of what they needed to know. I knew that they would often evaluate my words against those of a salesman. And I was quick to remind them that I wasn't selling anything.

Investing vs. Speculating

"I'm thinking of investing in the stock market . . . or stock mutual funds . . . or precious metals . . . or commodities . . . what do you think of my choices?"

The important choice here is the choice of one particular word: investing. My answer to the endless stream of questions on this subject was, "You can't *invest* in the stock market . . . or stock mutual funds . . . or precious metals . . . or commodities. You can only *speculate*, you can't *invest*."

That usually prompted an incredulous, "What are you talking about?" And I would then explain.

This is Rosefsky's Two-Word Vocabulary: investing and speculating. If I can teach you anything of value, it's the difference between these two words. If you understand the difference, and pay attention to it whenever you send your money off to work, you will be among the elite of money managers.

Perhaps the most common type of financial *mis*management involves people mistaking the difference between investing and speculating. The problem becomes clear when people find themselves with only a little bit of money when they thought they would end up with a lot of money. In short, they've lost when they had expected to win. That's because they *speculated* when they should have *invested*.

When you *invest* your money you know, with assurance, that you will have X or Y or Z dollars in so many months or years. You *know*. With *assurance*. Investment vehicles are federally insured savings plans and shorter-term IOUs—five years and less—issued by well-rated governmental units and corporations. (Later I'll explain why longer-term government and corporate IOUs can fall into speculative ranges.) You may not earn as much through investing as you could through speculating, but the important fact is that whatever you've invested, and whatever that investment has earned, it *will all be there* when you want it to be.

When you *speculate,* you *do not know,* you *cannot know,* and *no one can tell you* with *any* kind of assurance how much money you'll have in so many months or years. Speculative vehicles are those already noted: stocks, metals, and so forth. You may end up with alot *more* money by speculating instead of investing, or you may end up with alot *less.* But there's no way of knowing in advance which it will be, *no way.* And if you *must* have a certain amount of money in place at some specific future date, you *cannot* be assured of doing so through speculation.

If it's *important* for you to know how much money you will have at some future date, invest, don't speculate. If it *doesn't matter* to you how much money you have at any future date, have a fling at speculating. You may hit the jackpot, or you may lose your shirt. If it doesn't matter, you really won't care if you lose, will you? (Just kidding.)

Put another way, choose one from Column A and one from Column B:

A	B
I can't retire when I planned to . . .	. . . because I lost too much in the stock market.
We can't send Chris to college in two years . . .	. . . because I lost too much gambling on gold and silver.
We don't have the down payment to buy the home we want . . .	. . . because the mutual funds I put my money into were risky stock funds instead of safe fixed-income funds.
I won't be able to go into business for myself as I planned next year . . .	. . . because I took a fling in the commodities market and I crapped out.

Just a darned minute there, Bob! Are you saying that people should never put their money at risk? that they should never be venturesome?

No, I'm not saying that. I'm simply saying that your money should be put to work in line with clear objectives that you have set for yourself. If you have a *Must Goal,* that is, you *must* have enough money in place at a certain time for a certain purpose, then you *invest.* If you have a *Maybe Goal,* that is, if you have enough money, then maybe you can do such-and-such, then feel free to *speculate.*

The overriding rule is this: Once you have *clarified* and *committed* yourself to specific financial objectives—goals—and you have *embarked on a disciplined investment plan* to achieve those goals, then you can take some chances in the speculative arena. *Note:* I'm not telling you to wait until you've achieved all of your major objectives, such as education, housing, retirement, and so on, before you begin any speculating. I'm saying, and it's worth repeating, once you have *embarked on a disciplined investment plan.* If you stick to your guns with the investment plan, speculating can't cause serious harm. Can you stick to your guns?

(I beg one forgiveness: Now and then I may use the words "invest" or "investment" in the broad generic sense, such as in referring to the general act of putting one's money to work, be it in a conservative or a risky fashion. Whenever I do use the terms in the context of my two-word vocabulary, I do my best to make it clear that that is the case.)

Rosefsky's Age + 40 Rule

"I want to put money away for retirement. I don't want to take any unnecessary risks with the money, but I know that savings plans might not be as productive as the stock market and other speculative vehicles. What kind of mix between the two would make sense?"

First you must understand my own agenda. I'm very conservative fiscally. If everyone took my advice, the earth would stop spinning. But in every situation someone has to look at the worst-case scenario, and if you don't do it, I'm doing it for you.

To satisfy those who want to put some of their retirement money at risk I've devised a simple rule that allows you some leeway. I call it the Age + 40 Rule. Add 40 to your age. The total is the percent of your nestegg that should be *invested* (as above: federally insured savings and/or shorter-term IOUs issued by well-rated governmental units and corporations). The balance you can speculate with. In other words, if you're now 32, your age plus 40 equals 72. So 72 percent of your nestegg should be in fixed-income investments. The other 28 percent you can speculate with: stocks and the like. Even with that money, though, I'd urge you to stick close to the best-quality stocks that have good dividend payment records, or mutual funds that invest therein.

If you're now 50, your aim should be to have 90 percent of your nestegg put away safely, and speculate, if you wish, with the other 10 percent. After 60, take no chances.

Yes, many people will take issue with my position. That, as is said, is what makes horse racing. Yes, over long time periods the *broad averages* of the stock market appear to perform better than savings plans or bonds. Yes, there are also time frames in which specific stocks *and* groups of stocks *and* market averages come up *negative,* or don't otherwise perform as well as the dull and boring savings plans and bonds.

The catch is that you can never know the results in your specific time frame until that time frame has elapsed. And if it turns out that your stock, or your mutual fund, or your industry group headed south just when you were ready to cash in, you can't rewind and have another look at it.

Another important aspect of the Age + 40 Rule is that it is indeed age sensitive. One of the realities of life is that the younger you are, the more time you have to recover from mistakes, and the more resilient you are psychologically. A thirty-something can endure a speculative loss and bounce back, sadder but wiser, ready to tackle new challenges. A sixty-something certainly does not have the same amount of time to recoup from a speculative loss and probably doesn't have the energy to do so either.

Modify the Age + 40 Rule if you like—try Age + 30 or even Age + 20 if your speculative juices are flowing. But do so at your own risk.

Rosefsky's Law of Investment Dynamics

"My broker has told me about a stock that can't miss: National Pripichik and Gumball. He says it's a well-diversified megaconglomerate with strategic alliances in Asia and plate tectonics, and it's on the leading edge to be poised to race ahead on the information superhighway, and along the way its pharmaceutical division has the inside track on a cure for at least six as-yet-undiscovered viruses. It can't miss. What do you think?"

Try as I might to not let callers mention the names of specific companies, so as to keep self-promoting touts from polluting the air, some names did slip through. I gave the callers the benefit of the doubt, assuming that they really were innocent speculators who were seeking a second opinion.

My first response was to tell them that there are many thousands of stocks, and no one except for a handful of top executives at each company really knows all the salient facts upon which one could base a well-calculated risk. For that reason I did not make specific buy, hold, or sell recommendations.

I then invoked Rosefsky's Law of Investment Dynamics, which states, à la Isaac Newton: "FOR EVERY STOCK MARKET TRANSACTION THERE IS AN EQUAL AND OPPOSITE TRANSACTION."

This means, most simply, that for everyone *buying* 100 shares of National Pripichik and Gumball there is someone else *selling* 100 shares of National Pripichik and Gumball. The buyers are buying because they think that the stock has potential for gain. Why else would they buy? The sellers are selling because they think it does *not* have potential for gain. Why else would they sell?

Someone will be proven right, and someone will be proven wrong. In short, the chances are 50/50 that you're going to be a loser in any such transaction. Do you feel comfortable putting your money to work against those odds?

Some callers who asked this type of question really weren't seeking my buy/sell advice. They had already taken the plunge and were hoping that I might give them reassurance that they had done the right thing.

And some callers protested that I should be more forthcoming with specific recommendations.

But they all recognized the fact—which I emphasize here for your benefit—that any recommendation is only as good as the circumstances that exist *at that moment*. Within days, or even hours or minutes, factors can change that would turn a buy into a sell, a sell into a hold, a hold into a buy. Even if someone did have a magical ability to tap into the depths of information needed for a sound decision, that decision could be invalidated by subsequent events.

I didn't leave callers totally empty-handed. I did try to give them my read on some current broad general trends. But since I have no more faith in my ability to pick winning stocks than in my ability to pick winning roulette numbers or horses, I simply apologized for that shortcoming and suggested that they ask their brokers to admit to similar human frailties.

Shopping for Mutual Funds

"I've got some money to invest, and a friend suggested I put it into a mutual fund. Does that seem like a good idea?"

This certainly was one of the more frequently asked questions. And note well: The callers were not asking about any *specific* fund; they were seeking my advice on putting money into *a* mutual fund, as if it didn't matter which one they chose.

This apparent naivete was repeated so many times over the years that my concern remained high (and does to this day) that all too many people are treading in dangerous uncharted territory when they consider putting their money to work in mutual funds. I directed my response to the large number of people who need primary instruction, with apologies to the small number of people who are wise to the ways of shopping for a mutual fund. I do the same here and now.

My initial reaction to the frequent inquiry was, in a jovial but slightly chiding way, "That's like saying let's go to the supermarket to buy something to eat . . . what would you like, some filet mignon or some puppy chow?"

After the bemused silence I would go on: "You must understand that there are thousands of mutual funds from which to choose. Not only do they put your money to work in ways ranging from wildly speculative to staunchly conservative, but they all also have an extraordinary variety of costs and commissions that they will charge you. Indeed, it may be more tricky to pick one or two mutual funds out of the thousands available than to pick individual stocks out of the thousands of those that are available."

In many cases the callers had been exposed to a pitch from a mutual fund salesperson. Thus they already had a mindset, likely arising from having seen a presentation that showed how rich one might have become had they invested in a particular fund a few years ago. Despite attempts by government regulators to make sure that mutual fund advertising honestly and fully discloses all appropriate facts, the combination of a glossy sales brochure and a fast-talking salesperson can easily lead to misunderstanding by the customer. A simple diagram showing dramatic gains over a specific time frame can convince gullible investors that the same trend will continue on and on. What they don't show you are the trendlines during the time frames when the fund values went down.

Here, then, are the basic shopping tips, to help you separate the filet mignon from the puppy chow in the mutual fund industry.

   * *Your Starting Point.* Get a copy of the most recent copy of *Forbes* magazine's special annual mutual fund issue. It's published each September. Your library will no doubt have a copy. This is the single best source I've found for guidance in the mutual fund jungle. It rates thousands of funds as to their performance in rising and falling markets, and it has all the other initial data you need to *begin* your

serious research, including address and telephone numbers for each fund.

* *Your Objectives.* You must search your soul and examine your overall financial condition so that you can determine what your *objectives* will be in putting your money into mutual funds. I refer you again to our earlier discussion of *investing* versus *speculating.* Some of the saddest stories I listened to over the years were from people who put their money into speculative funds, not realizing that they were taking on serious risk, and they lost bundles. "But the salesman never told me . . ." was their common dirge. If your objective is to try to make a lot of money real fast, while at the same time *risking losing that money* just as fast, then you'd want to seek out the "growth" category of funds. Note the designation "growth." It would be more accurate and honest to call it "growth/shrinkage" but they wouldn't sell many funds that way. That's what you're up against. If you prefer to seek income, with your risk of loss much less, then the "income" category of funds is more up your alley. To compromise, you can explore the "balanced" category, which mixes the other two in varying degrees.

Please understand: Naming these three categories is like saying that the supermarket has meat, produce, and frozen food departments. We're still a long way from zeroing in on a *specific* nourishment to satisfy your hunger. That can only come from your own research, which assuredly will take a lot of time and energy. If you're not willing to make that investment, you'll be sending your money away and you may not know how to find it if it doesn't come back when you expect it to.

* *Your Costs. Outside the presence* of any mutual fund salespeople, study at least half a dozen proposals of different types of funds, specifically to understand how they charge you. Mutual fund companies do not handle your money for the fun of it. They're in it to make money, and there are three basic ways that they can do that:

1. They charge a commission when you first buy the fund. This is called a "load" or "loading charge." A loading charge might be as much as 8.5 percent of the amount you invest. In other words, if you put up $1,000, $85 of it will go to pay commissions, and the remaining $915 goes to work for you. In other words, your $915 has to earn $85—roughly 9 percent in the

first year—for you to just get back to Square One, to break even. And that's before even considering the other charges that might be imposed. Many funds charge a lesser load; some, called "no-loads," charge none at all. It's *mandatory* that you know these costs before you make a decision.

2. Funds all charge a variety of other costs to each customer to cover their expenses for making investment decisions, marketing of the fund, and other out-of-pocket costs. These expenses can range considerably, from about 0.5 percent to 1.5 percent of the value of your investment per year. A simple example: If a fund charges annual expenses of 1 percent, and your investment is worth $1,000, then the fund will take $10 off the top for that year, leaving you with $990 working for you at the start of the next year. As a general rule, no-load funds will impose higher annual expense fees than will load funds. Thus *timing* becomes critical: While a load fund may be more expensive up front, the no-load fund can become more expensive over a number of years, as the annual expenses begin to equal and exceed the amount of the initial loading cost that you paid. You must consider this factor in comparing load and no-load funds, in line with the length of time you reasonably expect to hold a given fund. Which type of fund performs better, load or no-load? How many angels can fit on the head of a pin?

3. Just when you thought you were done paying these costs you decide to cash in your mutual fund and you're hit with a redemption charge, which many funds commonly impose. Just to make it a little harder for you to figure it all out, these redemption charges may vary depending on how long you've owned the fund; generally, the longer you hold, the lesser the charge.

To help you with the projected calculations that you must do, let's look at an oversimplified example. Fund XYZ has a 5 percent load charge, a 1 percent annual expense charge, and a 2 percent redemption charge at the end of the third year of holding the fund. Let's say that you will own the fund for three years, and that it will grow by 7 percent each year. Your earnings will be reinvested in the fund.

You start off with $1,000, which is immediately reduced to $950 by the 5 percent ($50) load charge. During the first year your fund earns 7 percent, or $66.50 (that's 7 percent of $950). Add that to your initial $950 and you have $1,016.50 at year-end. Now slice off the 1 percent annual expense charge of $10.16, and you start the second year with $1006.40 (rounded off).

During the second year your $1006.40 earns 7 percent, or $70.45. Your nestegg has thus grown to $1,077, which is then reduced by the annual 1 percent fee of $10.77 to $1,066.23. That earns $74.63 in the third year, bumping your total up to $1,141, which is then reduced by the 1 percent annual fee to $1,129.60.

You then sell your shares and are hit with the 2 percent redemption charge, which would be $22.60, leaving you with the not-so-grand total of $1,107. In three years your $1,000 has grown by $107, or an average per year of $35.67. Your *real* rate of growth, then, is approximately 3.5 percent per year, despite the *apparent* annual increase of 7 percent. And that's before income taxes take their bite, assuming it's a fund whose earnings are taxable. Are we having fun yet? Do some noodling around with other numbers, higher and lower charges, to project possible outcomes for your planned adventure.

All of the specific data on mutual fund charges, as well as important information on a fund's management, objectives, risks, financial status, and performance records, are contained in the *prospectus* of the fund. It's *must* reading.

* *Your Choices.* Mutual funds can put money to work in a myriad of different kinds of securities—stocks, short-term IOUs (money market instruments), long-term IOUs (bonds), commodities, a variety of bets called *options,* mortgage-related IOUs, and many more. All of these different types of securities are subject to different influences. Some may be going up while others are going down (and vice versa).

If you get into a stock market fund when the market is on the rise, you may want to get out when the market turns down. At that moment the bond market might be poised for a rise (or fall). You may want to be able to switch easily and cost-effectively out of one fund into another. This is why the "families of funds" can be an attractive concept. Many big mutual fund companies operate a "family" of different individual funds, each one concentrating on a specific category of security.

These so-called families allow you to switch from one fund to another within the same family, usually by just making a phone call and paying a token amount to cover the transaction. Researching these families of funds can be very productive. The *Forbes* survey points them out, as do many other worthwhile mutual fund ratings services, many of which are as near as your local library.

* *Your Mantra.* The last aspect of this orientation training, before you go off on your own to do the real serious research, is to engrave one particular message—a mantra—in your mind. It's this: PAST PERFORMANCE IS ABSOLUTELY NO GUARANTEE OF FUTURE PERFORMANCE. That message may appear in small print on the mutual fund's literature. The salesperson may allude to it in a brief whisper in the sales pitch. But then the main thrust of the literature and the sales pitch may try to convince you otherwise. Don't deviate from the message—not one iota. It is as immutable as the Law of Gravity. Too many people get hooked on the prospect of endless gains because they shunned the message, only to learn to their dismay that the message *is* correct. "I wouldn't have bought the damned fund if I thought it could go down!" is the common outcry. Naive? Greedy? Vulnerable?—all of the above, and all too common.

Why So Negative?

Frequently I would have a caller interrupt the normal flow of questions and answers by asking me, "How come you're so negative, Bob? You always seem to take such a dim view of so many things."

I would point out that there were an ample number of positive messages among my precautionary negatives. But, moreover, I explained my role as "the worst-case-scenario guy." "Someone has to look at the downside in any venture, and if the salesperson doesn't do it for you adequately, I'll take that responsibility on myself. I'm telling you things that salespeople and brokers and agents and planners might not tell you, because I have nothing to sell. You can believe me, or you can believe them. But what if I'm right?"

Some would protest: "I'm not talking about being conned by a salesperson. I'm talking about taking advantage of the experience and knowledge of my friends, people who I trust, people who aren't trying to sell me anything."

Fine, I would say, as long as you understand the agenda of those well-wishers. They may not have anything to sell, but they might want to validate their own actions, for better or for worse, by convincing you to do what they have done.

Remember, too, that those who have been winners in the money game might tend to brag and exaggerate just a wee tad. And losers tend to keep their mouths shut, or fib a bit. You rarely hear anyone who's lost money pipe up at a cocktail party, "Hey, everyone, listen to me make a fool of myself while I tell you how I lost $5,000." In short, when you hear alot (of hot air?) from the winners and very little (of value?) from the losers, you may think you're missing out on something important.

Hold fast to your common sense in cases like this. It can be your best friend.

Forget about the Stock Market?

"Okay, Bob, I'm not the least bit interested in the stock market—never have been, never will be. I'm happy to just earn interest on my money. I'd just like to know what are the alternatives to bank savings plans. Where can I earn a better rate of return? And what risks would I be taking in order to get a better return?"

This seemingly simple inquiry, repeated in various forms constantly, lies at the heart of some of the most misunderstood facets of investing. The questions could prompt a book-length response in their own right, but we'll deal with them more economically. We'll cover the misunderstood facets after this necessary background discussion.

* *No one* can afford to be "not the least bit interested in the stock market." It can be foolhardy to ignore how extensively the stock market reaches into our lives. You may never actually make a direct investment in the market; that is, you may never write a check and deliver it to a stock broker in exchange for shares of stock in a company. But *indirectly* you may be more involved than you think, or care to think.

Some of your pension money is very likely invested in the stock market, whether you want it to be or not. Federal laws governing pensions mandate that employers put enough into workers' pensions to assure that the future obligations will be met. Sharp turns in the market can jeopardize (or enhance) the status of any given pension fund as well as the individual accounts that must be paid from it. If the company you work for has "unfunded pension liabilities"—not enough in the kitty to meet future obligations—you could feel it severely if the shortfall isn't corrected by the time you retire. (In fairness, stock market losses aren't the only culprits here. Some companies simply don't put enough into the kitty; others divert the pension money to improper purposes.)

If enough employees of a given company are concerned about the health of their pension fund, they can, as a group or through their unions, hold the pension fund managers accountable. If the pension fund is taking on too much stock market risk, pressure can be brought to lessen the risk and strengthen the fund.

Some life insurance policies and variable annuities are tied in part to stock market performance, and your benefits from those policies can rise and fall over the long term with the market's fates.

Perhaps most directly, your employment can be sharply affected by the stock market. If the company you work for is publicly traded—that is, it's shares can be bought and sold by the public on one of the stock exchanges—you will feel the ripple effects of the ups and downs in the price of the shares. Bosses may own a lot of shares, and their moods can swing in accordance with the price. You might be able to distinguish good days and bad days at work accordingly. Your boss, or the company itself, may have borrowed money and pledged shares of the company stock as collateral. If the price of the stock falls, the lenders may have to sell the pledged shares to protect themselves; or they may ask your boss, or the company, to ante up cash to reduce the lenders' risk. This can be quite traumatic for the boss, the company, and, subsequently, the employees.

Even if your company is not publicly traded, it may do business with other companies whose stock *is* publicly traded, and that can affect your well-being. If one of your most important customers suffers a sharp fall in its shares, that can impair their ability to do business, and the income your company receives from that company can thus be jeopardized, and jobs along with it (and vice versa).

Your options may be limited in circumstances such as these. But if you have knowledge of the market, and if you use that knowledge to keep yourself abreast of any conditions that can affect your well-being, you're in that much better of a position to take appropriate action should trouble, or opportunity, appear.

 * There are many different ways you can "invest" your money to earn a predictable rate of interest. You're a lender, and there are borrowers galore competing for your favor.

When you lend your money to a banking institution the IOU they give you is called a *savings plan*, usually either a passbook account, a Certificate of Deposit (CD), or some variation thereof. In a passbook account you can put in or take out money at will. The rate of interest they pay is relatively low and may vary from time to time, and too many transactions may result in service charges that will reduce your earned interest. (Checking accounts may also pay some interest.) A CD is a contract for a fixed amount of money, for a fixed amount of time, at a fixed interest rate. It's important to note that with these bank plans the interest you earn is automatically reinvested in your account, and as such it begins to earn interest. This is known as compounding; the effect of compounding can make a considerable difference in your financial status—more on that later. If you lend your money to a bank that is covered by the Federal Deposit Insurance Corporation, your accounts are insured by the government up to current limits.

When you lend your money to the federal government the United States Treasury issues IOUs that are called *Treasury bills, notes*, and *bonds*, depending on the length of time before the IOU becomes due. Short-term IOUs, payable within less than a year, are called treasury bills. Medium-term IOUs, payable within one to ten years, are called treasury notes. And long-term IOUs, payable in up to thirty years, are called treasury bonds. These are direct obligations of the federal government, and are considered to have the highest safety factor, along with federally insured savings plans. In addition to lending your money directly to the United States Treasury there are many agencies of the federal government that borrow from the public. All of these government and agency issues are listed daily in *The Wall Street Journal* section called "Money and Investing." The interest you earn on these securities is paid to you directly and does not compound. If you want your interest to earn interest, you must take steps on your own to reinvest the interest as you receive it. Interest earned on federal government IOUs is taxable on your federal return but exempt from state income taxes.

When you lend your money to a local government (state, city, county, and the multitude of subdivisions and agencies thereof) the interest you earn will be exempt from federal income taxes (with a few rare exceptions, which a broker can explain to you). If you invest in local government IOUs that are in your state of residence, the interest earned can also be exempt from your state's income taxes. These issues are commonly called *tax-exempt municipal bonds*, or "munis" for short. Most munis are long-term bonds. Interest is paid to you directly and does not compound. Since local governmental units can vary widely as to their fiscal status, munis are rated as to quality by such companies as Standard & Poors (from the top AAA on down). The higher the rating the better the quality, and thus the lower the risk and interest rate earned. Failures—wipeouts—in the muni bond market are rare, but they do happen.

When you lend your money to a corporation for a long term the IOU you get is called a *corporate bond*. Some corporations also issue shorter-term notes, and a few offer very short IOUs (90 days more or less) called "commercial paper." The variety of quality in corporate bonds is almost incomprehensible. Ratings are offered by Standard & Poors and other companies. Failures in the corporate bond market are not unusual. Interest is paid to you directly and does not compound. Income earned on corporate bonds is fully taxable, state and federal.

Any and all combinations of these securities can be available through mutual funds. In general, mutual funds that specialize in short-term IOUs are referred to as money market mutual funds; those investing long-term are called bond funds. Interest earned in all of these funds can be automatically reinvested if you so choose, or it can be sent to you by check periodically. Choosing the right interest-generating mutual fund can be as perplexing as choosing a stock mutual fund. Given the costs involved (similar to those noted earlier in the discussion of stock mutual funds) the net return to an investor may not be any better (if as good) as what investors could do on their own by buying individual securities directly. Funds, though, do offer diversification that individual investors may not be able to achieve as effectively on their own.

Other, more intricate, ways of lending your money include "securitized pools." Residential mortgages, car loans, and credit card debts are bought from the original lenders (mostly banks) by various private and governmental entities. These lumped-together personal

IOUs are then offered as collateral for loans. Don't enter this realm without doing plenty of homework. It can be very tricky.

* As to the issue of returns on investments: In general, federal government and agency issues will offer rates of return competitive with savings plans. But in addition to the rates offered you must also take into account the commission costs in buying and selling the government issues. Munis offer lower rates of return than corporate or United States government bonds, but since they are tax-free, you must calculate the after-tax return, as well as the costs involved in buying and selling. Corporates generally offer higher returns than savings plans, but entail higher risks, as well as buying and selling costs.

To complete this primer on interest-paying instruments let's look quickly at two essential elements, *compounding* and the so-called *yield curve.* Then we'll tackle the most common questions arising out of this whole realm of investing.

* Compounding, as noted, describes the situation in which the interest earned on your account is automatically deposited back into that account, where it begins to earn interest itself. For example: You put $1,000 into a compounding investment where the rate of return is set to be, say, 4 percent per year. At the end of the first year you'll have earned $40 in interest. That $40 is automatically added to your initial $1,000, so at the start of your second year you have $1,040 working for you, all of which earns the 4 percent interest. Without compounding, that is, if the $40 had been sent directly to you, your long-term earnings would be much less.

Example: You invest $10,000 in a plan that is set to pay 6 percent interest per year for 10 years. With compounding you'll have $17,900 in the account at the end of the 10 years. In other words, your original $10,000 will have grown by $7,900, or an average per year of $790. In effect, then, you will have had an average increase per year of 7.9 percent. Thus does compounding magnify your return. If you had invested the same $10,000 for the same 6 percent, but *without* compounding, you'd have earned $600 per year, giving you a total after 10 years of $16,000—that's $1,900 less than in the compounding plan. (If you *had* reinvested the $600 each year you could have improved your total, but it takes discipline and time to do that, and you're not as likely to be able to earn the same rate on the smaller amount being invested.)

If you're going to take out the earned interest each year and spend it, there's not much difference between an investment that compounds and one that doesn't. But if your goal is to accumulate the largest possible nestegg, compounding offers a distinct advantage over noncompounding, all other things being equal. Savings plans compound. Mutual funds can compound, but there are expenses involved in mutual funds, as explained earlier. Direct investments in bonds do not compound; you must take steps yourself to reinvest the earnings. What will you do with that semi-annual interest check—reinvest it, or succumb to the yen to go out to dinner with the proceeds?

(Many people who buy stocks can also take part in a form of compounding if the companies offer an automatic dividend reinvestment program. In these programs your quarterly dividends are automatically used to buy additional shares of stock. If you don't need the cash to spend, and if you have faith in the company over the long term, this can be an excellent and commission-free way to increase your holdings.)

Note that in any compounding plan, income taxes may be due on the interest you earn but don't actually have in your hand because it's been reinvested. Tax sheltered plans, such as IRAs, Keoghs, and 401Ks, are thus the most ideal way to take advantage of compounding, since the income in those plans is not taxed until the money is eventually withdrawn. In short, each full untaxed dollar goes to work for you rather than the after-tax dollars.

* The yield curve illustrates the rate of interest that can be earned on various investments over varying periods of time. For example, a yield curve for United States Treasury issues may show the rate of return for three months, six months, one year, three years, five years, ten years, and thirty years. *With rare exception, the shorter the term, the lower the yield. The longer the term, the higher the yield.* This is because long-term investors are facing a higher level of certain risk than short-term investors: Their money is tied up longer at a fixed rate, and they are therefore subject to the ups and downs of the marketplace. Those ups and downs can have a sharp impact on the value of a long-term investment, and they will be explored in more detail in the next section, which is titled, appropriately, "Ups and Downs."

Here is an example of a yield curve:

Rate	Term						
	3 mo.	6 mo.	1 yr.	3 yr.	5 yr.	10 yr.	30 yr.
8.0%							
7.5%							
7.0%							
6.5%							
6.0%							
5.5%							
5.0%							

5.0% 5.1% 5.2% 5% 7.0% 7.2% 7.5%

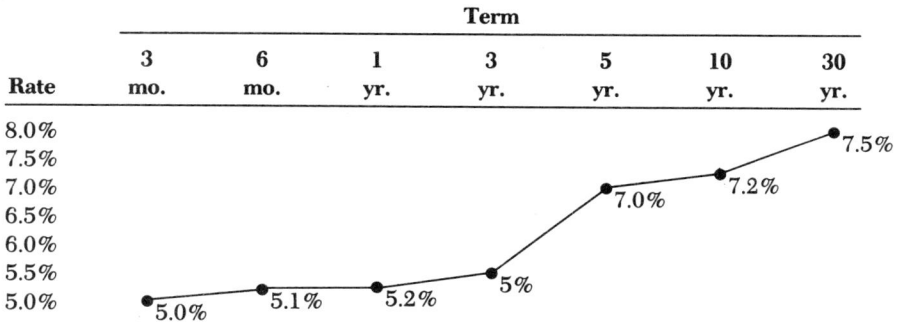

In any given category of securities, the yield curve will vary from day to day as interest rates fluctuate up and down. In this made-up curve you'll note that there's very little difference in the rate of return between a three-month IOU (5.0 percent) and a one-year IOU (5.2 percent). Then the curve begins to move sharply upward from the three-year level (5.5 percent) to the five-year level (7 percent), then to ten years (7.2 percent), and on to the thirty-year level at 7.5 percent.

In making investment decisions it's essential that you consider what the yield curve is telling you at any given time. *Any such decision must be tempered by your own view of whether interest rates will be going up or down in the foreseeable future.* If you believe that rates will be going up, you will want to maintain maximum flexibility so that you can move into better opportunities as they develop. In the above case, for example, there's so little difference between the three-month return and the one-year return that you might as well take the shorter run and retain your flexibility.

If you think, though, that interest rates will be heading down, you might want to lock in a high current rate for a longer period. The question is, how much longer? Is the .3 percent difference between one year and three years worth tying your money up for that long? Maybe not. But if you're willing to go for the three-year plan, maybe it's worth extending out for five years, where you'll earn an extra 1.5 percent for the whole time. If you were willing to stretch out for a full decade, you would earn only .2 percent more than you'd get for five years; it hardly seems worth it. And even less worth it is the thirty-year run, which pays only .5 percent more than a five-year plan.

These are the kinds of evaluations that wise investors make; and they review their conclusions periodically as the yield curve fluctuates. (On rare occasions there will appear a weird beast called the "inverted yield curve," wherein short-term rates will be *higher* than long-term rates. This is due primarily to large amounts of speculation on rate trends, wherein the speculators can literally bid the price of certain rates up and down. Such beasts are usually short-lived, but they can create havoc for investors, economists, and corporate financial officers.)

All of this is prologue—necessary background to enable you to spot and deal with perhaps the most perplexing and frustrating aspect of investing: the ups and downs of interest rates. That's what I gleaned from my callers, year in and year out. And the trend continues unabated.

Ups and Downs

"I can earn twice as high a yield on long-term bonds as I can on short-term bills. What's the catch?"

This is the *Catch* that perplexes not just the Mom-and-Pop investors, but also the Bean Counters who control many hundreds of billions of dollars in pension fund money, insurance company money, mutual fund money, corporate money, bank money, government (federal, state, and local) money, and Social Security money.

The *Catch* can affect the financial well-being of all the above entities (and the beneficiaries thereof, such as yourself) for they all invest heavily in long-term bonds, particularly those issued by the United States government. Indeed, the Social Security Administration invests *all* of the money it receives from taxpayers in Uncle Sam's long bonds. (Foreign investors, both individual and institutional, also invest heavily in United States treasury bonds, so many aspects of foreign economies can be impacted by the *Catch*.)

The *Catch* is this: INTEREST RATES AND THE VALUE OF BONDS FLUCTUATE IN *OPPOSITE* DIRECTIONS. An oversimplified example: You invest $1,000 in a bond that guarantees to pay you 6 percent interest per year for 30 years. If interest rates move upward after you've bought the bond, the value of your bond will dip. If interest rates move down, the value of your bond will increase. Either way, as long as you hold the bond you'll be earning 6 percent interest per year. Not a penny more, not a penny less.

This means that even though you've invested in what is perhaps the safest security in the world, a thirty-year IOU issued by the United States of America, you could still lose money on it. How? you ask. If interest rates move upward after you've bought the bond, and you want to, or have to, sell the bond at that time, you'll get less than you paid for it. On the other hand, if interest rates have moved down, you could sell the bond and reap a profit. In other words, despite the *long-term* security in the bond, it is still an instrument that *can* fluctuate in value, and thus becomes a fertile field for *short-term* speculators. They bet on every little twitch in the values of bonds looking for instant profits. And the more bets that are made on bonds, the more "action" there is, the more the prices will twitch, and the more speculative dollars will be attracted. A self-fulfilling prophecy if ever there was one.

The same rules pertain to bonds issued by corporations, only more so. It can be assumed that the quality of United States government issues will always be considered to be of the highest level. Uncle Sam will always pay his IOUs, even though he's incredulously in debt, because he can always tax his citizens to raise money to pay the bills. But corporations cannot tax their customers. Thus corporations that develop financial problems become riskier borrowers. So, a corporation's IOUs can fluctuate in value because of the financial status of the company, as well as because of the up and down trends in interest rates generally.

And *any* of this can happen at *any time* during a thirty-year period. Thirty years is a long time. A baby can be born, grow up, go to school, go to college, get married, and have babies of its own in a thirty-year span.

Here's a closer look at the details. Let's say that XYZ Corporation borrowed alot of money in 1993 and they issued thirty-year bonds as IOUs. They promised to pay investors 6 percent interest per year, or $60 for every $1,000 invested, in two installments of $30 each every six months. This rate of return, 6 percent, is referred to as the "coupon rate." That was the interest rate that XYZ had to pay to be able to borrow what it needed. Corporations with a lower credit rating would have had to pay a higher rate (and vice versa).

Five years later, in 1998, interest rates have crept upward. At that time XYZ would have had to pay 8 percent if it wanted to borrow money in the corporate bond market.

Let's say that you invested $10,000 in XYZ bonds when they were first issued in 1993. You'd earn $600 per year, and you intended to hold onto the bonds for the foreseeable future.

Lo and behold, in 1998, you face an unexpected need for cash—an emergency perhaps, or a terrific deal on a new car, a cruise, whatever. You consider selling your XYZ bonds to raise the cash, and you come to me and say, "Bob, I have here a perfectly good $10,000 IOU from the XYZ Company. It pays 6 percent, or $600 per year. I'd like to sell it to you for the same $10,000 I paid for it."

I would reply, "Why should I pay you $10,000 for that IOU when I can buy a brand new bond today from a company of comparable quality that will pay me 8 percent, or $800, per year? If I can earn 8 percent on my money today, why should I settle for the 6 percent that you're offering me, which is what I'd earn if I paid you $10,000?"

I can see that you're dismayed. You had invested in this bond in good faith, having been told that it was perfectly safe. And now, five years later, you can't sell it for what you paid for it. I'm a good sport, though, so I make you a fair offer:

"I'll buy your $10,000 IOU from you for $7,500. I'll earn the $600 in interest each year. $600 is 8 percent of $7,500, which means that I'll be earning an 8 percent return on my investment of $7,500, which is what I could get in the open market at today's rates. Take it or leave it."

Your bottom line is that you're looking at a loss of $2,500 on your original $10,000 safe, secure investment *if* you sell *now*. Yes, if you hold onto the investment, you will still earn your promised 6 percent interest per year. Yes, if you continue to hold the bond until it matures—in the year 2023—you'll get your full $10,000 back from the XYZ company. But 2023 is a long way down the road, and what will $10,000 be worth at that time? And do you want to hang onto the bond for another quarter-century to find out?

On the flip side, if interest rates moved down from 1993 to 1998, you could sell your XYZ bond at a handsome profit. If that happens, should you take your profit and run? Or should you hold on and hope for a bigger profit? Well, you may not have a choice. Welcome to another bond market gremlin: the call privilege. Borrowers are no dummies. They know that interest rates will move up and down over time, just as the tides go in and out. They protect themselves by putting a call privilege in their IOUs. This says, in effect, "As of a certain date we reserve the right to pay off this IOU in full, even though the promised maturity date is still decades away."

So, there you sit hoping to sell out at a fat profit, and before you know it, whoops, the issuer pays you off at a prestipulated price that could be far less than market potential. Or, you're sitting on what you consider a nice fat yield that you're going to ride with happily over the years and all of a sudden, whoops, the issuer pays you off in full and you find yourself having to reinvest the money in a much lower interest rate environment.

Not all bonds have call privileges, and those that do have specific terms and dates applicable only to that particular issue. You must know about call privileges before you invest in bonds lest you receive a rude awakening at some future date.

So much for the long-term bond market as a nice happy safe haven for your money. It isn't, unless you're iron-willed and fearless. Regretfully, the aforementioned factors give a casino-like image to what used to be regarded as a conservative and secure way of putting your money to work. How come it "used to be" but no longer is? A few decades ago interest rates didn't fluctuate nearly as much as they have in the past ten to twenty years; speculators were less active and there were fewer speculative vehicles upon which bets could be placed; call privileges were more rare; the overall quality of the bond market was much less distorted by "junk," or low-rated bonds.

In short, the market has changed drastically from what it used to be. But we haven't changed our habits in tempo with the changing realities. Countless Moms and Pops still plunge deeply into long-term bond investments (directly or through mutual funds) without appreciating the peculiar risks they're taking on. Corporations, banks, pension fund managers, insurance companies, and governmental treasurers do the same, but they're more aware of the subtleties and pitfalls in the market.

Nonetheless, even those pros can and do make mistakes, because Rosefsky's Law of Investment Dynamics is at work here as well as it is in the stock market: For every transaction there is an equal and opposite transaction. For all professional money managers who are selling bonds from their portfolios, there are others who are buying the same bonds. One-half will be proved right, the other half wrong.

Is there a happy medium? There can be. Look again at the yield curve chart from a few pages ago. Reasonably often you'll find securities that have three to five years to run that pay a decent return and are, because of their short span, relatively immune to the fluctuation and call privilege problems. You might find that time frame to be a comfort zone for your intended investments. You won't earn the highest possible return, but you'll have flexibility and you'll be much less exposed to market risk and to the dangers inherent in interest rate ups and downs.

Take it a step farther and stagger your nestegg into different time chunks. For example, if you have, say, $10,000 to invest in the fixed-income arena, consider breaking it up into three or four equal amounts, each for a different length of time. Example: Invest $3,333 for three years, $3,333 for four years, and $3,333 for five years, or whatever other combination seems suitable for the circumstances. This will increase your flexibility and liquidity, and will enable you to be able to take advantage of the new opportunities that the market is always offering.

Don't get caught by the *Catch.*

The Tax-Exempt Catch

"I can get almost the same rate of interest on municipal bonds as I can on bank CDs. But I don't have to pay income taxes on the munis, and I do on the CDs. What's the catch?"

This is an extension of the prior section, but with some important additions: The lure of tax exemption is powerful; so are the sales pitches that most of my callers had already been subjected to; and there's a lot of hanky-panky out there in the realm of muni sales.

Indeed, the majority of callers on this point had already taken the plunge, and they were calling me after the fact to find out if they had done the right thing.

Yes, I pointed out, tax-exempts may pay close to the same rate as CDs. But the CD runs for a short time—six months to a few years, which gives you a lot of flexibility. On the other hand, the tax-exempt muni runs for *thirty years!* That can lock you into circumstances that might prove quite uncomfortable.

Most of the inquiries came from retirees, for whom thirty years may exceed their life expectancy by twenty years. (If you are young enough to not be bothered by these considerations, that's fine. But your parents might be caught in the trap. Help them if you can by heeding my cautions and passing them on to your parents.)

There's alot that can happen in the next three years, let alone thirty years, and it can be foolhardy to tie up your money for such a long period, particularly if you've put your money into a bad deal.

"How bad can they be?" they'd ask me. "Behind these bonds is the full faith and credit of the state/city/town/school district/sewer assessment agency/hospital authority. . . ." I could just hear the echoes of the salespeople as my callers repeated the spiel almost word for word.

How bad can they be? Very bad! Here goes worst-case-scenario-Rosefsky again. But remember, if I don't show you the dark side, will the salespeople?

Here is a quick checklist of the potential problems in municipal bonds:

* Thirty years is too long, particularly for seniors. The main reasons are those stated in the prior section, Ups and Downs: Interest rate fluctuations put your money at greater risk than you may realize. This is particularly so for seniors who well may have to cash in these bonds before maturity, and might have to do so at a loss.

Of course it's possible to invest in bonds with a shorter life span than thirty years. Most new bonds are issued for that time span, give or take, but there are countless bonds in the secondary market—bonds that were issued many years ago and have been performing ever since—that offer a multitude of choices. Most of the bonds that are aggressively sold by bond dealers are the new issues.

* The tax advantages may be minimal, especially for seniors, many of whom are in the lowest tax brackets. Munis can be fine for the fat cats in the top income tax brackets. But when you get into the lower brackets the advantages diminish rapidly. Let's look at an example. A one-year CD pays, say, 5 percent interest, or $50 per $1,000 invested. A thirty-year muni pays, say, 4.5 percent, and the interest is exempt from federal taxes. A CD investor who is in the 15 percent marginal tax bracket will pay 15 percent of $50, or $7.50 in federal

income taxes on his investment income, leaving him with $42.50 after taxes. The muni investor in the same bracket will earn $45, and that's what he'll be left with after taxes—a difference of $2.50 per year per $1,000 invested. And that's before any commission the muni investor will have to pay to buy and sell the bonds. If you take these commission costs into account, the muni investor could well end up with less than the CD investor, who pays no commission for his investment. And the muni investor is exposed to market *and* quality risks for thirty years.

*   The quality of the muni may be far less than that of the CD, which means that it's riskier. CDs at federally insured institutions are protected up to the current limit by the federal deposit insurance program. That's tops for safety. But the quality of munis can range from AAA down to garbage. There is a lot of garbage out there, particularly in rural areas that are susceptible to economic downturns.

A quick lesson: There are two basic types of munis—general obligation bonds and revenue bonds. General obligation bonds are issued by the taxing authority of the given location. That means that the government has the power to tax its citizens to get the money it needs to pay its debts. Revenue bonds are issued by entities that hope to raise revenues as a result of their operation: hospitals, airports, toll roads, and so on. The ability of these entities to repay their debt depends on the revenue they raise. If they don't raise enough revenues to pay interest and/or principal on their debts, those debts can go into default.

All too often innocent investors don't know, don't ask, and aren't told about these distinctions. Nor are they aware that municipal bonds are rated as to quality (Standard & Poors and others). And if they *are* aware of the quality ratings, they may not be aware that the quality can change over time, as it can with corporations, and what might have started out as a AAA, AA, or A rated bond may sink to a C level, or worse, because of bad management. Revenue bonds carry higher risk than general obligation bonds as a general rule. But general obligation bonds can have their problems as well.

Can defaults happen in muni bonds? Oh, yes, indeed they can. In the mid-1970s the municipality of New York City, no less, came to the brink of default. It was ultimately rescued, but holders of New York City bonds sat on losers for a very long time. The granddaddy of them all was the Washington Public Power Supply System—WPPSS, or "Whoops" for short, and very appropriately so.

Though the Pacific Northwest has an abundant supply of hydro-power for electrical generating purposes, a group of eighteen public utility companies in that region—mostly rural, small, and unsophisti-cated entities—thought they could improve on Mother Nature. They proposed to build a series of nuclear generating stations, and suc-ceeded in convincing some of America's major brokerage firms to underwrite and sell (i.e., borrow from the public) bonds worth billions of dollars so they could build their plants.

But nobody ever asked, "What if we build these nuclear power stations and no one wants to buy the electricity we generate?" That's what happened, and WPPSS whoopsed to the tune of $2.25 *billion.* That is to say, they defaulted on that amount of bonds. The investment world went topsy-turvy. Major brokerage houses were embarrassed beyond description. Lawsuits have been going on ever since the late 1983 debacle, and will likely be going on for years to come. *That's* how bad munis can be. And for every Whoops, there are little hospital, sewer, and industrial development districts all around the nation that are going bankrupt every year, leaving investors holding the bag. And those now-empty bags in many cases used to hold all or much of the investors' life savings.

* The problem is compounded by overly aggressive sales outfits who sell bad bargains. Another quick lesson: There are two basic types of entities from whom you can buy muni bonds. First is the garden-variety stock brokerage firm, which has a department specializing in munis. As brokers, they find someone who wants to sell what you want to buy, and they arrange the transaction and take a commission from the parties for their efforts. Dealing in this way you are more likely to get a fair market price for any given issue.

The other type is the dealer, who has acquired a supply of bonds for his own account, just as a shoe store acquires an inventory of shoes. If you want to buy a bond from a dealer, he will sell you what you want out of his inventory and he will charge what the traffic will bear. His profit is the difference between what he paid and what you pay him. This type of transaction is likely to distort the fair market value. You might pay a lot more for a bond than you would through a broker. Sometimes the line between brokers and dealers is blurry. But few people I've ever spoken to have done one simple thing to protect themselves: Get a second opinion, or price quote, from someone other than the initial pitchman.

The process can be reversed when you want to sell your bonds. The broker will seek a willing buyer and you make your best deal. The dealer will buy it back from you at a price he's willing to pay, which may be far below the true market value. But if you bought it from him you're likely, aren't you, to go right back to him to sell it. You can get clobbered getting in, and you can get clobbered again getting out if you're not careful and if you don't shop around for the best price both when you buy *and* when you sell.

Some muni dealers and brokers will employ hard-sell telephone techniques. Some will be less than forthcoming about the risks involved. Some will decline to discuss the true tax advantages, if any, in your specific case.

If you're in a high enough tax bracket, and *if* you're willing to take time to study the quality and risks inherent in various muni issues, and *if* you are willing to shop around for prices, or have found a reliable broker in whom you have implicit faith, then munis can be good for you. But don't get caught by the muni *Catch* as so many well-intended but easily distracted other investors have.

"I've Never Had To Do This Before . . ."

"My husband died recently, and I'm completely befuddled about managing my money. My husband had always taken care of everything, and I never learned about all the ins and outs of financial matters. Everyone—family, friends, strangers who call on the phone—tell me what I should be doing. I'm totally confused. Please help me!"

Hardly a week went by that I didn't get calls from recent widows who were facing utter frenzy over having to assume the duties of money management. I don't mean this as a sexist thing. It's just a plain fact of life. I *never* got a single call along these lines from a man.

Today's younger generations are more sharing in their family roles than their parents were; maybe the women in these families will be more adept at handling finances than their mothers were. I hope so, because it was heartbreaking to hear so many widows suffering doubly—from grief, and from the staggering task before them of remaining solvent.

You may not feel that this dilemma is possible in your own immediate family. Are you certain of that? Don't take anything for granted. Even if you feel that you and your spouse can handle such concerns effectively, is the same true of your parents? If a widowed parent of yours has to confront this issue and can't handle it, *you'll* feel the repercussions, and they may be financial as well as psychological. Tackle the problem before it becomes acute by starting an education program today for anyone who can be thusly afflicted.

Some simple facts before we go into the advice mode:

1. Life expectancy at birth of women in the United States is about seven years longer than men's. At age fifty the spread is about five and one-half years. That means, simply, that the odds are very good that *any given wife will be a widow for about six years.*

2. The life insurance proceeds that widows receive upon their husband's death is all used up within two years. Part of the reason for this is that the average amount of insurance on the husband's life is about equal to two years' worth of his income. But it doesn't necessarily follow that the insurance benefits should be all spent within two years, since there are no longer any expenses for the deceased husband. The more overriding reason that the money disappears prematurely is that it is lost, stolen, or otherwise squandered.

Despite the best of intentions, many widows make poor investments. They allow themselves to become victims of greedy family members and friends, unscrupulous con artists, and "financial advisors," and/or they simply spend without awareness of how long their finite supply of money will last.

The dearly beloved would turn over in his grave if he could hear some of the pitches that are thrown at his widow:

* "Mrs. Jerome, I'm J. Fairly Nicely. I was your husband's stock broker for the last 27 years. Please accept my condolences over your loss. Howard was a wonderful man. I know you have other things on your mind just now, but we must realize that life goes on, and so does the stock market. In fact, the market

is in quite a turmoil today, and I want to protect you for Howard's sake as well as your own. I know you're not familiar with the market, so I'd suggest you sign some simple forms that will give me full discretion over your account. That way I won't have to bother you, and you won't have to worry about a thing. Howard told me, just a few days before he passed on, 'J., I know you'll treat my widow with the same honesty and loyalty and integrity that you've shown me all these years.' So, Mrs. Jerome, why don't I stop by your place tonight with these forms for you to sign, and then you can rest easily. . . ."

* "Hi Aunt Helen. We were so sorry to hear about Uncle Howard. He was such a wonderful person. He taught my Ralphie all he knew about the dry-cleaning business. Speaking of which, Aunt Helen, you know Ralphie has been talking about opening his own place, and he needs a little money for down payment and equipment, maybe about $40,000 or so, and we were wondering if maybe you could help us out a little bit. Of course we'll pay everything back plus interest. We'd sure be grateful, Aunt Helen. You know, Uncle Howard was always our favorite uncle, and he loved Ralphie so. . . ."

* "Good morning, Mrs. Jerome. My name is Isaiah Benevolent. I didn't know your poor husband personally, but I read his obituary in the paper today. My company, Widows and Orphans Lifetime Fiduciary, specializes in setting up conservative financial trust funds for people in their time of need. It will cost you nothing for all of the documentation. Our only fee is a tiny percentage—just one-twentieth of one percent— of your assets for our management and investment expertise. Might I make an appointment with you so you can learn more about how WOLF can be of benefit to you. . . ?"

Bad enough the wheedling stock brokers and whining relatives, but a pox upon the vultures who actually sift through obituaries looking for victims for their nefarious "investment" schemes! I've heard stories like this that would turn your blood cold. The obituary vultures can tell from the deceased's age, address, occupation, and survivors just where the choice victims are. They home in like laser-guided missiles heading for Baghdad.

So, what to tell these confused and often weeping folks? First and foremost: For at least one full year, and even better for two years, *do not put any money into anything other than federally insured accounts at a local bank.* I know, J. Fairly Nicely and Mr. Benevolent will moan that you're making a big mistake settling for puny bank interest when they could be making you *wealthy!* And nephew Ralphie will be beside himself with agony that you're not doing what his Uncle Howard would have wanted you to do. And the fact is that maybe you *could* earn more than bank interest with Nicely or Benevolent or Ralphie. *But you could also lose a lot!* Stay away in droves from brokers seeking full discretion over your account, from greedy family members, and from the likes of Isaiah Benevolent!

Your mind is clouded by grief. That's the *absolute worst* condition you could be in to make financial decisions, particularly when your financial skills are wanting in the first place.

Your money in the bank will be just that: money in the bank. *It will be there when you need it.* Take the time during that year or two to let your grief subside—and it will—and as you feel comfortable, begin to do some studying on money management. You can take basic investment courses at local colleges and adult extension programs. You can read financial books from the library. Inquire about what may be available through local social service agencies and outside entities such as the American Association of Retired Persons (AARP). Be wary of seminar programs offered by financial companies; much can be learned from them, but they are putting on the seminars to win customers, and you might get more of a hard sell than would be healthy for you.

After your year or two of "training" you'll be ready to proceed on your own, cautiously but confidently. If you're not, then just wait another year. For all those who tell you that you're missing out on so many good deals, simply remind them that there'll be more good deals later on, when you feel more confident about tackling them. Don't worry about hurting anyone's feelings. If anyone does get ruffled by your attitude, blame me. Tell them, "Rosefsky made me do it." That'll get you off the hook.

Bear in mind that *conservation of capital* is your primary goal. That's the case, as well, for *all* folks in their senior years. The years of *accumulating* capital are from the thirties into the late fifties or early sixties. Then comes the time to *conserve.* You must then use investment techniques (as opposed to speculative) consistent with your own circumstances. See the discussion at the start of this chapter on investing versus speculating.

To all those who offer you advice during your first year or two of widowhood, while your money is safely working for you at the bank, be cordial and appreciative. You don't want to offend them, nor do you want them to finagle around with your money. Simply tell them to put their specific suggestions in writing, and then look at the results of their recommendations a year or two later. That could be quite an instructive exercise.

If you happen to be reading this while your spouse is well and thriving, take time now for the necessary information and attitudes to be shared. That way you can prevent this whole sad problem from happening at all.

"Financial Planners"

"I've been talking to a financial planner about taking over all of my investment and insurance matters. That way I won't have to worry about whether I'm doing the right thing at the right time. The planner will do it all for me, and it'll be worth it to me to know that everything is being taken care of properly. Any advice?"

As the years went by this inquiry became more and more frequent, if for no other reason than that there were more and more "financial planners" out there soliciting business. I'm all in favor of financial professionals getting more education, which is required by some associations that confer "financial planning" designations on their students. But I have some serious concerns as well.

We are still years, if not decades, away from there being any kind of uniform standard governmental licensing or regulation of so-called "financial planners." Lawyers and accountants are licensed under the laws of their states. Banks, insurance companies, and brokerage firms are subject to state and/or federal regulations. Even barbers and manicurists are licensed. With all of these entities, violation or abuse of privilege can mean revocation of the right to continue in business. That provides at least a modicum of protection for the public.

But in the main, "financial planners" *per se,* are not so regulated. And they can do you a lot more harm than a barber can. Indeed, virtually anyone can call himself or herself a "financial planner," without having to worry about being governmentally licensed or regulated. (Lawyers, accountants, insurance agents, and stock brokers may be regulated as such within their own industries, but as "financial planners" they are not so regulated.)

I've heard too many stories of slick salespersons posing as "financial planners" so as to appear more authoritative and credible to customers. And I've heard far too little about any kind of effective self-policing by the "financial planning" profession when abuses do occur. Until I stop hearing so many of the former stories and start hearing more of the latter, I'm going to have to be very precautionary about the whole phenomenon. During my years on the radio I heard an endless stream of complaints about "financial planners." To be as fair as possible, I continually invited listeners to call in or write to me with stories of success they had had with "financial planners." I never got a single response to this offer.

If you are inclined to seek the services of a "financial planner," perhaps the following guidelines will help you choose wisely:

* Know well the difference between the two major types of planners: those who charge a fee for their services and make no commission on products they sell you (these are called "fee-only" planners) and those who earn their living from sales commissions. The former should be more objective: They have nothing to gain from any financial products you might obtain as a result of their advice. The latter must be carefully interviewed before your client relationship begins. You must discern exactly what kinds of commissions they earn from what types of products. It certainly is legal and proper for planners to earn commissions, but to the extent that potential commissions sway their advice to you, you must know that up front.

* Conduct prehiring interviews, at which you must determine the extent of services you'll receive. What services will the planners provide, and what services will be farmed out, and at what cost? These various services—all of which should be

optional for you—can include tax planning and preparation, legal documentation (trusts, wills, contracts, etc.), loan documentation (financial statements, business plans, etc.), and overall personal financial planning documents. You must also (note I keep saying "must"; that means mandatory) learn about the planners' educational and professional credentials, and obtain reliable personal references from other clients. If there is any agency in your state that reports on complaints against planners, contact them for a status report. It can't hurt, also, to get credit reports and bank references on them as evidence of how they handle their own personal finances. If they're not doing well for themselves, do you want to trust them with your money?

* Think long and hard before you actually turn over any money to them to manage. What protection do you have if they go bust?

* Beware of overload. Some planners are trained to get very extensive data from you which they then run through a computer and give you a very extensive printout, a lot of which may be of relatively little importance. But it looks impressive. Much of it may be tweaked to convince you (more than necessary) that you need so much life insurance or so much of a certain kind of mutual fund or annuity. Get a second opinion on any recommendations. Some of this you can do just by researching at your library: look for articles or books that discuss the pertinent issue and evaluate those other views. You may want to get opinions from other planners, stock brokers, insurance agents, or accountants. Be aware, of course, that they might have something else to sell you, but at least you'll get another view that you can analyze. It can't hurt. If there's enough at stake, it might be worth it to pay a fee-only planner for a hopefully more objective opinion.

* Even if you find the best planner in the whole world, *never* abdicate your own personal financial responsibilities. You must continue to be on top of current trends and opportunities if you want to be able to choose the best for yourself. And you must do this if for no other reason than to know that your planner is on top of everything. A planner is not a substitute

for your own intelligence. A good planner is a professional who can help you shape and carry out what's best for you, as your own intelligence dictates. If you maintain your ongoing education and keep your intelligence honed, you can easily get a glimpse of the best planner in the whole world: Just look in any mirror.

Don't Retire . . . Regenerate

"I'm beginning to think of retirement. I have a good pension plan from work, my home is all paid for, and I've stashed away a tidy nestegg that should be able to see us through almost any situation. Yet when I look out there at that looming date my stomach does flip-flops. Frankly, I'm scared, but I don't know of what. Have I made any financial mistakes? What am I doing wrong that leaves me so fearful of the future?"

If you're in your twenties or thirties and think that this subject doesn't apply to you, please think again. You will, someday, have to face the same issue, and it can't hurt to put some deep-background frame of reference in place right now. More important: Even if you're not facing this crisis today or in the near future, your parents might be. If you care about them at all, you can be of great help in listening to their concerns and talking them through the traumas and uncertainties. Whatever peace of mind you can help them attain can rub off on you. If continued trauma is to be their fate, that can rub off on you too. In short, by helping them you can help yourself. At the same time you'll be preparing yourself for a more secure future.

Hopefully, the following thoughts can help to dispel the fears and guide you to a secure place in your own mind.

Fear is often an irrational thing. If you analyze what's causing your adrenalin to pump so furiously, you'll often find that there's really nothing to be afraid of, and that you *can* deal with the ogre.

Consider, then, the fear expressed so often over the uncertainties of retirement. The root cause of that fear, as I've discerned in countless conversations and consulting sessions with would-be retirees who have sought my advice, is over the *cessation of work*. Most folks focus on the more obvious surface problems: loss of income, loss of personal power and influence, self-doubt about how they'll get along without the long-habituated work routine, worry over what they'll do to fill all the hours in the days, and even dread of their own mortality. But cessation of work lies at the heart of it all.

Work has an incredibly deep and far-reaching influence in your life. With rare exception it's the wellspring of all the money you will ever acquire. Whether you love it or hate it, it's the one activity in your entire life that commands most of your attention and energy. For a great many people the workplace is a primary source of social activity, as co-workers so often become fast friends. For those poor souls who are addicted to power—the ability to control the lives of other people—they will likely find that the only opportunity to indulge in this obsession is through work. Overall, work offers continuing opportunities to find a sense of achievement, of greater responsibilities, of progress, of self-esteem, of personal growth.

No wonder then that when the concept of *cessation of work* begins to flicker murkily in one's mind a sense of dread starts to arise. The manifestation of the fear is often disguised by more visible symptoms. You'll see or know people who have recently retired, and you'll be saddened to note that they've turned to the bottle out of boredom; or that they seem to be unhappily struggling to get by on a reduced income; or that they seem to have aged terribly quickly; or that they have become miserable curmudgeons who bitch and moan about absolutely everything; or that they spend all their time indulging their grandchildren and playing shuffleboard, mah-jongg, and gin rummy, thereby convincing you that their once fertile and creative brains have turned to mush. And so you wonder and worry, "There but for the grace of God go I?"

These are all very negative aspects of what we commonly call "retirement." The word itself has negative connotations: done, finished, out of it. Sad to say retirement is, in fact, a negative experience for too many people. But that is so, I've found, mainly because *they have not properly prepared themselves for this potentially enriching stage of life.*

I conducted a survey of recent retirees, seeking to discover their attitudes toward retirement. I had over 1,500 responses nationally, which puts the survey into the Nielsen category in terms of representing a cross section of reality. The single most frequent cause of malcontent with retirement was this: "I failed to get ready for the day, and when it came *I had nothing to do.*" My listeners and readers throughout the years have verified this over and over again. (The survey also asked, "If you had it to do over again, what would you not do, and what would you do?" The most frequent "not do again" was invest in the stock market. The most frequent "do again" was acquire more whole life insurance. Out of fairness to the stock market, the survey happened to coincide with a downturn in the market; responses might have been a bit more positive if the market were moving upward.)

Another fact of life: On the verge of retirement age the average person has a life expectancy of *fifteen to twenty years,* and that span is getting longer as health care technology advances. That's a hefty chunk of time that can be put to productive and enjoyable use. How sad to regard oneself during that time as done, finished, out of it.

Instead of retirement, then, consider *Regeneration* as that actual phase of life. Work, as you've known it, may be ceasing, but your *post-work career* is just *beginning.* And this can be as rich and as varied as you want to make it. Or it can be as fallow and depressing as you allow it to be. The choice is yours and no one else's. You can reach out to new challenges or you can atrophy. You can become a mentor or a grump. You can taste new flavors of life, or you can let your mouth go dry.

"Easy for you to say, Bob, but this kind of freedom can be expensive. It takes money."

Funny you should mention that. Let's look at the hardcore financial side of it. Yes, it takes money. Just staying alive takes money. Adjustments may have to be made, and the sooner you become cognizant of what adjustments you may have to make, the easier it'll be for you to make them.

Those adjustments can include:

* Cutting back a bit on your style of living well in advance of the *Regeneration* years so that you can put aside more money now to be enjoyed later.

* Earning more money now, if you can, to add to your *Regeneration* kitty.

* Devising an intelligent workable phasing-in program now that will begin five to ten years prior to *Regeneration,* and which will involve embarking on a gradual diminution in your living expenses and debts so as to minimize any budgetary shock that may come from switching from paycheck to pension check.

* Lastly, but as important as any of the above, devoting some
serious hours each week to the activities you'll be wanting to
fill your time with when work ceases.

"No, Bob, you don't understand. I'm talking serious money. I just
came from a session with a financial planner, and when he told me
how much money I'd have to start saving now just to maintain my style
of life and keep up with inflation on retirement, I about flipped!"

Okay, let's work on this often misleading, fear-inspiring concept,
which often is little more than a sales pitch for some kind of investment or annuity plan. I've heard it myself more times than I care to
remember, and droves of listeners have sent me copies of what they've
been pitched.

A common come-on in selling long-term retirement investment
plans is to show the prospect a mystifying chart representing "the
future value of money." While this is, indeed, a valid and important
concern in many areas of the economy, it can play games with the
minds of ordinary folks. In essence, the future value of money refers to
how much you can buy tomorrow with one of today's dollars.

The pitch may sound something like this: "If you need six dollars
to buy a movie ticket today, you might need twelve dollars to buy one
when you retire. That's inflation for you. If you're earning, say,
$50,000 a year now, you will need $100,000 a year when you retire to
continue living in the same style you're now enjoying. How can you
generate that kind of money when you're no longer working? You start
putting it away now in our Variable Adjustable Guaranteed Universal
Eternal plan. Once you sign up for VAGUE and start stashing those
dollars, your future will be secured."

And so will the salesperson's.

The concept is fine: To be able to continue living in your present
style even after income from work ceases. The problem, though, is that
if you want to do that you may have to put away so much money now
that you'd seriously impair your current life style.

But you don't have to punish yourself now in order to live comfortably later. And you don't have to take on needless risks to accomplish your goals.

Harken to some of the realities of *Regeneration* time.

You will not need the same relative income to continue living in
your present style. That's mainly because you will find a *new style* of

living that won't require as much money as you now spend. These factors will reshape your financial situation:

* Your dwelling needs will diminish. The kids will be grown and off on their own. The family house will be too big for two people. You'll sell the family home, thereby freeing up a substantial amount of capital that you can put to work earning extra money for you. You'll find new quarters that will be less expensive to maintain. Even if you decide to stay in the old home, your mortgage will be paid off. If it isn't, you can likely refinance it and cut your monthly payments considerably. All of these factors can make a huge difference in your spendable income. (Being able to do all of this requires that you don't load yourself up to the hilt in homeowner debt; it's part of the advance phasing-in program I mentioned earlier.)

* Your transportation costs will diminish. There may have been a time when you were a three- or four-car family: one each for you and the spouse, and a couple for the kids. When *Regeneration* kicks in you'll become a two-car, and maybe even a one-car, family. Just cutting commuting costs can mean a difference of thousands of dollars per year.

* Your custodial costs will diminish as your kids become self-sufficient. (See Chapter 28, "Getting the Kids Off the Payroll.")

* Your "social" costs will diminish. This encompasses a variety of expenses you incur in your working routine that will phase out as your work ceases. You spend more on clothing, cosmetics, and accessories when you're working than you will during *Regeneration*. Work-related entertainment, lunches, and similar indulgences (a couple of drinks after work with your pals?) will be reduced if not eliminated. And the buying of "toys"— having the newest and best electronic gizmos, and so on, so that you can keep up with the trends—will fade away as the foolishness of "keeping up" becomes more clear.

* Some insurance costs may diminish. Obvious savings can be on your home and auto coverage as noted above. If you carry income disability insurance, there'll be no further need for that once you've stopped working. If you've been paying for some of your health insurance—and more people will be doing so as

employers shift more of that burden onto employees—you can be relieved of that load, though some of the savings may go to pay for Medicare supplementary coverage. You may be able to realize some major savings in your life insurance portfolio. (See Chapter 29, "That Was Then, This Is Now.")

Not all people will realize all possible savings, and none of the savings are automatic. You have to make a conscious effort to attain the savings, but you can do so without making any tangible sacrifice in the quality of your life. By making these timely conscious efforts you can offset much of the effect of inflation on the future value of money.

Before you embark on a VAGUE plan, you must evaluate if you truly will need as much disposable income at that future time as the projections indicate. The above steps can help you inflation-proof yourself to a considerable extent. Your other earning assets—home equity, life insurance equity, pension, investments—can provide a handsome cushion that a VAGUE plan might not take into account.

Please do not misunderstand me: I'm not telling you that you don't have to put away money for your future security. You do. And that's most emphatic. But do so using your common sense and acquired knowledge. (See Chapter 23, the section on Rosefsky's Age + 40 Rule.) Some sales pitches might scare you into a program that has unseen pitfalls. Worse yet, once in such a program, the cost of getting out might be punitive, particularly if there was a heavy up-front loading commission plus a redemption charge.

*
**   *
**   *
**

There will also be many who will not plan to retire, or *Regenerate,* at any time, for any reason. They're going to keep on working, come what may, until the bitter end. So be it. That is their choice. To which I can only say that no one ever lay on their death bed saying, "I wish I had spent more time at the office."

How Are Debtors Like Ostriches?

"We're running behind in all of our debts. We just can't seem to catch up. The collection agencies leave messages for us every day. If we talk to them, they just dun us all the more. How can we get out from under? Please help. We're getting desperate!"

If I had a dime for every one of these calls I got, I'd never have to worry about my own debts. The most distressing part of these calls was that they all had one similar feature: The debtors were hiding. They had their heads buried in the sand hoping that the problems would just disappear. Oh dear, what a sad mistake . . . and how easy it can be to avoid the problems altogether.

Herewith, Doctor Rosefsky's Remarkable Remedies for Common Credit Ailments:

* The *absolutely worst* thing you can do if you're in debt trouble is to bury your head and hide. That's true for any and all kinds of debts: credit cards, charge accounts, rent, home loans, bills, car financing, and so on. Take my word for it that no grantor of credit wants to have to worry about delinquents; I learned this first hand in the years I spent in banking, and more years in real estate. Do not wait until trouble is at hand. At the earliest possible time you sense trouble looming, you *must* visit with your creditors *in person* and start to work out a program that you both can live with. I said in person, and I mean in person. Phone calls and letters will not do. This *must* be eyeball-to-eyeball if it's going to work. (Obviously, if you're dealing with an out-of-town lender, the personal meeting might be impractical; in such a case speak with a credit supervisor on the telephone.)

Creditors *will* try to help you develop a payoff schedule that gives you some breathing room. It may be something as simple as altering your monthly payment date from, say, the first to the fifteenth. They may be able to allow you to skip payments for a month or two. They may be able to rewrite your debt so as to reduce the monthly payments. (But beware the trap that Pat and Fran fell into in the Captive Borrowers section of Chapter 9.) And they may even waive late charges if you ask them to. (See Rosefsky's Rule #738b.)

If you do hide from creditors, they will *rightfully* assume that you do not want to correct your delinquent status, and they will treat you accordingly. That means the dunning letters, the collection agencies, a bad record on your credit history that can stay with you for many years, and extra interest and costs.

I know you're scared and embarrassed to face these people and discuss your problems. But they don't bite. It's in *their* best interest to meet with you and help you. So please, *just do it.*

There are other places you can go to get credit problems corrected. The *wrong* kind of place is what I call a "credit repair clinic."

Abuses by these privately owned companies have been going on for years. While there may be legitimate operators among them, the bad apples pose serious danger to the unwitting consumer. They promise that they will solve all your credit problems—for a fee. Once you've paid the fee they promise to work out a new payment schedule with your creditors. You're told to send an agreed monthly total to the clinic, and they will parcel it out to the creditors in accordance with the revised plan. Worst-case scenario: They keep your fee and/or monthly payments and disappear. Your creditors never see a penny, and you're in deeper than you were before.

On the other hand, virtually every community has a Consumer Credit Counseling Bureau, or a similarly titled agency, that is a non-profit entity funded by local merchants and lenders, with possible additional support from the government. These agencies provide a counseling service, usually at no cost, and can also work out a new payment plan with all of your creditors. There may be a nominal service charge for handling the payments. Every bit of feedback I've ever gotten from folks I've referred to these agencies has been positive.

* There are some federal laws that you should be aware of whether you're having credit problems or not. Knowing how these laws work can keep you out of trouble. Any lender or credit bureau should be able to provide you with details of the law, as can your local reference librarian.

* *The Truth-in-Lending Law.* It sets forth the legal way lenders must quote borrowing costs so that you can get an accurate comparison of costs from various lenders. It also establishes a three-day "cooling off" period during which you can cancel certain agreements, particularly with reference to those that put liens on real estate that you own or are buying.

* *The Fair Credit Reporting Law.* It sets forth rules on what local credit bureaus and lenders can and cannot do with regard to credit information on individuals. It gives you specific rights to know what's in your credit file, to be able to correct wrong information in your file, and to insert your own version of any disputed item in your file.

* *The Equal Credit Opportunity Law.* It prohibits discrimination in lending with respect to sex or marital status.

* *The Fair Debt Collection Practices Law.* It defines what debtors and debt collectors can and cannot do with respect to collecting money owed them, and it sets forth remedies for debtors who suffer abuses under the law.
* *The Fair Credit Billing Law.* It sets forth your rights if you receive an erroneous billing on a credit account, and describes how to protect yourself in such an event.

Many states may also have laws that duplicate or overlap these federal laws.

Please be aware that the feds will not come riding to your rescue if your rights under any of these laws have been violated. *The burden is on you* to recognize that your rights have been violated, and to take the necessary steps to protect yourself. Once again Rosefsky's Rule #738b comes into play.

* Self-abusive practices account for a great many credit problems. Two of the most frequent are known as "pyramiding" and "consolidating." A brief look at each: Pyramiding occurs typically in auto financing. You buy a new car and finance it with a four-year loan for, say, $10,000. Three years later, when you still owe about $2,500 on the first loan, you decide to get another new car, for which you'll need a loan of $12,500. But because you still owe $2,500 on the prior car, your new loan has to be increased to $15,000 (plus all the interest that's added on). You are pyramiding one debt on top of another, and in a few years you're going to be in deep trouble.

There is one commanding rule that you must follow if you want to avoid the dangers of pyramiding: *Any installment loan should be paid off before the need recurs to borrow again for that same purpose.* In other words, if you obtain a four-year car loan, don't get another car loan until the initial one is paid off, and so on. The rule is broken all too often by folks who later regret having done so. Don't be one of those troubled people.

Consolidating, which was referred to briefly in Chapter 9, involves taking out one big new loan to pay off alot of smaller debts. If this is done prudently and infrequently, it might ease up your credit problems. But the temptation is there to do it too frequently, in which case you end up needing one giant consolidation loan to pay off all of your former big consolidation loans, and that's the day that the camel's back breaks.

These potential problems can be minimized by having frank discussions about your overall credit situation with a loan officer at your bank or with a counselor at your local Consumer Credit Counseling Bureau. Needless to say, you should have these consultations before you take on any substantial load of credit. After may be too late.

* The granddaddy source of most credit problems is plastic: the credit card. I thought that certain people might be immune to such problems, particularly if they had a father who was an acknowledged authority in matters of personal finance, and who saw to it that his children were regularly cautioned on the dangers of easy credit. I was wrong. At least three of my four kids all ran into the plastic demon at one time or another. They've all been able to bail themselves out, but we had some delicate moments.

I recall with amusement the plight of my oldest, Debbie. During her college years I offered to co-sign for her on a Visa card. She had a part-time job, and knew that it was her responsibility to make her own payments. I lectured her sternly but affectionately about how treacherously simple it can be to run up unmanageable debts, particularly if she paid only the minimum amount required each month.

A few years went by during which I heard nothing about any credit card problems she might be having, so I assumed (foolishly) that everything was okay. Then one day she called me, quite elated, and said, "Guess what, Dad."

"What?" I asked.

"I'm getting a MasterCard!" she enthused. "On my own!"

"That's fine, dear," I replied. "But what's the matter with your Visa card?"

"It's full."

I cautioned her that, as with automobiles, you don't get a new one because the ashtray is full, nor do you get a new credit card when the old one is full. She's been dodging bullets ever since, and I think she'll survive, but it's been dicey now and then.

Credit can be an addiction, and the cards are the paraphernalia, the needles and the razors and the clips. I think the worst case I ever heard of was the couple who couldn't resist taking every new credit card offer that came in their mail. When I found them they had close to twenty different cards with debts in excess of $40,000! Interest alone on the debt was costing them over $8,000 per year. It was a long hard climb out of that hole.

Here are some easier-said-than-done-but-you-can-do-it-if-you-put-your-mind-to-it tips to keep you from falling into the most common credit card traps:

* Pay off your credit card debt in full each month. How are you supposed to do that, you may be asking me? Simply, wisely, prudently, and intelligently by *not* charging any more in a given month than you can afford to pay off! If you do this, I guarantee you'll never again have to worry about how much interest it's costing you to keep your credit card accounts up to date. Just how does one manage this? Two ways:

* Go through your budget and determine just how much each month you can afford to charge on your credit cards. Post that amount on a sheet of paper in a conspicuous place, such as on the door of your fridge. Every time you use your credit card write that amount on the paper and keep a running total. When you hit the total for the month, put the credit card *into* the fridge and leave it there until next month. Seriously: Keeping a visible running total of the amounts you've charged can serve as an excellent reminder of when it's time to stop. Most people never have a foggy clue from week to week as to what their charges for the current month are totaling.

* Better still: Each time you use your credit card write out a check to the bank for the amount of the charge. Put the accumulated checks into an envelope, and at the end of the month you've already paid your debt in full. (Just be sure that in doing this you don't overdraw your checking account.)

* Every budget has a "miscellaneous" bulge. That's a cause of a lot of credit grief, because it's tough to trace where all the money went. Cure: Go on Dr. Rosefsky's Dollar Diet. It's free, and it works! Carry a pad and pen with you, and for sixty days, each time you're about to spend *any* money (cash, credit card, or check) stop *before* you spend to write the item and the cost on your pad. In the few seconds it takes you to think about it, you might well decide not to incur the expense. But if you do spend the money, you'll have a clear record at the end of each month as to where every penny went, and what constitutes

the miscellaneous bulge. Then you can reflect, discipline yourself, and take action. You'll shed excess debt quicker than you thought possible.

* As I mentioned earlier, credit is an addiction, a dumb craving. But you must realize that no credit card yet invented can, on its own, jump out of your wallet and onto the stamping machine. You can't blame the card for your excess debts and overpowering interest costs. It's you that does it. Stop feeling that it's the bank or the store or the advertising that causes your debt. It's you. Take responsibility for your own actions. You're smarter than some dumb craving. Prove that to yourself, and be proud of yourself.

Complications

Woven throughout all of these common problems were common complications that made the problems harder to solve. You are heir to the same problems. Let me illustrate them so that you can spot them and avoid them. They are: Jargon Trauma, Rosefsky's Rule of Thumb, and The Greater Fool Theory. In order:

* *Jargon Trauma.* With rare exception, my troubled callers had picked up a dose of jargon—language that they didn't really understand, but whose meaning was critical to their concerns. They may have heard professionals use the language of their trade, such as when stock brokers glibly refer to "p/e ratios" or "ex-dividend dates," or "convertible debentures." Or when insurance agents unthinkingly use terms like "waiver of premium" or "incontestible clause" or "double indemnity." Or when bankers talk about matters such as "margins" and "the cost of funds index" and "due on sale" clauses.

Or they may have read the jargon in an article, or picked it up over drinks, or adapted it as the latest trendy buzzword. In whatever way they've come in contact with it, they really don't understand it. Failing to understand it, they could make a serious financial mistake.

All professions have jargon—mumbo-jumbo, gibberish, bafflegab, econobabble—words and phrases that they are accustomed to using so often that they are unaware the public might not understand them.

Lawyers and shrinks are the worst. I know, I'm the former and my wife is the latter. It's a wonder we were ever able to get together long enough to have four kids.

What was most frustrating to me was that people who were suffering from Jargon Trauma *knew* that they didn't understand what those particular words meant. More important, they *didn't know* the consequences that could follow if they took action based in part on jargon. As in (with the jargon *in italics,* as if you didn't know):

"My financial planner tells me that if I want my money to grow, I should put it all into a *growth* mutual fund."

"Do you know what a *growth* mutual fund is all about?"

"Uhhhh nn . . . no, not really. It's where your money grows?"

"No. A growth mutual fund puts your money at risk. In a growth mutual fund, you could lose money. In an *income* mutual fund your investment should grow at a slow but steady pace, with little risk of loss. Isn't that what you prefer?"

Or:

"The seller's real estate agent told me that I don't need to have a *financing contingency clause* in my contract to buy the house. It'll just slow things down, and I want to move fast."

"Do you know what a *financing contingency clause* is all about?"

"Uhhhh nn . . . no, not really. It's where you might be able to get a mortgage loan?"

"No. A financing contingency clause states that if you can't get a home loan at a certain rate of interest, you can get out of the contract to buy the property. Without that clause, you may have to end up paying a higher rate of interest than you can really afford. Is that what you want?"

Or:

"A plumber did some lousy work on my house, and I refused to pay him. He says if I don't pay he'll slap a *mechanic's lien* on the house. He can bluff all he wants, but I'm not paying!"

"Do you know what a *mechanic's lien* is all about?

"Uhhhh nn . . . no, not really. It's an auto repairman standing at an angle?"

"No. A mechanic's lien is a legal claim against your property. In most states, most tradesmen can place a lien on your property if you fail to pay them for work done. Once a lien is on your property, you may not be able to sell or borrow against the property until the debt is paid. And it could be reflected in your credit history. This is no bluff. Resolve your dispute—perhaps through mediation or small claims court—or be prepared to suffer along with a mechanic's lien against your property."

What's the solution to Jargon Trauma? I'm as prone to using jargon as anyone, but I do my best to be aware of it and avoid it. (My apologies if any has slipped out in this book.) I have done this countless times on the radio, and in private consultations as well: I tell my listeners to stop me if I say something that they don't understand. Just simply say, "Stop . . . you just said something and I don't know what it means. Please explain." I do my best to comply.

I want you to do the same thing whenever you talk to anyone, or read material anyone has given you that has financial implications you don't understand. Say to them, "I don't understand what you just said (or what I just read). Please go back and explain, and *keep* explaining until I'm *certain* that I know the meaning of the words *and* their specific importance to me." If they don't comply, look for someone else selling the same thing who will comply.

One other aspect of Jargon Trauma:

Every so often I will accidently let some jargon slip, and soon thereafter I see my client's eyes glaze over. That tells me that they heard my jargon but did not stop me. So I stop myself and say, "You didn't understand what I just said, did you?"

"No."

"Then why didn't you stop me like I asked you to so that I could explain what I was talking about?"

"I forgot." Or, "I was too embarrassed." Or, "I didn't think it would make any difference."

Don't forget. You do so at your own peril. *Don't* be embarrassed. You're entitled to explanations; it's the person using too much jargon who should be embarrassed. *Don't* think it makes no difference. It can make a huge difference.

 *   *Rosefsky's Rule of Thumb.* This is the essence of simplicity: All Thumbs Are Different. Failure to recognize that can lead to financial danger.

A frightfully large number of people make financial decisions that simply mimic decisions that other people have made, for better or worse. Note the following examples:

"My cousin Dave and I are very much alike. We're the same age, and we both have two kids in their mid-teens. I know I need to have a will drawn, but rather than spend good money on a lawyer, I'm just going to copy the will Dave just had prepared."

"My co-worker Vinnie and I are very much alike. We both have been on the job here for 15 years, and we belong to the same bowling team. Vinnie's stockbroker just gave him a great tip on a company that has a patent on something he calls a transferable digital multiplexing fractionator. You know, a TDMF. I don't have a stockbroker of my own, but if this is good enough for Vinnie, it's good enough for me."

"My neighbor Shirley and I are very much alike. We both live on the same street, and we both have each other as neighbors. Shirley just refinanced her mortgage. She got a great interest rate on a thirty-year adjustable loan. I could save $300 a month compared to what I'm paying now, so I'm going to get the same deal that Shirley got."

I am not making this up! Oh, yes, the names and the particulars are fictional, but the basic situations are all too common—ridiculously so. You and your cousin Dave are *not* alike for purposes of estate planning, and copying his will could leave your family in a shambles. You and your co-worker Vinnie are *not* alike in financial terms, and sending your money down the same road that he is could be catastrophic for you. You and your neighbor Shirley are *not* alike with respect to your housing budgets, and by aping her you could be in for a bruising, particularly when the initial come-on rate for that adjustable mortgage starts climbing, and your assumed $300 a month savings soon turns into a higher payment than you're now making.

My Rule of Thumb is ignored because people want shortcuts, bargains, and cheap thrills. But things just don't work that way, friends. Despite any and all outward similarities, you are *unlike* everyone else. If only just your dreams and aspirations are exclusively yours (and they are), that puts you into different circumstances for your major financial decisions. You must evaluate *your own condition,* as it is *now* and *as you want it to be,* and make the important decisions accordingly. If I ever catch you being a copycat in matters such as these, you'll be sorry. You'll be sorry even if I don't catch you.

*   *The Greater Fool Theory.* This represents mankind's futile attempt to reject the Law of Gravity. The Greater Fool Theory states: "If I buy something, no matter how high the price, sooner or later a

Greater Fool than myself will come along and buy it from me at an even higher price."

In short, this is a belief that what goes up will not necessarily come down.

The Greater Fool Theory does work much of the time. But one important fact is overlooked by those who subscribe to the theory, and it's this: There is a *limited supply* of Greater Fools. When you run out of them, the theory no longer works.

I heard innumerable psalms to the glory of the Greater Fool Theory. This is what they sounded like:

"I know that property values are sky high, but if I don't buy that dreamhouse right now, it could cost me thousands more in just a couple of weeks."

"I know that the stock in National Pripichik and Gumball is selling at an all-time high, but there's still plenty of room for it to go higher. I'm jumping on the bandwagon while I can."

"I know that Mickey Mantle baseball cards are going through the roof, but the supply is limited and the demand is phenomenal. You know what that'll do to the price? I'm buying all I can."

"I know that the time-share condo is expensive, but there'll always be a booming tourist industry in Miami Beach. So let's take the plunge. We can always unload it at a huge profit."

The Greater Fool Theory is most evident during times of buying frenzies. A buying frenzy takes place after all the insiders have grabbed up the best deals, and after the insiders' relatives have picked the meat off the bones of what's left. Then comes the frenzied public, having learned too little too late about what once was a good deal. They buy the bones, and then wait and pray for the Greater Fools to come along to bail them out. But there are none left.

*
**   *
**   *
**

Jargon can be defined.

Rosefsky's Rule of Thumb can be easily explained.

But the Greater Fool Theory is an imbedded mindset that is very tough to dispel. It's even tougher to restore common sense when a salesperson is involved, fanning the flames of the frenzy in the mind of the would-be buyer. What makes matters worse is that there's no absolutely reliable way to predict the exact moment when the supply of Greater Fools will dry up, so people continue to defy the odds until the last bitter moment of truth. There are even those who, *after* the bubble has burst, will say, "That's only a temporary setback. The potential for profit will come raging back."

So I can't give you any hard-and-fast solution for the dilemma posed by the Greater Fool Theory. Everyone, sooner or later, falls prey to it. Many of us have enough common sense to recognize the pitfalls and pull back before it's too late. And many don't. But armed with just your basic intelligence and awareness of this phenomenon you should do quite nicely when temptation rears its ugly head—which it will, often.

After some 10,000 phone calls over almost a decade, it came time to give my final sign-off and move on to other things, such as this book. I was proud of my work, and I knew from my listeners' responses that I had helped a lot of people. The same problems and frustrations and fears persist in the minds of the public at large, and will continue to do so for decades hence. I wish I could offer some magic formulas or get-rich-quick potions that would cure all these ills. There are already too many out there who do that; the field is overcrowded. I can offer only more modest nostrums: common sense, a willing-to-learn attitude, a healthy skepticism of deals that sound to good to be true, and a continuing quest for knowledge. Thanks for listening. I'll be back after these messages.

Chapter Twenty-four

Jests and Jibes

✔ *Fooling Around with the IRS and Living to Tell About It*
✔ *Physician, Heal Thyself, and a Lesson You Can Take to Work with You*

How about a little dessert after that heavy meal in the last chapter?

Fooling Around with the IRS and Living to Tell About It

I'll keep my promise now to tell you about an incident with the IRS that took place on my radio show; that plus an instructive little lesson that I was able to give to one of the bigger banks in Los Angeles, and which might be of value to you, too.

As I mentioned, I rarely had guests on the radio show. One exception was a gentleman from the Internal Revenue Service named Abe Carnow. Abe was an agent—he did audits—and I wanted someone with that background to help me answer appropriate questions at tax filing time and during a regular year-end tax planning program that I did each November. Abe had been referred to me by the IRS Public Affairs office in Los Angeles, which was headed by Rob Gianangeli. Abe had been a frequent guest on the show. Rob had been with me just once, but he was the heavy hitter when most of the local newscasts needed an IRS person to explain something current. They both did an excellent job, and they both had a delightful sense of humor.

That particular year there had been a lot of new income tax laws put on the books and filing season looked to be rather hectic for taxpayers. I decided to take a double-barreled approach and have both Abe and Rob guest on the show. Between the three of us, I felt, no tax question could go unanswered.

Sunday, the day of my show, happened to fall on April 1. I wondered, "Do I dare play an April Fool's joke on the Internal Revenue Service, with 100,000-plus people listening?"

I'll tell you what happened, just as it happened.

Abe and Rob arrived at the station about fifteen minutes before showtime. Both had had plenty of experience in broadcasting so there was not a trace of nervousness about them. They were armed with enough tax books to fill a small library, and they were ready to deal with any and all questions that came their way. We chatted amiably until the start of the show. Before we took any calls Abe and Rob explained the major changes in the laws and the forms that taxpayers would be facing in the weeks ahead.

Then I opened the lines for the first call. It was from a young woman named Deb. The following is as close to verbatim as I can remember.

Deb: "Good evening Abe and Rob and Bob. I have a question about deductions. Is drinking beer deductible?"

Abe, grinning confidently, answered this seemingly naive question most politely: "Not really, Deb. The cost of food and beverage that you consume is not tax-deductible. The only exception might be if the beer was consumed as part of a business meal or meeting. If it was related to business, then its cost could be deductible."

Rob, authoritatively, but equally polite: "Of course, you'd have to have proper receipts if you wanted to claim the deduction for business purposes. Does that answer your question?"

Deb: "No, not actually. It isn't me that drinks the beer, it's my Dad. And I'm not sure if he drinks it for business purposes or not."

Me: "Well for what purpose *does* he drink the beer?"

Deb: "He collects beer bottles from all over the country and all over the world. Most of the bottles he gets have beer in them, obviously. But he doesn't want to collect the *full* bottles. He wants to collect *empty* bottles because they're easier to handle. So, naturally, he has to get rid of the beer in the bottles. And rather than waste it by pouring it out, he drinks it."

Abe, getting serious as he starts to flip through the pages of the tax reference books: "So your Dad drinks the beer in conjunction with his collecting beer bottles. That's his hobby, right?"

Deb: "Right."

Abe: "If it's part of a hobby activity, that is, a non-income-producing activity, it wouldn't be deductible. Hobby expenses aren't deductible."

Deb: "But what if you separate the cost of the beer from the cost of the bottle? The bottle collection isn't any good unless he disposes of the beer. So could just the cost of the beer inside the bottles be deductible?"

Rob, joining Abe's seriousness over this increasingly perplexing question, the nature of which has obviously never come to their attention in all their years with the IRS: "No, Deb, Abe is right. You can't separate the cost of the beer from the cost of the bottle. It's all one cost, and as long as it's a hobby the cost is nondeductible."

Deb: "Well, what if he *sells* the beer bottle collection and makes a *profit*. Wouldn't that be a taxable gain? And if the gain is taxable, wouldn't the cost of making the collection saleable—that is, getting rid of the beer—be deductible?"

Abe and Rob, both befuddled now at the seeming logic of the question, even though the entire subject was completely off the wall: "Yes . . . I'm not sure . . . Maybe. . . ."

Deb, insistently now: "Well I happen to know that last year there was a decision in the Second District United States Circuit Court that said when a collector of coins sold his collection at a gain, all the costs involved in putting the collection into the most saleable condition could be subtracted from his profit, thereby adjusting his cost basis upward, which in essence establishes the deductibility of those expenses. If the Second United States Circuit Court says that about coin collections, wouldn't the same thing hold true with beer bottle collections?"

Abe, flustered: "Under those circumstances you might be able to get away with the deduction for the beer, but your Dad might have to prove that he couldn't have sold the collection at the same price if the bottles were full instead of empty."

Rob, equally flustered: "I'm not familiar with that case. Further, we happen to be in the Ninth Circuit of the United States court system, and I'm not sure if a decision in the Second Circuit would have the same binding effect on us as would a Ninth Circuit opinion. Also, that Second Circuit opinion might be appealed, and it could be overturned. So I'd wait until after that time has elapsed before feeling comfortable with claiming the deduction."

Me, seemingly vexed with this persistent call of very narrow scope: "Young lady, just who do you think you are, and who does your Dad think he is, taking up our valuable time with a question like this? We have lots of other callers waiting to ask more pertinent questions!"

Deb, who is actually calling from an engineer's booth adjoining our studio, about ten feet away from where we're sitting, and who now becomes visible through the glass partition as the light in her booth is turned on: "Who do I think I am? I think I'm Bob Rosefsky's daughter, and I'm here to wish Abe and Rob and the entire Internal Revenue Service and all of Bob's listeners a happy April Fool's Day."

Gotcha! Abe and Rob burst into laughter as they quickly realized our little prank. As gentlemen, they took it all in good humor as callers throughout the evening chuckled at the incident.

I had scripted the whole thing for Debbie, and I was lucky in anticipating every response that Abe and Rob would give. Taxes aren't funny, but people can be. It added a bit of lightness to what was otherwise an evening of heavy-duty tax matters, and the flavor stayed on for many weeks as callers continued to recall the episode.

Do not try this at home.

Do not claim the cost of your beer as a tax deduction.

Do not send me beer bottles, empty or full. I don't really collect them.

Do not otherwise try to fool the Internal Revenue Service.

Physician, Heal Thyself, and a Lesson You Can Take to Work with You

I always tried to keep a good mix of questions on the program. It's not good to get bogged down for too long on one subject. Variety keeps listeners tuned in.

But one particular night I must have hit a raw nerve among my listeners. One caller brought up the subject of how rudely she was treated by her bank, and this opened a floodgate of similar complaints.

That's all the callers wanted to talk about, so I let them all spill their anger into the airwaves.

The next day I received a phone call at my office from the head of public relations of one of the city's larger banks. I was expecting to be chastised for allowing so much antibank venom on the air, and I was certain that the caller would ask for equal airtime to defend his industry.

To my surprise, however, I was told that the complaints on my program were justifiable, and that it was high time that bank employees who deal with the public were given some training in good public relations. He then asked me if I would conduct a series of seminars for his bank to do just that. The seminars would be attended primarily by branch managers.

I quickly recalled my years in banking: how hard it was to attract new customers and how easy it was to lose one for the slightest reason. I welcomed the opportunity to do the seminars, and the scheduling was soon underway.

Coincidentally, at that same time, the federal government was loosening controls on the kinds of accounts banks could offer the public. One such new account that was just going into effect was the thirty-month (two-and-a-half years) Certificate of Deposit. Prior to that time CDs were not permitted to run that long. As part of my regular radio and TV commentaries I reported on interest rate trends at various local banks, and this new account added a feature to my so-called "interest rate scoreboard."

When the new account debuted—at all local banks simultaneously—I phoned most of the major ones to learn what rates they'd be paying on those plans. Because of some inexplicable habit or quirk of mine, I referred to the new plans as "two-and-a-half-year CDs," rather than thirty-month CDs. The responses I got were to become a major focal point in my educational seminars.

The first seminar was underway, and it went well. I pointed out some of the ills that cause public relations problems: tellers who are so intent on keeping track of their window transactions that they don't always extend the simple courtesies that customers expect; branch managers who could—but don't bother to—smooth the ruffled feathers of customers waiting in long slow-moving lines; other personnel who will allow themselves to get into petty arguments with customers rather than apologizing for their lack of knowledge and calling for a superior to help solve the problem, and so on. We discussed some of the cures that could remedy the ills—education, communication, some minor rescheduling of lunch hours to minimize bottlenecks, and the like.

Then came time for the midmorning break, and this was when I was going to drive home the most important lesson of the day. I gave all of the branch managers an assignment during the break: They were to call their branches anonymously and ask what interest rate they were paying on the new two-and-a-half-year accounts. They were to pay close attention to the manner in which their calls were handled and their inquiry answered.

They asked me, almost in unison, what point there was in them calling their own branches. I told them that they'd get the point when they made their calls.

When they returned from the break their expressions ranged from angry to perplexed, and all points in between. They had received the same kind of responses I had gotten when I made my survey calls, which they described as follows:

* "The person who answered the phone was downright rude; I was astonished. If that's the way customers are treated, we're in big trouble, or else that phone receptionist is."

* "I asked about the two-and-a-half-year account and I was told that they didn't have such an account. They did, however, have a thirty-month account. I couldn't believe it."

* "When I asked what rate they were paying on the two-and-a-half-year account she said to me, 'Is that the same as the thirty-month account?'"

* "He put me on hold; it was interminable. I've never called our branch before anonymously; it was terrible."

* "I asked what rates they were paying, and he just rattled off a list of all our various accounts, so quickly that it was a jumble. When I asked him to repeat the rate on the specific account he just read the whole list to me again. I felt like I was talking to a robot."

* "I was put on hold, then I heard a lot of clicking sounds, and then I was cut off. I called back and it happened again!"

* "Whoever answered the phone couldn't answer my question so she went to find someone who could. Then someone else came on the line, but he didn't know the answer either, and he then went to find someone who did. At that point I gave up. I thought we had instructed all of our employees adequately about this new account."

* "The person who answered the phone said, 'Just a moment please, I'll let you speak to our manager.' Ours is a small branch. Everyone can see everyone else. I can't believe she didn't know that I wasn't there all morning. Then she came back on the line to tell me that I must have stepped away from my desk, and asked if I wanted to leave a message. No one else was asked if my question could be answered."

A small minority were satisfied that their calls had been properly handled. The rest were mortified at how improperly they had been treated. That was the lesson of the day, and it had been right on target.

A few weeks later I called a sampling of the bank's branches and asked what rate they were paying on two-and-a-half-year accounts. Without exception I got a crisp, polite, and accurate answer, followed by, "Can I help you open an account, sir?"

When was the last time you called your place of work, pretending you were a customer or client, and wanting to have a simple question answered? Try it. It could prove to be an incomparable learning experience.

Chapter Twenty-five

Going Broke by Going for Broke

Enthusiasm is wonderful in a business venture, but beware of an excess of it. Lessons for entrepreneurs, investors, lenders, employees, suppliers, and others whose financial well-being is at stake.

✔ *Breaking Free*
  . . . in the realm of the impossible there are too many possibilities
✔ *Breaking Rules*
  . . . high-hopes showdown by guided missile?

The familiar rallying cries are hard to ignore:
  "Go for it!"
  "Give it your all!"
  "Gangbusters!"
  "All or nothing!"
  "Give it your best shot!"
  "All the marbles!"
  "Go for broke!"
  "The whole nine yards!"
And so on. (I could never understand that last one. I thought it took ten yards to make a first down. Am I missing something?)

Far be it from me to dampen anyone's genuine enthusiasm, but I must tell you that there is danger in going overboard on a venture: Going for broke in the wrong way can break you.

Business ventures, particularly new ones, can get caught up in the rush of inflated expectations, with the result that too much money and too much energy are thrown into the project at the outset, and not enough is kept in reserve for a fallback position.

Had enough money and energy been held back, a prematurely failed venture might have become a success—later than sooner, but a success rather than a failure.

Whether you're an entrepreneur, an investor therein, a landlord or employee thereof, or a supplier or lender thereto, you can get hurt if a "go for broke" effort fails to pay off. It's incumbent on you to monitor any such situation, and take whatever actions are appropriate in order to protect your own interests. If someone in whom you have a financial stake appears to be going overboard, and you fail to stop the plunge, your money could go overboard as well.

I've seen many ventures fail because of this excessive initial enthusiasm. I've often been called in as consultant, but usually (and unfortunately) after the fact.

I've also been personally involved in some insane situations along these lines, so my cautions to you are tempered by my own experiences.

Breaking Free

I had written a book some years earlier titled *Getting Free: How to Profit Most Out of Working for Yourself*. It was, as the title makes clear, a how-to guide to becoming successfully self-employed. It was published by Quadrangle/New York Times, and, like the vast majority of hard-cover books, it had its brief life and then went to Book Heaven.

Years later its ghost came back to haunt me. As you've no doubt seen, late-night television is chock-a-block with various kinds of "infomercials"—half-hour (and longer) programs that are really nothing more than one long sales pitch for convection ovens, diet plans, computer lessons, and assorted other nonnecessities.

Of special interest are the money-related pitches that offer secrets known only to the promoters. But now the promoters are willing to share their secrets with you if you pay them enough money. You know the ilk: Make a fortune in real estate, a killing in the stock market, a bonanza trading commodities. The fact is that the only people who make a bundle are the promoters, and then only when they come up with a clever enough pitch. Didn't you ever wonder, "If those secrets are so good, how come they're willing to sell them for a price?" The answer, simply enough, is that *the promoters can make more money selling you the secret than they can by using the secret*. Otherwise, they wouldn't be willing to sell it! If the secret was really that good, they'd keep it to themselves.

To this day I've yet to hear a single legitimate story about anyone who ever bought any of these get-rich plans who ever made any legitimate money from them. (Note my choice of the word "legitimate"; phony stories abound.)

Thus, when I was approached to create a television "infomercial" home-study course based on my self-employment book I was both aghast and curious. I was aghast at the thought of lending my good name to this form of hucksterism. And I was curious to see if I could create a truly legitimate home-study course that could deliver what it realistically promised, and be good value for the consumer's money.

How did they happen to approach me to take on this project? It's yet another example of karma: how fate can work its devilish ways. In the *Getting Free* book I had related a number of personal case histories, based on extensive interviews, telling how previously employed people had taken the initiative to leave the ranks of the employed and go off on their own. One of those stories involved a fellow who had worked for an advertising agency. He had grown tired of the grind and the politics and opted for the exciting insecurity of starting his own one-man agency. Through his agency he became, in time, one of the pioneer producers of infomercials. And he made a lot of money doing so. When he was looking for new subjects to turn into infomercials he remembered his own "getting free" experience, and my interview with him, and the story that became part of the book. Thus I was contacted to create my very own infomercial for him.

I met at length with the producers and the investors who would be putting up the money for the actual production costs (the video plus the print and audio materials that would comprise the home-study kit that they'd be selling). There was promise of good money in it for me, and the producer was willing to accept my strict terms. I was to receive a substantial amount of money up front, as an advance, plus further money later as a percent of sales. I was to have complete editorial control over everything—the content of the infomercial itself and all advertising relating to it, as well as the print and audio tapes that I'd be writing and voicing. There were to be no misrepresentations; no promises that could not be fulfilled to the letter.

We signed a contract and work got underway. The actual infomercial was shot in a single day, and it then took a few months to write and record the course material, plus another few months to manufacture the tapes and the printed matter.

Meanwhile the late-night infomercial phenomenon continued unabated. The public was seemingly buying anything and everything in enough numbers to assure a continuing flow of new products. Based on projections of my producer's own experience with his other products, and with what he knew about the market, he estimated that there would be a profit of many hundreds of thousands of dollars to be divided among us: the producer, the investors, and myself.

Did I begin to have inflated expectations about this prospect? You had better believe I did. Did I start to spend the money I hadn't yet earned? No. (I knew I was going to write *this* book someday and I had to be true to my own advice.) Did I have any inkling about the incredible event that would eventually occur that would determine the fate of this venture? I'd be kidding if I said I did. So would everyone else involved in the project.

Before we get to that incredible event—and at this point you couldn't possibly guess what it was—a few words about the marketing of these infomercial products. Like most books, home-study courses had a very short shelf life. In the first few days of a good new program the sales could be phenomenal. Then, within a few weeks, as the audience became saturated, the sales would taper off. When they reached a point when the income from sales was not enough to pay for more airtime, the product would be pulled off the market. Some products would be revived months later seeking a new audience. But given the rapid decay rate, new products had to be constantly introduced. That's why I was able to dictate such good terms for myself: New products with good potential were becoming increasingly hard to find. I was paid handsomely up front. But the real bonanza would come from my share of sales.

Generally, infomercial producers would introduce a new product with a weekend blitz on as many cable TV channels as they could afford. The reasonable expectation, based on their continuing experience, was that the income from that first weekend's blitz would pay for all production costs and the first week's advertising, plus enough left over for an ongoing advertising campaign, from which would come the profits. So the first weekend was critical.

Our infomercial was a mock "seminar" using paid actors as the participants. This fact was made known to our viewers. (Some infomercials use a "studio audience" who cheers wildly for the product and its pitchpeople. Know well that those audiences are rewarded for their seemingly genuine enthusiasm, and clever editing heightens the appearance of enthusiasm even more.)

Just as a regular television program is interrupted regularly by commercials, infomercials are interrupted every ten minutes or so by a sales pitch for the product. Viewers who are motivated to buy the product could call a toll-free 800 number and place their orders with a credit card. Most of the home-study courses were selling at that time in the $300 to $500 range.

Most of the cable channels used the same 800 numbers, which actually are fulfillment companies that processed all the orders. The producers, not the cable television companies, made arrangements for these 800 numbers.

In all cases, viewers were given unconditional money-back guarantees if they didn't like the product. This was offered even by the producers with the most ridiculous products. (Also in the ridiculous category was the number of viewers who did demand their money back: It was so small as to be insignificant.)

Our product was slightly retitled as *Breaking Free* to give it a more dynamic flavor. It consisted of twelve one-hour motivational audio tapes, a textbook that included material from the original *Getting Free* book plus detailed information from the Small Business Administration and other comparable sources, and a self-testing aptitude program that I had a psychologist create for the project. If anyone wanted the basic informational and inspirational tools that they'd need to embark on self-employment, I was proud that I had delivered what was being promised.

I also included an ongoing theme that my producers didn't like: I told viewers that if they wanted to become self-employed but couldn't hack the requirements I set forth, then my course could save them from making a catastrophic mistake that could cost them many thousands of dollars and cause untold disappointment. In short, even if my course convinced them that self-employment was *not* right for them (and it isn't for everyone, though some folks need a trial-by-ordeal to be convinced of the fact), then the expense would have been well worth it. My producers didn't like this because they thought it was negative. They wanted everything positive, but it stayed in the pitch.

Our infomercial had its opening weekend blitz on five cable TV networks, coast-to-coast and dusk-to-dawn. The producers had an advertising kitty of $50,000 and they allocated it all for that opening salvo. But with sales for the first weekend reasonably anticipated at 500 to 1,000 kits, at $395 per kit, we'd be at breakeven, including all production costs, by Monday morning. Even if the first weekend sales were only 300 kits—a number too low to believe, based on past experience with other products—we'd still be healthy, albeit a bit wary.

They were going for broke. The future looked incredibly bountiful.

The program really did air. I saw it. Lots of times, on different cable stations. So did family and friends, all of whom thought it was a good, solid, value-for-money offering. It took forever for Monday to arrive so that we could get the sales tallies from the 800 service.

On Monday morning the word I heard from the producers sent icewater rushing through my veins: "None." Zero. Zilch. Nil. Nada.

We had not sold a single solitary kit.

None.

Impossible? Impossible!

What had happened? The program had aired as scheduled. The 800 number had appeared on the screen as scheduled. As best as could be determined (cable television audience ratings were sketchy at best) the program had typical audiences for the time periods in which it aired. Nationally, over the course of the weekend, hundreds of thousands of people, if not a few million, had to have seen the program. I had some name recognition and good credibility from my other broadcast and newspaper exposure. Could it possibly be that *not one single soul* out there would have been interested in buying a very instructive home-study course on how to leave your boring job and go off on your own? with a money-back guarantee no less?

Have you guessed what happened? I doubt it. In the realm of the impossible there are too many possibilities.

This is what happened: *Nobody had informed the toll-free 800 order-fulfilling service that there was a new product being advertised that weekend called Breaking Free.*

Nobody!

So, when people called in to order, credit cards in hand, the 800 service had *no record* of its existence. Thus they could not take any orders.

Yes, there were lots of orders. We found that out later (too late to help) when the 800 people surveyed their operators. But no one took the names of the buyers because they had no order number to attach to the names. It was not in the computer. It didn't exist. And the 800 service didn't know how, or didn't think to contact the producers in the middle of the night to ask about this nonexistent product.

That part of the problem was compounded by the fact that the 800 operators wouldn't have any way of knowing which of the many producers out there had created *Breaking Free* because they were all sitting at their telephones taking calls for dozens of different products, not watching the sales pitches on television.

Further, over the course of the sixty to seventy hours that the program was airing, there could have been eight to ten different shifts of operators, with each shift having dozens or hundreds of operators. Realistically, then, there could have been upward of 1,000 operators on the phones over the course of the weekend blitz. Each one of them might have received *one* order for *Breaking Free*, and, having not found it on the computer, thought it was just a mistake and promptly forgot about it, and there could have gone the 1,000 orders that would have set our bells ringing.

Finally, during the *daylight* hours of the weekend no one, neither the producers (who had no reason to think there was a problem) nor the 800 people (who couldn't have known there was a problem) identified the glitch, let alone taken steps to correct it.

So, "none" it was, and "none" it was to remain. The producers had shot their wad on that first weekend blitz. They had gone for broke, given it their all, all or nothing, the whole nine yards. Now they were about $200,000 in the hole, counting production, advertising, my advance, and overhead. Each of their products had to stand on its own. They couldn't borrow from income on one successful product to buy airtime for another one. Contractual agreements by all the various parties prevented that.

Impossible? Incredible? Unbelievable? Never mind. It happened. Not only were they left with a stinging loss, but they had no fallback, no reserve. They had no choice but to let the project die aborning. I was the only one to come out ahead, but considering the time I had invested it was far from a bonanza.

This had happened before my very eyes. I had trusted their judgment, their experience, their skills. I didn't question. I didn't doubt. I didn't ask any "But what if" questions. And I'm supposed to know how to do all of that. If I can get caught like this, so can you. Except that now you're armed with some forewarnings.

End of story . . . but not the end of impossible happenings.

Breaking Rules

I was fated to have another confrontation with the Go-for-Broke syndrome. This time I was alert to the potential danger and I tried to stop it from happening, but I was helpless to change the course of events.

In 1989, after having left the radio and television stations in Los Angeles, Linda Sue and I decided to spend half our year (May through October) living in London, and the other six months in Los Angeles. Having sold my L.A. real estate investments at a handsome profit, and having packed my self-employed pension plan to the brim, I was in the enviable position of being able to choose what work, if any, I wanted to do. The first six months in London presented me with two opportunities: one for this chapter and one for the next chapter.

The Economist is the premier magazine on business in Britain, if not in the whole English-speaking world. I had always been a reader and admirer of it, and I longed to do some writing for it. While in London I made inquiries about writing assignments, only to find that with rare exceptions the entire magazine is written by staff. The rare exceptions were reserved for special articles by VIPs.

However, there was a subsidiary of the magazine called *Business International (BI)* that did publish a variety of works by freelancers such as myself. I stuck my neck out (see Chapter 12) and asserted myself into some meetings with the chief editors of *BI*, hoping to wangle myself some kind of assignment. I was what the British call a "cheeky Yank." We here in the former colonies are regarded by our former overlords as pushy, aggressive, and overly-competitive. Maybe that's why we've moved ahead so dramatically while their national spirit has been on the wane for decades. At any rate, if it took being cheeky to get an assignment, I was willing to risk carrying that stigma.

One category of *BI*'s publishing was a series of what they called "research reports." This was a most unusual publishing venture. These reports were, by any other name, simply books. They were large-format (8" by 11") soft-cover books that ran about 200 pages. The subjects were very narrowly focused for their international business clientele, dealing with high-level management and marketing issues, and laden heavily with specific case histories of worldwide business successes and failures. The key to the success of these publications was that the information in them, in addition to being very timely, was not readily available from any other source.

Further, the manner in which these reports/books were marketed gave them a very special veneer of exclusivity. They were sold *only* by direct-mail advertising. Over the years *BI* had developed an extraordinary mailing list of top corporate executives around the world who were able to buy expensive research publications for their companies without having to get any approval from anyone else. In short, the mailing list consisted of people who could write checks on the company accounts and thus buy items on impulse.

It was *BI*'s firm policy to put their all—go-for-broke—into one initial mass worldwide mailing for each report. If the mailing was successful, they would follow it up with another a few months later. If the initial effort failed, they would abandon the project. Having faced a similar situation in the past, I vowed to monitor this matter more closely. (But who was I to question one of the world's most successful business publishing firms?)

Pricing these reports had become an art in its own right. Take a stack of paper with words printed on each page and put the stack into a binding: If you call it a "book," people might be willing to pay $20 or $30 for it, maybe a bit more depending on the subject. If you call that same stack of paper a "research report," and you market it in the guise of being "for your eyes only . . . secrets of other businesses that are revealed only within these exclusive pages," you can charge a lot more for it. That's particularly so if you pitch it cleverly enough to executives with the right kind of liberal expense accounts and the ability to write a check for it without getting committee approval.

Are you sitting down? *BI* was charging between $400 and $500 for these research reports! That is not a misprint. At those prices, they didn't have to sell a whole lot to break even, and they were selling them—about six titles per year, and about 500 to 1,000 copies per title. This is all perfectly legal, mind you. It's called "charging what the traffic will bear." Without any doubt, if businesses wanted to acquire on their own the information that was in the *BI* reports, it would have cost them many tens of thousands of dollars in research time.

The editors I met with told me that they would be interested in a report that dealt with the American market. Almost all of their publications dealt with European and Asian issues; they felt that they had ignored the United States and that there was good potential for a report covering some aspect of American business.

I had in-depth knowledge about marketing in the United States, having worked in the print and broadcast media for about twenty years. Having spent a great deal of time in London and other foreign cities I knew that marketing was drastically different at home than it was abroad. We Yanks are indeed pushy and aggressive; the rest of the world, by comparison, is very shy about foisting products on the public.

I asked many of my British business friends how might non-Americans go about selling their products in the United States? Where could they get valid information on how to advertise cost-effectively in the United States? How could they get into an efficient distribution system? How could they learn to deal with United States laws and regulations? In particular, how could they begin to understand, let alone cope with, the vastness and diversity of the United States as a marketplace?

I did my own research and found that there was no single comprehensive source for this information. So I proposed to *BI*'s editors that I create that source: a research report titled *Selling to Americans . . . Successful Sales and Marketing Strategies for the United States*. I had pitched a strike, right down the middle, and they made me what they called their standard offer.

It was an offer I couldn't refuse. I would receive the advance I had requested, plus their normal royalty. Stay seated, their normal royalty was 20 percent of the selling price (compare that with the normal royalty on a regular bookstore book of 10 percent). Further, their anticipated selling price was $450 per copy! Some quick arithmetic: 20 percent of $450 is $90. Sales of 1,000 copies (their initial target) would thus generate $90,000 in royalties for me. The spinoffs—lecture dates, and so forth—could generate a lot more on top of that. I signed a contract without delay, lest they change their minds.

Did I have inflated expectations? You'd better believe it (shades of *Breaking Free*). Did I start to spend the money I hadn't earned yet? The answer still, thank heaven, was "no." (And I hope you're learning your own lessons from my experiences with inflated expectations.)

Before we proceed with this saga, a quick look at the direct-mail business might be of interest to you. It is a *gigantic* business: about $22 billion per year. That's almost as much as is spent nationally on television advertising. Though many people refer to direct-mail advertisements as "junk mail" it can be a very powerful way to sell a lot of products and services.

It's a business with some *very strict rules:* When an advertiser comes up with the precisely right combination of words and images in a direct-mail campaign, and that combination successfully generates profits, *you don't tamper with a sure thing.*

Finding the precisely right combination of words and images requires a lot of trial-and-error experimentation. A mail-order house might try many different pitches for a given product before coming up with something that clicks. Some experiments can be very subtle. Sometimes an accident can turn a blah campaign into an unexpectedly successful one.

In one venture an advertiser used postage stamps instead of metered postage on the mailings. Some of the stamps were put square into the upper-right-hand corner of the envelopes. Some of the stamps were slightly off-kilter, at a bit of an angle. The advertiser tracked the results and found that the envelopes with the off-kilter stamps brought noticeably better sales results than did the envelopes with the perfectly placed stamps!

Why? Market research revealed that people who received the off-kilter mailings tended to notice the eccentric stamp, and that gave them the *impression* that a real person had licked and placed the stamp on the envelope. That in turn gave them a more *personal feeling* toward the advertiser, and they were thus more receptive to the sales pitch inside the envelope, with the result being higher sales. Subtle experiment or lucky accident? Go figure. In any case, they used off-kilter stamps very successfully thereafter.

The success of direct-mail advertising also depends very heavily on the *timing* of a mailing. Obviously seasonal and holiday-related pitches *must* be mailed in a timely fashion, often through a very narrow window in time. Certain shifting trends *must* be observed, such as selling stock market advisory services in the right sync with market

cycles, and timing fund-raising efforts to coincide with periods of local-
ized economic strength as opposed to recession.

The direct-mail industry had one of its long-standing rules of timing etched in granite on the weekend of November 22, 1963. That was
when President Kennedy was assassinated. Every direct-mail pitch
that had been—innocently enough—mailed at that time had disastrous
results. The rule *never* to be broken by direct-mail advertisers is: *Never
mail into the face of catastrophe.*

Now back to my adventure with my book for *BI, Selling to Americans.* By the time I had delivered my manuscript—and it was a good
one—in the summer of 1990 there had been a few major changes in
the world's economic outlook that, unfortunately, were beyond my
control. The communist empire was collapsing, which put alot of
question marks on certain aspects of world trade. The United States
was heading into a recession, which would lessen its appeal as an
export market for anyone who might otherwise be interested in my
book. The most ominous and imminent sign of trouble was the fact
that Saddam Hussein had invaded Kuwait and the threat of all-out war
hung over the Middle East. Even the editors at *BI* were aware of this,
I think.

The editing of the manuscript was complete by the fall of 1990, and
the book was off the presses in late November. *BI* was anxious to get it
out into the market. I urged them to delay the one-and-only worldwide
direct-mail solicitation until after the Christmas season, during which
period even executives have other things on their minds than buying
$450 research reports. By early January of 1991 *BI* was champing at
the bit to send out the go-for-broke all-or-nothing mail-order solicitation. Concerned with the mounting crisis in the Middle East, and with
the United States economy, I begged them to wait still more. A few
extra months wouldn't make a difference. I was willing to wait even
until spring to make my fortune . . . maybe even summer. I could not
convince them.

Perhaps they had not heard of the immutable law of *never* mailing
into the face of a catastrophe. Or maybe the Brits thought it was an
American rule that didn't apply to them. Or perhaps they were aware
of the rule and thought that they could break it with impunity. Or
perhaps they had no foggy idea what they were doing when they broke
that rule of rules.

Our all-the-marbles give-it-your-all one-time-only mailing piece was sent out *at the same time* the full-fledged air war against Iraq broke out. The envelopes must have been dodging Patriot missiles as they winged their way toward corporate headquarters around the world. Or maybe they were shot down by the missiles.

What happens when you break the rule about *never* mailing into the face of a catastrophe? In this case, you don't sell 1,000 copies of *Selling to Americans.* You sell sixteen copies. And you tell your author, "Sorry, old chap." And you hope you've learned about not breaking the rule next time.

BI had no fallback after this debacle. They were geared for one and only one mailing. As with *Breaking Free*, each *BI* product had to live or die within its own budget; there was no borrowing from other publications to pay for another round of mailings. At least I had gotten my advance and the chance to write for *The Economist* group.

My earlier caution bears repeating: If you are involved with an entrepreneurial venture—as a lender, investor, supplier, landlord, employee, or as the actual entreprenuer—you must be on the alert for the Go-for-Broke mentality. It can devastate even the most carefully laid plans, and your financial stake with it.

The problem isn't limited to entrepreneurial activities. You must avoid the Go-for-Broke mentality in many other areas of your finances:

* When buying a home, can you afford to go overboard with furnishings, appliances, and luxurious extras? This can drain all your available funds, leaving you without a reserve, a fallback. Wouldn't it make more sense to proceed slowly, taking on extras as you can afford them, and keeping a healthy reserve in place for other needs that will inevitably arise?

* The same holds true for buying automobiles. The total cost is far lower than for a home, but the payment schedules are much shorter, which means much higher monthly payments. Too heavy a commitment on a car loan can be a real crippler if you bump into hard times and find yourself without a reserve to fall back on.

* Investing or speculating with your money can prompt a Go-for-Broke splurge, particularly if you think (or are finagled into thinking) that a given bet is the once-in-a-lifetime sure-

fire winner. "Why diversify?" you'll ask yourself. "I've found the be-all-and-end-all, and I'm going to go the whole nine yards with it." Bye-bye reserve . . . bye-bye fallback position. It's time to pray.

The best defense against succumbing to the Go-For-Broke syndrome is to keep asking "but-what-if" questions. Then seek the answers. Even that may not help you if you're up against an egomaniacal attitude that can cancel out all common sense. The lessons I learned on those counts are in the next chapter.

Chapter Twenty-six

Ego Trips Have High-Priced Tickets

How ego can get in the way of sound financial decisions, and how that can hurt you.

✔ *What if It's Broke and You Can't Fix It?*
... an ego-driven fiasco

✔ *Got Them Radio Station Blahs*
... just because you're good at one thing doesn't mean you're an expert at other things

Very often, perhaps more often than you may realize, your financial well-being is in the hands of someone who has more ego than is healthy. If you work for, or lend to, or invest in, or provide supplies or services to a business that is run by such a person, there are a few things you might want to keep in mind:

* Keep your resume up to date.
* Keep networking.
* Keep your interests well-diversified.
* Keep your bag packed and near the exit.
* Keep your savings account well stocked. You may need it to tide you over if the oversized ego causes oversized problems.

This is strictly an unscientific conclusion, but it's based on decades of observation of how businesspeople function: Problems come quickest to those whose egos get in the way of sound business principles and solid common sense.

Business publications, notably *The Wall Street Journal*, frequently run articles on businesses that have run into serious trouble. And I've come across many more such situations in my own experiences on the air, as a consultant, a banker, and even as a participant in ego-driven ventures.

At the heart of the troubles you'll usually find top executives whose egos have gotten the best of them. Sometimes the hyperego masks basic business incompetence. Sometimes it's a cover-up for fraudulent activities. Sometimes it manifests itself in a tyrannical style of dealing with employees. Sometimes it is simply an expression of the executives' beliefs that they really are superior beings who can neither do anything wrong nor make any bad judgments.

Don't get me wrong. Ego has its place in the world of money and business. Indeed, it's a critical ingredient—in the right dosage. Leaders must have a positive sense of self-esteem and self-confidence. Without those qualities their business, their employees, their lenders, their investors, and their suppliers are doomed to take a financial whipping. But when the ego goes over the top, the dangers are equally imminent.

Following are two stories of business failures that were the result of excess ego. They contain other human frailties we've discussed in previous chapters, such as inflated expectations, go-for-broke reckless abandon, and lack of knowledge. But the prime flaw that caused the wreckage was a surplus of ego. I was involved in both situations, and I report them to you as I observed them.

What if It Is Broke and You Can't Fix It?

At first I thought I had lucked out again by being in the right place at the right time. On the very day that I handed in my resignation at KABC Talk-Radio I was contacted by someone who asked me if I wanted to take part in a nationwide financial radio network that was about to be launched. I was told that I could write my own ticket.

This new network was starting out with a bank balance of some $6 million and was in need of people with good radio experience and financial credentials. I could have my own talk show. I could do commentaries. I could do whatever. And the pay would be excellent. Too good to be true? Of course. Did I get inflated expectations? No, to be honest. At this point I had become so hardened to hype (and my own finances were in good enough shape) that I could take it or leave it.

But there was one ticket that I did want to write for myself: Though we had made up our minds to spend six months a year in London, I did want to keep my finger in some kind of creative activity. Being on the air live had no appeal to me—I'd been doing that for almost a decade, and that was enough. But if I could tape commentaries at my own convenience, from wherever I happened to be, that would be ideal.

Thus, I proposed to this new radio network that I be their London correspondent: I would prepare ten commentaries per week and would phone them in (collect, of course) all in one cluster for them to air the following week. I admit to excitement over the prospect of heading each commentary with "I'm Bob Rosefsky . . . Money Talks from London." The network agreed to this proposal. They offered no money up front, but a generous split of any advertising revenues they generated. The prospects were fine. I had an agent negotiate the terms of the deal for me. Before I had even left for London they had sold sponsorships to Bank of America and Los Angeles' biggest Cadillac dealer. My split of the revenues, which was to take place quarterly, looked to be quite rewarding.

Again I digress. This is not my story. It's the story of the Financial Broadcasting Network (FBN)(RIP) and its founder, Chief Executive, Chairman of the Board, Glenn T.

Glenn, as I was told, had been instrumental in the late 1970s in creating the Financial News Network for cable television. FNN was later absorbed by NBC-owned CNBC, and the FNN format of stock market reports and interviews then became the daytime portion of cable's CNBC schedule. Glenn had long since exited the FNN scene.

Now, in the late 1980s, he was back and ready to try his hand with the same subject, finance, on a different format—radio. It was, I readily admitted, an excellent idea if it could be executed smartly. Glenn's brainchild, FBN, would be based in the Century City office center in Los Angeles, and its objective was to sign up affiliate stations around the country that would receive the daytime programming from FBN via satellite. Interest in financial broadcasting was keen, and this would allow small local stations to offer programming that they couldn't afford to create on their own.

The basic concept—as is the case with broadcast networks generally—is that local affiliate stations would agree to air the network's commercials and would still have ample time to air their own local commercials. By this arrangement, a network can offer its sponsors a nationwide audience, for which it charges accordingly higher fees. The local stations get good-quality programming at little or no cost, which in turn attracts local sponsors who want to be in that quality broadcast environment.

Glenn had been successful in convincing investors to ante up the $6 million in initial working capital, a good deal of which went into building state-of-the-art facilities in their posh Century City offices, and into hiring high-priced talent for both on-air and administrative functions.

Glenn seemed a low-keyed sort, pleasant enough to have a brief chat with. But as the weeks progressed it appeared to me that his vision of FBN far exceeded what could be realistically achieved. This was most evident in the Excessive Executive department. From the outset, long before the network went on the air, and even longer before advertisers were paying money to be on the air, there were Vice Presidents and Senior Vice Presidents of Everything: of Network Affiliates, of National Advertising Sales, of Local Advertising Sales, of Programming, of Personnel, of Operations, and of the Publishing Division (yes, the radio network had a full-fledged publishing division whose job it was to produce booklets, magazines, flyers, and any other print items that could be marketed to listeners on the air). Many of these vice presidents had given up other jobs to move to Los Angeles. And, as I was told, they were all enjoying fat paychecks and lavish expense accounts, all coming out of the initial working capital, since revenues were still months away.

There was not a hint of "crawl before you walk" thinking in this venture. It was grandiose. It was fanciful. And it was doomed.

As I met this assortment of high-level executives, before I departed for London, I couldn't help notice that they seemingly had no egos of their own. They had deferred to the boss's ego: "Glenn knows what's best . . . Glenn will do what's right . . . Glenn makes the big decisions . . . Glenn's in charge. . . ." And, of course, Glenn authorized all of their paychecks.

In short, FBN was a kingdom that was being run by an Absolute Ruler who held the reins on his assortment of Barons and Dukes, each with his own little fiefdom.

There was a suffusion from the top of so much self-importance that pesky little problems seemed to get ignored. "Somewhere on down the line, *way* down the line, some underling will take care of that." Then along came one particularly pesky problem that may have been ignored for too long. It had to do, of all things, with being able to *hear* FBN when it went on the air.

The nuts and bolts of radio are simple enough: Sound signals go from the announcer's mouth to a transmitter, from which they are beamed through the air and into people's radios. In order to beam radio signals from a transmitter you must have permission (a license) from the Federal Communications Commission. In most places in the United States, especially Los Angeles, the FCC does not hand out new licenses readily because the airwaves are already overloaded.

The Los Angeles operation was to be the flagship station for the network. It was also to be the primary source of advertising; most major American advertising agencies have offices in Los Angeles. With 20+ million Southern Californians within listening range of the Century City station, the L.A. market was certainly important as a trial venue for potential national advertisers.

FBN could not get a new broadcast license in Los Angeles. But *that* was not the pesky little problem. "Not to worry," came the voice of authority from on high.

Nor could FBN take the next best step, which would have been to buy an existing local station in order to get access to its transmitter. Riding the crest of the late eighties boom, even low-powered stations in Los Angeles were selling for millions of dollars. FBN had already spent so much on its Excessive Executives that it didn't have enough left in its kitty to buy another local station. But *that* wasn't the pesky little problem either. "Not to worry," resounded the voice of authority from on high.

But people *were* beginning to worry, even when they were told not to, particularly those who had quit other jobs to come to FBN, and were now starting to wonder if there really would ever be an FBN. Radio stations that aren't on the air aren't much good.

What FBN *could* do, lacking the ability to get a license or buy an existing station, was to get creative, and creativity lay 130 miles to the south in Tijuana, Mexico, just across the border from San Diego. There was a high-powered Mexican station in Tijuana that could bounce a signal loud and clear all the way to Santa Barbara, 90 miles north of Los Angeles, and *most* places in between. The operative word here is *most*. Now we're getting to the pesky little problem. Stay tuned.

FBN approached the owners of the Mexican station with an offer they couldn't refuse. FBN would pay handsomely to take over the Tijuana transmitter. They would then send their signal from Los Angeles to Tijuana (by wire, not over the air), and the Mexican station would, in turn, bounce the signal back north into California. (This got around FCC requirements legally. Also, yet-to-be-signed-up local affiliate stations on the FBN system would be getting their signals via satellite, so the transmitter problem didn't apply to them.)

Now, with a signal that could be heard throughout *most* of Southern California, all that had to be done was find those few little nooks and crannies where the signal *didn't* come in loud and clear, and then adjust the Tijuana transmitter to fill in the nooks and crannies with a crisp signal.

"No problem," said FBN's leadership, cocksure that this minor nuisance would soon be resolved and that the station would, at long last, be up and running.

"No problema," echoed the Mexican station owner, anxious to start getting his income from FBN.

Well, there *was* a problem. Even after repeated attempts to fine-tune the signal from Mexico, there was a little nook and a little cranny in which FBN'S signal could *not* be clearly received. The little nook ran from Century City to downtown Los Angeles, an area that's surrounded and bounded by tall buildings. Within the confines of that little nook are the offices of virtually *all* the major corporations and financial institutions—all potential sponsors—*and* the major advertising agencies in Southern California!

The little cranny stretched from the hilly, posh suburbs of Brentwood and Pacific Palisades all the way to Malibu, all places where a lot of the decisionmakers of the advertisers and the advertising agencies *lived.*

Radio waves can get beat up pretty badly by tall buildings and hills, particularly when they've shlepped all the way from Mexico. The problem was, in the final analysis, that people who absolutely needed to be able to hear FBN if they were going to become advertisers, *could not hear the station* either where they worked or where they lived. *That's* a problem.

Why couldn't this mess have been avoided? As I perceived it there was an overpowering attitude emanating from FBN that they could do nothing wrong, that anything could be fixed with a little money and a little salesmanship. "No problem. The engineers will fix the signal and the sales force will convince the sponsors that the crackling sound they hear on their radios is really the FBN station coming through loud and clear."

Why didn't they first determine whether they could deliver a clear signal *before* they leased the luxurious space and *before* they bought expensive equipment and *before* they hired the highly paid vice presidents and *before* they spent virtually all the money that was in their startup kitty? Why? Because there was a belief that they were above human error.

What happened then wasn't pretty. The transmitter problem wasn't being fixed quickly enough to suit FBN, so FBN started to withhold the payments it owed to the Mexicans. In retaliation, the Mexicans began to *un*fix the transmitter problems, hoping thereby to scare the back payments out of FBN. This helped convince advertisers to stay away in droves. No advertisers means no revenue for the network. Lack of advertisers also impaired the credibility of the network, which scared away potential affiliates. Lack of affiliates further clobbered any chance of signing up national advertisers. The investors' seed money was all gone, with little or no hope of them ever seeing a penny back. With the money all spent, and none coming in, FBN started issuing rubber paychecks to employees, who, needless to say, eventually stopped working.

Chapter Seven bankruptcy ensued for FBN less than one year after it first went on the air. Not Chapter Eleven, which gives a debtor breathing room to reorganize while keeping the creditors at bay; Chapter Seven—kaput, down the toilet, and the creditors suck wind.

People picked up the pieces of their lives and carried on. Secretaries and announcers and investors and stationery suppliers and the telephone company, and the landlord and the wire services and the janitorial company and the banks and the furniture stores and the electronics salesmen and the unemployed gaggle of vice presidents all licked their wounds and went on to other things.

I sat in Glenn's office just a few days before FBN's Chapter Seven proceedings were announced. I heard him speaking to someone on the telephone: "Don't you worry about a thing," he told the other party. "We're going to turn this around and everything will be just fine. I've put alot of the company's stock in your name, and some day it's going to make you a very rich lady."

After he hung up he told me that he had been speaking to his daughter.

*
**   *
**   *
**

My own personal P.S. to this woeful tale adds yet another bizarre note. FBN had been covering my expenses, but I hadn't been paid anything. As the date of my first quarterly split of the advertising revenues approached I phoned my Los Angeles agent from London to alert him to the due date, asking him to swoop in and get my money before it was spent on Excess Executives or otherwise wasted. I knew that trouble was brewing.

On *that* day, the day the payment was due, my agent suffered a heart attack and was in the hospital. By the time we could regroup, my money had been swallowed up in FBN's black hole of lost dollars.

My agent recovered, but my money wasn't. This was still many months before FBN's downfall. I continued to do my commentaries from London because I was enjoying it and didn't need the money. I had no faint hope of ever seeing any of it anyway. And, as I suspected, I didn't.

But little did I suspect that within one year I'd be back in the ex-FBN studios ready to head into another ego-driven venture.

What am I, a masochist? Never mind if I am or not. Don't you be one. Learn from me.

Got Them Radio Station Blahs

In mid-1990 I was contacted by one of the old FBN people who had stayed around. There was to be a reincarnation! Someone had taken over the old FBN lease and all the equipment that had been sitting idle, and was going to start a new business-format station. Did I want to be on the air?

This time it was just going to be a local station, not a network. It was going to be solid, well-financed, lean, and trimly run. No frills, no Excessive Executives, no publishing division. And most important, no Tijuana transmitter. The entrepreneur had been able to buy another Los Angeles station cheap, and so he could take over their license and use their transmitter.

The entrepreneur was a real estate mogul named Fred S. I had never met Fred, but I knew he had an excellent reputation as a real estate broker: His firm was one of the largest and most successful in Los Angeles. I'm sure that he did *not* have an excellent reputation as a rocket scientist or as a brain surgeon or as a criminal defense lawyer. That's because he was a real estate person. It takes more than a leap of faith to think that because you're good at real estate you can also be good at rocket science or brain surgery or criminal defense, or, for heaven's sake, running an all-talk radio station.

But let's give Fred the benefit of the doubt. Let's say he could have successfully transferred his skills in real estate to talk-radio. But what do we say about the recession that was, at that time, descending upon the United States in general, and Los Angeles in particular? And what do we say about the fact that two of the industries being most hurt by the recession were advertising and real estate? If Fred's new-found radio skills could survive a general recession, what would he do when advertisers cut back sharply on their expenses with long-standing proven-successful media, let alone a new upstart radio station?

And how strong would Fred's capital base and financial resilience be if the Los Angeles real estate market went down the tubes because the USSR had suddenly decided to call it quits, so we no longer needed so many defense workers, tens of thousands of whom owned homes in Fred's Southern California domain?

In short, it was clear that Fred was bucking incredible odds. Nonetheless he invested a reported couple of million dollars (cheap at the price compared with the $6 million that his predecessor had dumped), and like a phoenix from the ashes a new radio station, Business Los Angeles, came into being in the old FBN digs. Call letters? Well, in the western part of the United States all broadcast stations' call letter must begin with K. (It's W in the East.) So, to K we add the initials of Business Los Angeles, and we come up with Fred's own personally chosen KBLA.

"K-blah?" the pundits mused. It was not a name destined to inspire awe among such potential advertisers as banks, insurance companies, stock brokerage firms, and the like, but KBLA it was.

I made my deal with my eyes wide open and my expectations lower than a sewer rat's toepads: I would record five commentaries a week and I would split advertising revenues with the station. Fortunately my segment was quickly sold to a good sponsor, Great Western

Bank. They had sponsored me for years on KABC radio, and the relationship was still warm. The checks did come in, and I did get paid as agreed. And I enjoyed doing the commentaries.

I didn't enjoy seeing the station, and the nice people that worked there, go steadily downhill. The advertising recession and the real estate recession worsened weekly. Sponsors were very difficult to sign up. And as Fred's real estate business suffered, his ability to carry the station through seemingly endless red-ink months strained him to his limits.

People were let go, first here and there, then in clusters. Future programming plans were curtailed. Then current programming was cut back. As the end neared the station was a mere shadow of itself. Staffers would have to search their souls as to why they let one man's ego (and drive, and money, and guts) lure them in. And the same goes for the people who were lured in by Glenn at FBN, and for anyone else who suddenly finds grandiose plans shattered, and dreams of success turned into personal and corporate nightmares.

* Was it their awe of another person's ego?
* Was it a lack of their own ego and a concurrent need to have someone else hold a banner aloft for them?
* Was it a naivete that blinded them to the realities of the venture?
* Was it a lack of lessons learned in the school of hard knocks?
* Or was it, plain and simple, the money?

Those are hard questions to answer. But they must be asked.

*
**   **   **

KBLA still lives, as of this writing. In early 1992 Fred very suddenly announced that he had leased his interest in the station to another radio operator, and the remaining staff had to clear out swiftly. The new operator was going to cater to one of Los Angeles' many burgeoning ethnic groups, and under their management it appears to have become a great success. Many years from now Fred may recoup his investment.

The irony is that the blah call letters that may have sullied KBLA's image and thus contributed to its downfall are providing appropriate glitter for the new people: Korean Broadcasting Los Angeles.

*   *   *
**   **   **

You pay a costly premium to take an ego trip. I strongly advise against striving for frequent flyer points.

Closely related to the ego-driven business is the one that is powered by a volatile combination of greed and the stock market. It can be even more explosive than the ego fuel.

Many companies are owned, in part, by the public. That is, shares of stock in the company are owned by outsiders. Insiders—those who own a major chunk of the company and run the company on a day-to-day basis—can become obsessed with the value of the company's stock.

The insiders' personal wealth goes up or down with each twitch in the value of the stock. They may have pledged their stock as collateral for loans at their bank or with their stock brokers, and if the value of the pledged stock falls too far, the insiders could be in deep trouble: They may have to quickly come up with more cash or stock to avoid having to pay off the loans immediately. These concerns, and others of a more technical nature, can make for a lot of tension within the business.

The problem boils down to this: Are the bosses paying too much attention to the stock values, and too little attention to the profitable running of the business? Ah, you ask, doesn't sound business management result in higher values for the stock? Not necessarily. Besides, the insiders might not want to wait and see if that's the case.

This anxiety can result in subtle, possibly illegal, manipulations of the company's books, which in turn can create a false valuation for the shares in the company. The welfare of investors and employees is thus jeopardized. If you sense any of this greed/stock activity in any business with which you're associated, heed the advice I gave in the first page of this chapter: Stay near the exits, and so forth.

*   *   *
**   **   **

One other spin-off of the company-in-danger syndrome: Excessive debt can be a big spoiler. If a company is having cash flow problems, it might borrow temporarily to get over its crunch. This is a perfectly normal and acceptable business practice, but the practice is subject to abuse. If the temporary borrowing is renewed rather than repaid, it then gradually becomes a long-term debt. Eventually another "temporary" borrowing becomes necessary, and then that too is renewed instead of repaid. The time comes when the debt load—and the interest cost—is too much to bear, and collapse can occur.

This demonic problem is not reserved for businesses. Individuals in vast numbers also succumb to the same temptations . . . a word to the wise.

Chapter Twenty-seven

"How Could You Believe Me when I Said I Loved You when You Know I've Been a Liar All My Life?"

You're in for heartache if you place too much trust or reliance on the wrong people
- ✔ *Ripple Effects*
  . . . how a distant event can spread troubles to unsuspecting victims
- ✔ *You Can't Bank on Some Banks*
  . . . what can you do when your lender slams the door in your face?
- ✔ *If You Can't Rely on Mommy and Daddy, Then Whom?*

The title of this chapter is also the title of an old country-western song. Its message is clear: You're in for heartache if you place too much trust or reliance on the wrong person.

You could also be in for a financial debacle.

We are basically a trusting people. We come into the world that way. Some miraculous infantile instinct assures us that Mommy and Daddy will take care of us. When we doubt that, we test the theory by crying. With rare exceptions we receive quick proof—a breast, a hug, a clean diaper.

As we grow, our sense of trust is reinforced. We rely on our parents for continuing basic care and guidance. We rely on our teachers to give us the essential knowledge we need to function in the world. We rely on our clergy to instill within us a sense of morality and spiritual well-being. And we rely on our fellow human beings to act in a decent and civilized manner, which they more or less do most of the time.

At some point we also learn to become self-reliant: We acquire confidence that we can provide for our own livelihood and for our childrens' well-being.

All of this reliance in our lives is fine. Without being able to rely so much on so many others, life would be chaotic. The law of the jungle would be paramount. Our complex system of mutual trust is, indeed, the foundation of our society. But it is not a perfect system. There are flaws and weaknesses, particularly where money is concerned.

We can easily become overly dependent. We can place our trust in people or institutions when there have been signals that they may no longer be deserving of our trust. Financial chaos can ensue from such actions.

As you read the following stories, ask yourself whether you might have misplaced your trust. If so, what might be the ramifications? Is there still time to take actions that can minimize problems? For the future, refer to these lessons to help you avoid falling into a trap of overreliance.

Ripple Effects

One question that you must periodically ask yourself is: "How much do I depend on so-and-so for my income, and what would I do if that income was cut off?" If you're always prepared with a practical solution to that possibility, you may never have to worry about dipping into your nestegg to tide you over rough times.

As the following wide-reaching incident illustrates, you must look beyond your immediate source of money. You must consider the distant ripple effects.

The Sears Roebuck mail-order catalog was an American institution dating back to the nineteenth century. It was known as the "Wish Book"; in it's earlier days it was the only way most rural Americans could see and buy the huge assortment of products that was readily available to their city cousins.

Even as Sears retail stores proliferated around the nation the catalog continued to be a fixture in millions of American homes. Eventually the catalog fell on hard times, a victim of new trends in retailing such as the megadiscount stores, the shoppers' "club" stores, and even the shop-by-television channels. In the "downsizing" of the retail industry that took place as the free-spending eighties became the penny-pinching nineties, word began to circulate that the Sears catalog might be headed for extinction.

A lot of people didn't pay attention to those rumors, to their detriment. They may have been thinking that you can't terminate such a long-standing tradition. But they were wrong. Thousands of .Sears employees lost their jobs when the catalog was killed. But beyond those direct job losses there were vast and frightening ripple effects.

The Wall Street Journal did a survey on non-Sears people whose livelihoods were severely hurt by the catalog's demise. Following is but a brief summary of the ripple effects in just two parts of the massive catalog. First, the furniture section:

* Nugent Wenckus was a photography studio in suburban Chicago that took a lot of the pictures that appeared in the furniture pages of the Sears catalog. Their Sears business, on which they had relied for a long time, was worth $80,000 per year before they lost the account.

* Selene Wacker was the interior decorator who did the room arrangements of the Sears furniture for Nugent Wenckus to photograph. Selene had long relied on Nugent Wenckus for her work. She lost her job.

* Des Plaines Lumber supplied the wood that built the room sets which Selena Wacker arranged for Nugent Wenckus to photograph for the Sears catalog. The account had been worth $25,000 a year to Des Plaines Lumber . . . gone.

* Kennicott Brothers supplied the flowers that decorated the room sets that were built of wood supplied by Des Plaines Lumber and arranged by Selene Wacker to be photographed by Nugent Wenckus. Kennicott Brothers had relied on an income of about $8,000 per year from the account . . . gone.

* Hoos Drug and Photo Center sold the film that captured the flowers that decorated the sets that were built of wood from Des Plaines Lumber that Selene Wacker arranged for Nugent Wenckus to photograph for the Sears catalog. Hoos Drug lost a $10,000-a-year account.

Meanwhile, in the fashion section:

* Kelly Anderson modeled young women's apparel for the Sears catalog. She lost 70 percent of her annual income when the catalog folded.

* Clair Rich had been making $450 a day as Kelly Anderson's stylist when Kelly was modeling for the Sears catalog . . . no more.

* Commercial Graphics, the production company that photographed Kelly Anderson and other fashion models, lost an estimated $1 million in revenue per year as a result of the catalog's termination.

* One particular fashion shoot that was scheduled in Baton Rouge, Louisiana, had to be canceled when the catalog's closing was announced. The photo processor for Commercial Graphics would have processed some 800 rolls of film that would have been used at that shoot, but cancelation meant a loss of $16,000 that would have been earned by the processor.

* The hotels and restaurants of Baton Rouge lost about $200,000 in income that Commercial Graphics had planned on spending there before the cancelation.

Finally, lest you think that *you* weren't affected by the demise of the Wish Book, the United States Post Office estimates that it will lose upward of *$100 million per year* in revenue that it used to get from delivering the catalog. Guess who gets to make up that deficit.

How safe are you from any kind of ripple effects? Who do you rely on, and for how much? And how can you protect yourself if the grounds for your reliance get shaky?

You Can't Bank on Some Banks

Closer to home, a very dear friend learned a harsh and life-altering lesson when his local banker turned demon on him. What happened to Bill also happened to thousands of small businesses—and their employees, investors, landlords, and suppliers—in the late eighties and early nineties.

Bill had been in business in Phoenix for many years, and he had long ago arranged a line of credit with one of the biggest local banks. He borrowed against the line as needed for various business purposes: to finance inventory, to expand or remodel his plant, to meet other obligations. It was a normal, standard garden-variety arrangement that thousands of businesses have with their banks. It had been set up in the days when a credit check, a financial statement, and a signature on the IOU were all that was needed. There was no collateral, no assignment of accounts receivable, no co-signer. It was just a straight IOU from Bill to the bank. Bill relied on this access to credit, and it had always been there when he needed it.

He had met all of his payment obligations promptly. He maintained an excellent personal relationship with the loan officer. His credit rating was impeccable. His financial condition was solid. Unfortunately, the bank's condition was not solid.

As happened to so many banks in the rip-snorting eighties, and particularly in such wildly speculative areas as Phoenix, Bill's bank got overloaded with bad loans. That caused the government regulators to step in and demand that the bank clean up its loan portfolio pronto. If the bank failed to do so, the government would have taken it over.

This couldn't have happened at a worse time for Bill. He was anticipating an early retirement in just a few years, and he had stashed away a princely sum of money in his pension account to enable him to do just that.

Bill's loan was one of the many that the bank demanded be paid off, or in the alternative, collateralized. He was given just thirty days to solve the bank's problem. What was wrong with his loan? Nothing, by earlier banking standards—it was what's known as a signature loan. But in the rocky banking environment that now prevailed, just a signature on an IOU was not good enough. To be considered a good-quality loan it would have to be collateralized with valuable assets, or paid off.

Bill sought the help of the loan officer who had been his buddy for so many years, but found to his dismay that the loan officer had departed. In his place was what Bill called "the loan officer from Hell" who would not bend an inch to help Bill out of his dilemma.

Bill had planned to sell the business on the advent of retiring. The proceeds from the sale would have paid off the bank loan. The only asset Bill could have pledged as collateral for the loan was his pension fund, but he dared not put that money at any risk, for that represented his source of funds for the rest of his life. If the business should, by some long shot, fail before he was able to sell it, he would lose the pension money if he had pledged it as collateral. The bank was apparently concerned about that too, but there was not an iota of compromise in their demands. "Pay the loan *in full,* or collateralize it 100 percent, in thirty days, or else." The "or else" could have amounted to a lawsuit that would have jeopardized Bill's entire pension fund.

His only viable option was to sell the business. But a forced sale could mean a much lower price than he'd get in more relaxed circumstances. Or it could invite a buyer to offer as little as possible cash down payment, and as much as possible to be paid to Bill over a long period of time.

Scrambling to save himself from disaster, Bill was able to find a buyer on short notice. There was enough cash in the deal to satisfy the bank. The rest was to be paid out over a multiyear arrangement. To protect himself—to assure that the business generated enough money to afford Bill his payments—Bill had to continue working for years beyond his anticipated retirement date. And no job is tougher than the one you thought you wouldn't have to be doing.

I know how badly Bill was tasting his retirement years, and my heart broke for him. Eventually he did start seeing the light at the end of the tunnel, but the pain of those lost years—years that he had planned to be enjoying rather than working overly hard—may never subside.

He had relied on his bank, reasonably and justifiably. Yes, when it became apparent that the bank was having serious troubles Bill might have done a better job of anticipating how that might impact on him personally. But he didn't. And the consequences were rough.

There have been lawsuits in recent years in which borrowers sued their banks for terminating their loans, or otherwise changing the terms of the loans in a fashion that the borrowers deemed punitive. Borrowers have won some of these cases: Their rights as debtors entitled them to a reasonable continuity in the lending practices of the bank, and when those practices were sharply altered, the rights of the but it has been upheld numerous times. I don't recommend, though, but is has been upheld numerous times. I don't recommend, though, that you consider this as your defense against getting cut off by a lender. It takes very deep pockets to bring such a suit, and the outcome is never assured.

If you are a borrower dependent on a continuing source of credit for either business or personal purposes (and who isn't?), your best course is to maintain lines of credit at more than one bank, and to switch your borrowings back and forth between them periodically. Banks prefer this also; they like to know that you have the capacity to pay them off in full every so often. You're a better credit risk for them when you can do that. And that might translate into lower interest rates for you when you borrow.

Also, try to have something you can pledge as collateral, or a co-signer waiting in the wings, should you be asked to provide one or the other.

The flow of credit from banks goes through cycles. In the 1980s it was a torrent, and our grandchildren will still be paying for the *hundreds of billions of dollars'* worth of the bad loans that were made in those years. (Taxpayers have to ante up to pay off the insured depositors who had their money in institutions that failed because of excessive bad loans.) After the eighties, and the Savings and Loan debacle that capped that decade, credit slowed to a trickle as banks tried to improve the quality of their loan portfolios. That's where Bill got caught, along with countless others. Credit will expand again. And it will contract again. You don't want to be in need of borrowing, or owing more than you can readily pay off, when the banks get tight-fisted again.

How would you get along if your otherwise reliable sources of credit got turned off? *Now's* the time to plan for such contingencies, not the day it happens.

If You Can't Rely on Mommy and Daddy, Then Whom?

Nothing can come between friends or family members more sharply and divisively than a dispute over money . . . sad but true.

If anyone can be relied on, we tend to think, it would be our family and close friends. Yet fierce battles can rage even within seemingly close-knit families, and money is generally at the core of the troubles. In recent years there have been some high-profile wars among families whose names and/or business empires are household words:

* The Haft family, owners of Crown Book Stores and other chain stores, has been devastated by internal squabbling over who would run the family empire.

* The Schoen family, owners of the U-Haul Company, has been destructing itself in courts and boardrooms over matters of power and control.

* The Robbie family, owners of the Miami Dolphins football team and its stadium in Florida, have had their wealth and cohesiveness destroyed by disagreements over financial matters.

And that's just a small sampling.

Arnold and Suzanne, husband and wife, were small potatoes by comparison with the above dynasties. They had a wholesale clothing business, importing high-priced fashions from Europe and selling them to boutiques around the United States. They visited Florence and Paris and Rome scouting for chic items that would set the cash registers ringing in their retail customers' shops. They hung out with designers and models, stayed in the best hotels, and ate at the trendiest restaurants.

It all sounds like a very glamourous business. The fact was that they were so caught up in the glamour that they didn't pay proper attention to their business. Indeed, the business was floundering. They were able to stay afloat only on borrowed money. Why would a bank lend them money if their business was so shaky? Because Suzanne's father, who was very well-to-do, was willing to co-sign for them, and the bank was pleased to go along on that basis.

Arnold and Suzanne were more than just reliant on Daddy's co-signing. They were utterly dependent on it. Without it they'd go bust in a hurry. Their borrowings had started out in the $50,000 range, but over the years had grown to more than ten times that. Not only were they not paying off any principal; they were increasing their borrowing on every loan renewal date to pay the interest. That's one of the worst borrowing traps there is.

Why didn't Daddy cut them off when he saw how deeply—and irretreivably—in debt they were? Because he was Daddy. Hindsight dictates that he should have cut them loose to fend for themselves at the early stages of their business. But he didn't. Maybe, as happens in some families, this was Daddy's way of assuring himself of his daughter's continuing devotion and affection?

The problem was compounded when Daddy died. His estate planning was a mess. He had not made any provisions regarding his obligation on Arnold and Suzanne's debt, so the debt became a debt of his estate, which meant that all of his survivors—his wife and son, plus daughter Suzanne—would have to share the responsibility for the debt if and when it had to be paid. And that day of reckoning was on the near horizon.

If Daddy had made proper provisions, then on his death Suzanne's share of the estate would have been responsible for her debt, and Mommy's and brother's shares would be left intact.

Mommy was not keen on having to be responsible for that debt. Nor was she keen on the way Arnold and Suzanne were squandering what little money they did earn. But when the IOU came due Mommy was caught between a rock and a hard place; that is, between a bank and a son-in-law. She could either co-sign the loan for another go-round (the bank was willing to accept her signature in place of Daddy's), or she could refuse to co-sign, in which case the debt would have to paid, and the money would come from Mommy's inheritance, which she needed to live on.

For reasons best known to herself, Mommy chose to co-sign the renewal of the loan for Arnold and Suzanne. And, as had been the habit, the new loan was for a still larger amount to pay off the accrued interest that was owed. Part of her reason for co-signing may have been her fond hope that, given more time, they could turn the business around and the loan would eventually be paid off out of earnings from the business. But that was wishful thinking.

At the second renewal date she co-signed again, admittedly against her better judgment. And again, the loan amount increased. It was now more than $100,000 higher than it had been before Daddy died. This time Mommy warned her daughter and son-in-law that this co-signing could not go on forever. Some day, the sooner the better, it would have to end.

The tension grew as the third renewal date approached. Brother had now entered the fray, pleading convincingly to Mommy that they were on a never-ending spiral, and that the debt would ultimately consume Daddy's entire estate. "Cut them off now," Brother urged, "and limit your losses before it's too late!"

Suzanne, on the other hand, argued that there had been such a long-term reliance on the co-signing that it would be catastrophic to refuse to do so again.

Catastrophic it was. . . . Mommy refused to co-sign. Arnold and Suzanne then *sued* Mommy for damages arising out of her refusal to co-sign, claiming that irreparable harm had been done to their business! (See the brief discussion in Bill's case, earlier, about how some borrowers have successfully sued their lenders for cutting off their access to credit.)

Here now was a family in a state of total and apparently irreparable chaos. The venom that flew was horrendous. The battered psyches were beyond repair. The bitterness will likely go with all of them to their respective graves.

It took years, and *hundreds of thousands of dollars* in legal expenses, to finally settle matters. At least the financial matters were settled. The personal scars will probably never heal.

The whole mess could have been avoided if Daddy had prepared some simple legal documents clarifying whose responsibility the debt would be upon his death.

But Daddy didn't do that.

And Daddy was a lawyer.

Everybody, no doubt, had relied on him to do the right thing in that department.

*
**   **   **

So, who can you trust? Who can you rely on? In the real world, happily, you *can* trust most of the people most of the time. But you still always have to cut the cards. I'm just back at my worst-case-scenario tricks, hoping that I've instilled a little signal beacon in your memory banks, and that it will flash to warn you if you're about to place too much faith—or money—in the wrong person, place, or thing.

Chapter Twenty-eight

Getting the Kids Off the Payroll

Why some parents never seem to be able to stop shelling out the money for the kids, and some workable ideas to help solve the dilemma

You thought it was tough raising the kids? Starting with the obstetrician and on through the diapers and the braces and the proms and the car insurance and the tuition bills and the weddings, do the bills never cease? How do you turn off the treadmill? As one dear friend of mine asked so plaintively, "How do you get the kids off the payroll?"

If you thought there was a divergence of opinion on which stocks to buy, or which kind of life insurance is best, or whether to go with a fixed or adjustable rate mortgage, try a debate on how to wean the kids off parental support.

I've heard more opinions on the subject and have watched more families go through the paces than I care to remember. I've been going through the process with my own four kids—a process for which we laid the groundwork long ago—and despite some lurches and jolts now and then, I think we've been doing a pretty good job.

I've provided well, through college, the first car, and then some. And as a loving father I've always wished I could say to my kids, "Here's a blank check. Fill in the amount, and let it be enough so that you never have any financial worries for your entire life." Of course I couldn't do so, nor would I if I could. Such an act of largesse could be terribly destructive to them (although they might argue that point).

Then I look at what other families have done, and I realize all the more that there is no single right way. What is the right way for one family can be the wrong way for another. Even within a given family, Method A might work fine for Child A but could be a disaster for Child

B, and vice versa. These scenarios may be familiar to you, ranging as they do from one extreme to another:

* Parents throw their young chicks out of the nest at the earliest possible age, letting them fend for themselves from their mid-teen years and onward. That includes earning *all* their own spending money, earning *all* their own college expenses (by work, by scholarship or by loans, or any combination thereof), and earning *all* of their own automotive expenses (including insurance). Does this create hardened, tough, self-sufficient pioneers who are ready to hit the ground running when it comes time to enter the real world? Sometimes; it can also create resentful adults who missed out on opportunities to pursue their own natural talents because they couldn't earn enough on their own to get the needed education. Those would-be concert violinists and rocket scientists and cancer researchers just never had the inbred entrepreneurial spirit that their parents assumed everyone had, and they were too young at the time to know the difference. So whose responsibility or fault or problem is that? It depends on who you ask, the parents or the kids.

* Parents dote on their little sprats throughout their adolescence, young adulthood, and beyond, protecting them from having to fend for themselves. This includes providing them with ample allowances, abundant budgets for all college expenses, well-insured automobiles, a cornucopia of clothing, vacations, table settings (china, crystal, *and* silver) for twelve, and starter condominiums. Does this create grateful, well-adjusted and devoted adults who are ready to hit the ground running when it comes time to enter the real world? Sometimes; it can also create spoiled, selfish, spendthrift maladjusted dolts who are unable to function productively, let alone raise their own kids in a sane and civilized manner. So whose responsibility or fault or problem is that? It depends on who you ask, the parents or the kids.

Fortunately for the real world, most parents come down somewhere between these two extremes. For the kids in the former case, there's no problem about getting them off the payroll because they were never on it. For the kids in the latter case, there may never be such a thing as getting them off the payroll. It's for the millions of in-between cases that these issues are presented here and now.

Your ability to get your kids off the payroll and securely on their own will be a direct function of the guidelines and motivations you will have given them as they grew up. There can be a number of attitude conflicts underlying these considerations. Ponder where you fit between these various opposing viewpoints.

    A. "I'll raise my kids the way my parents raised me; it was good enough for me and it'll be good enough for them."

          Versus, "I wouldn't raise my kids the way I was raised; I don't want to inflict the mistakes my parents made with me upon my own children."

    B. "The more I support my kids (financially), the closer and more devoted they'll be to me."

          Versus, "The less I support my kids (financially), the more independent they'll be, and the less they'll come bothering me for help."

    C. "The sooner I get my kids to become self-sufficient, the sooner I'll lose their closeness and affection."

          Versus, "The longer I can keep my kids dependent on my financial support, the longer I can control them."

    D. "I'm going to spend every penny I earn on myself, and let the kids worry about themselves."

          Versus, "I want to leave a nice inheritance for my kids, and I'm willing to sacrifice some of my own pleasures if need be to do that."

    E. Variations on D, above, are endless: "My folks didn't leave me a penny, so I'm doing the same with my kids" . . . or, "My folks had a bundle and left me without a cent and I don't want that to happen to my kids" . . . or, "My parents left me well off, and I look back now and see that it spoiled me, and I don't want that to happen to my kids so I'm cutting them off" . . . or, "My parents left me well off, and I feel I owe it to my kids to do for them what was done for me" . . . and so on.

It has been one of the recurring themes of this book that attitude awareness must precede behavioral change. I thus present these point-counterpoints not to take sides, but to prompt your awareness as to how your own attitudes may be skewed. You can thereupon make any behavioral adjustments you deem necessary.

Some Workable Ideas

Far be it for me to tell you how to raise your kids. But do allow me to offer some ideas that may be productive in the right circumstances. These are culled from decades of experience of my own, of friends and family, and of many from my audiences who shared their concerns with me over the years. The ideas are geared to the needs and concerns of young adults—from their mid-teens to their late twenties or even early thirties. These are years during which youthful enthusiasm can use constructive support in some circumstances, and can benefit from some gentle (if not direct) toning down in other circumstances.

* *Even-handedness.* Kids compare notes. Your kids will discuss their financial status—allowances, chores (required and voluntary, paid and unpaid, etc.)—with their siblings and friends. This can cause some tightrope-walking on your part: keeping peace in the family by treating all the kids equitably, and keeping peace in the neighborhood by recognizing reasonable and acceptable standards of the community. The key is awareness: Pay attention to your kids' expressed concerns and react promptly and fairly. Silence by a child on the subject of money does not necessarily signal satisfaction on the child's part. The child may be holding in a grudge, afraid to speak out, and the end result may be detrimental behavior—snitching money, shoplifting, or worse. Don't take anything for granted. Inquire in a friendly and understanding way. Be prepared to listen and respond fairly. And keep your tightrope shoes handy.

* *Matching funds.* Every case is different, of course, but there's alot to be said for providing incentive to kids by offering to match what they earn with a contribution of your own. If they want to buy a car or a CD player or an airplane ticket, you might want to offer to kick in $.50 or $1.00 or $1.50 for every dollar that they earn on their own. Or you might offer to lend them that amount, to be repaid at some

specific future date. Aside from the money itself, the lesson learned in setting a goal and then reaching a goal can be invaluable.

 * *Setting limits.* To whatever extent you do want to help your children with their financial needs, set clear and understandable limits at the earliest possible time. For example: "I will pay XYZ dollars toward your car insurance until your twenty-fifth birthday, after which time you're on your own." Or, "I will help you defray your rent (or mortgage payment) by XYZ dollars for two years, after which time you're on your own." Or, "I will provide you with XYZ dollars for spending money in college until the end of your junior year, after which time you're on your own." It can't hurt to put these items in writing; anyone can easily foret such specifics. Setting limits is a mature, responsible, businesslike, and intelligent way of dealing with financial matters. *Not* setting limits can result in frustration and chaos at some future date. The earlier in a child's life you begin setting limits, the easier it will be for you to establish limits later on, and the easier it will be for the child to work within them.

 * *Health care.* Let your conscience be your guide as to how much backup you want to provide for your children with regard to health care. Most group health policies will cover dependents only until they reach a certain age—usually between 21 and 23—and this limit may depend on whether or not the children are in college. The advent of a governmental health insurance program may convince people that they don't need separate coverage, but any such governmental program may be in a state of extreme flux for many years. So regardless of Uncle Sam's protection, the wise family will evaluate their risks in a most conservative manner. Young people are far less prone to high medical costs than are older people, but maternity, sports injuries, and unexpected accidents can result in some whopping bills. Many young people may have coverage gaps that you will want to help close. You might want to contribute something to their insurance costs, either by chipping in some of the premium or by having them take out a high deductible policy, with you paying part of the deductible if and when the need arises. The ultimate question you have to answer is this: If your children do face major medical costs for which they are uninsured, will you be content if they have to turn to a welfare program, or will you want them to have more choice in getting the care they need?

* *Life insurance.* See the next chapter for a pertinent discussion.

* *Automobile insurance.* From all my discussions, this seems to be the one element of continuing expense for parents that hangs on, and on, and on. This is often due to the fact that the kids' cars remain registered in the parent's name(s), which in turn is due to the fact that the kids may not be eligible to have auto policies in their own names. Once the kids are able to qualify for their own policies—both through age and good driving record—the family often overlooks having the kids do just that.

But there is one compelling reason to move swiftly to switch both ownership and insurance into the kids' names as soon as possible. If the kids are on your policy, and they have an accident that causes losses that exceed your policy limits, *your assets are at stake.* You could legally be forced to pay any damages out of your own pocket to the extent they exceed the policy's limits. If you want to protect yourself, either increase your coverage limits or get the ownership and insurance on the kids' cars into their own names. Discuss this in detail with your auto insurance agent at the earliest opportunity. If your kids can't afford their own insurance, help them out if you choose, but do so on their own policy.

* *Co-signing.* You may get the kids off the payroll, but you may never convince them to stop asking you for a loan now and then. If you do want to help them with these occasional needs, you'll be doing them a favor, and yourself as well, if you offer to co-sign for them at the bank rather than lend them the money directly. Or, in the alternative, you may be able to pledge some collateral on their behalf. In doing either, you relieve yourself of having to part with your own money and then worry about having it repaid. And you're giving them a boost toward getting an enhanced credit rating on their own. (Note: When you do co-sign or pledge collateral you can ask to have your name removed as co-signer once the payment progress on the loan appears satisfactory. The bank won't volunteer to do this, but if you ask them to they might oblige. Rosefsky's Rule #738b.)

* *Maturity.* Kids tend to lack it. That's why they're called kids. They're all too often fueled by impulse and the desire for kicks. (So are a lot of adults.) Those habits, left unchecked, will result in grown-ups with financial problems. You can help them to learn—and thus make it easier to eventually get them off the payroll—by apprising them of some of the traps that impulse and the desire for kicks can lead to. Chief among these traps is excessive debt and the bad credit rating that accompanies it, not to mention the sleepless nights and the angry phone calls from debt collectors. In their innocent youth they may not be able to imagine what those dire circumstances are like. Were you able to when you were their age? Don't flaunt your maturity; they won't respect you for that. But don't be embarrassed to tell them how your own lack of maturity once caused you problems. They'll identify with that. And didn't you have some excess spending/debt problems along the way? Come on, 'fess up.

One other problem that can arise from impulse and the desire for kicks—and it's a problem with incalculable financial and emotional ramifications—is an early death from AIDS. Don't assume that your kids know *and do* all that conventional wisdom dictates. Help them. Coach them. Convince them that they may never *reach* the maturity that you have if they ignore the clear warnings. My wife professionally counsels people before and after they have their HIV tests. The pretest counseling is fairly routine. The posttest counseling, especially for the positives, is harrowing. She is continually shocked at the number of young people who come through the clinic who believe they are immortal and have no need for precautions. There's a crying need for a whole lot more maturity out there.

* *Communication about your respective financial conditions.* People talk about their sex lives more openly than they do about their financial situations. Parents keep secrets from kids. Kids keep secrets from parents. That goes for all ages, from the golden-agers to the teeny-weenies. It applies from day-to-day business matters to estate planning concerns (which will be dealt with in more detail in Chapter 30).

If parents are on the financial rocks, mature kids have a right to know early on so they can make their own plans accordingly. If kids are in a jam, shame may prevent them from seeking guidance from their parents until it's too late. Mom and Dad may spend like drunken sailors, anticipating that a future inheritance will bail them out. When it doesn't; they're ruined. Or, Mom and Dad may sacrifice unduly to give a kid a higher education, only to learn later that there was more than enough money in an inevitable inheritance to have paid those bills. They can't go back and catch up on what they sacrificed. These things happen when people fail to communicate. It's a dangerous habit to get into. Please avoid it strenuously.

* *The safety net.* Like all other matters discussed here, this is a judgment call. Once you do get the kids off the payroll, how much of a safety net do you then want to provide for them? How much cash and how much counsel? How much can they count on you, come hell or high water, to bail them out of trouble? No obligation here, of course. It's strictly up to you. You can do all you want. Or nothing. But if you do hold out any kind of safety net, you and the kids should both clearly understand its limits.

It is certainly proper to offer a safety net in some circumstances and not in others: "If the grandchildren need medical attention, we'll be there for you. But if you put your money into that cockamamie scheme and lose it all, don't come running to us for any support." It is certainly proper to terminate the safety net whenever you feel you can no longer provide it. Just let them know in clear and uncertain terms just what the facts are as time goes along. Imagine the artistry of the trapeze performers when they know there's a safety net underneath them. And imagine what a crime it would be to remove the net without telling them.

Chapter Twenty-nine

That Was Then, This Is Now

Looking back on some major decisions regarding life insurance: how the concerns of twenty- and thirty-somethings impact on the financial well-being of fifty- and sixty-somethings

A long time ago I bought a lot of life insurance on myself, on my wife, and on my children. I committed a major chunk of my disposable income to those policies, and I wondered if I was doing the right thing. The agents told me not to worry. "Years down the road," they said, "you'll be happy with your decisions." I was young, I trusted them, but I had my doubts.

That was then: Over the ensuing years I sent a lot of checks off to the life insurance companies. That was money that I could have easily put to much more tangible enjoyments.

This is now: After paying on those policies for anywhere from twenty-five to forty years, and after having taken action with respect to the choices available to me in those policies, I can honestly say that the agents back then were right. I am happy with my decisions. Indeed, in many respects I'm thrilled.

I'm not here to sell life insurance. I'm not being paid a penny by any insurance company to tell you of my experiences. I just want you to know what worked for me, because maybe it can work for you too.

I'm also not here to engage in the interminable debate over which kind of life insurance is better, whole (or, as it's also called, "straight" or "ordinary") life insurance on the one hand, or term insurance on the other hand. A quick summary for those not familiar with these terms:

* Whole life provides a fixed amount of coverage at a fixed annual cost for an indefinite period of time. As long as you make your

payments every year the policy will remain in force. The longer you make your payments, the more values build up within the policy. These are commonly known as conversion values. They allow you to convert the form of your protection to another form.

Here's a very conservative and oversimplified sample of how conversion values work. Say you have a whole life policy with a face value of $10,000—that is, the policy will pay $10,000 to your named beneficiaries on your death. You were twenty-five years old when you started the policy . . . that was then.

This is now: After paying on the policy faithfully—the same amount every year—for twenty years, you now have the following conversion values from which you can choose.

1. You can cash in the policy for about $3,000. That is, after having had the $10,000 worth of protection for twenty years, you can cancel the policy and get back $3,000 in cash.

2. You can borrow about $3,000 against the policy at a favorable rate of interest. That is, you can borrow that amount by simply notifying the company that you want to, and you don't ever have to pay it back. (You do have to keep paying your annual policy costs, plus the interest, and if you die before the loan is repaid, the policy will pay the face amount less the loan, or about $7,000.)

3. You can stop making annual payments altogether and convert your coverage to about $5,200 of "paid-up" status. That is, you never have to make any more payments, but you remain insured for the rest of your life for $5,200.

4. You can stop making annual payments and convert your coverage to "extended term" status. That is, you never have to make any more payments, but you remain insured for the *full* $10,000 for a limited period, in this case about twenty-three years.

5. You can continue making your payments as you have been, and in another five or ten or twenty years evaluate your choices all over again. At those future dates your conversion values will be much greater than they were in the above example.

(Check with your agent to find out about the simple paperwork that needs to be done to accomplish any of these conversions.)

*   Term life insurance provides a fixed amount of coverage for a fixed annual cost but for a *limited* amount of time. A term policy may run for one year, or for a longer term, such as ten years. During *that specific term* the annual cost will stay the same. But when the term ends, if you wish to continue with the insurance, you will have to renew it at a higher annual rate.

While at any given starting age a term policy will cost less per year than a whole life policy of the same amount, eventually the *annual* cost of term insurance can exceed the annual cost of a whole life policy that was commenced on the same starting date. Over a long period, the *total* out-of-pocket costs of term insurance can exceed those of a whole life policy.

Further, in general, term insurance does *not* build up conversion values. These factors make it quite difficult to compare the true value of term versus whole life insurance. They're really very different creatures, and they both can have their rightful place in an individual's portfolio. (Another form of life insurance, universal life, offers a combination of whole life and term elements.)

My role now is not to contemplate what might have happened if I had made other choices along the way. It's merely to tell you what choices I did make and how they worked for me.

Simply put, I chose all whole life policies at the very outset, and I let the years go by, and by, and by, and slowly but surely my conversion values grew and grew. Two other factors came into play.

1. As medical science allowed life expectancies to increase, the life insurance companies changed their mortality tables (from which they calculate how much you have to pay for life insurance) to reflect longer lifetimes. Longer lifetimes means that the insurance companies have a longer time to reap earnings on your money that they have invested, which in turn reflects in lower annual costs for policies issued based on the newer mortality tables. Insurance companies make these adjustments only every few decades; it will happen again.

2. In the 1980s the insurance industry invented "second to die" insurance. This is basically a life insurance policy covering

two people instead of one. The policy pays off when the second person dies. As with extended mortality, this gives the insurance companies a longer time to work with your money, which in turn brings down the cost to the policyholder. A two-person policy can cost quite a bit less than a one-person policy.

New kinds of policies are invented infrequently, but there will be more as the years go by. I benefited from both of these factors. There will be other new factors emerging in the future from which you can benefit.

As noted in the discussion on Regeneration in Chapter 23, a time may come when you want to cut down on some of your ongoing expenses, such as life insurance. In most cases, the conversions referred to above can accomplish quite a lot. But you can go one giant step farther and *exchange* old policies for new ones if you're physically fit. I found by doing so I could not only *decrease* my out-of-pocket expenses, but I could also *increase* the amount of protection. Most of the policies on my wife and myself I exchanged for two-person policies. The substantial values that had been built up in those policies allowed us to end up with much lower costs and much higher protection. The policies on my children, which had commenced when they were very young and therefore had many years to accumulate values, allowed them to be exchanged for new policies that more than doubled the amounts of coverage at a fraction of the cost.

The ability to make these changes made an *enormous* difference in my overall financial structure, and in my frame of mind—all very much to the good. And no, I never did look back and wonder what might have been if I had put all those insurance dollars into the stock market or government bonds, or the race track. I've always found that living life to the fullest doesn't allow for very much, if any, "what might have been" thinking.

(Note for tax wonks: All of the exchanges referred to qualified as so-called "1035 exchanges" for federal income tax purposes, which allows old policies to be replaced by new ones with minimal, if any, income tax consequences. Also, the larger policies on my wife and myself were transferred into a "life insurance trust," which minimizes estate tax liabilities. Consult your own insurance agent and tax advisor for specific details as they might apply to your own case.)

When we are in our twenties and thirties we are ripe plucking for life insurance sales pitches. We often resent these pitches—often for good reason, because they can be off-putting and uncomfortable. But the fact is that that is the ideal time to acquire life insurance: youth assures lower rates, and good health should be taken advantage of while it's at hand to allow qualification for policies. Neither youth nor good health last; capitalize on them while you have them.

As I wondered about the wisdom of my choices when I was in my twenties and thirties, the same goes for you and your children. It's admittedly very hard to look decades down the road and sense what benefits will be in hand as a result of the decisions made in youth. But take it from one who's been there and who has nothing to sell: Yes, I questioned my judgment back then. And yes, I finally know, here and now, that I did the right thing.

A Fitting Ending

Do's and don'ts of estate planning: An array of case histories that had
unhappy endings, and what you can do to keep that from happening to you

All of the following situations happened to real people. Similar chaos could happen to anyone . . . even you perhaps?

     * Alfred and his wife Elaine were having marital problems. A separation seemed imminent, if not a divorce. Much of their problem was due to the fact that Alfred's aging widowed mother lived with them, and Elaine didn't like the old lady one bit. Elaine was constantly haranguing Alfred to put his mother into a nursing home. That way she'd be out of Elaine's life. Alfred died suddenly. He left no will. Had he left a will, he would have provided comfortably for his mother. As it was, the *laws of intestacy* in his state dictated that his spouse, Elaine, was entitled to *all* of his estate, and his mother was entitled to *none*. Elaine treated her mother-in-law brutally and abusively, and sent her off to live in a squalid home for the aged.

     * Marvin and Freida's only child Nate was a ne'er-do-well. He was in constant trouble with the law, and his parents were always having to bail him out. He borrowed from them constantly, always squandering the money on gambling and drinking. He had even stolen from them to support his habits. Marvin died suddenly. He left no will. As it was, the *laws of intestacy* in his state dictated that his surviving spouse was entitled to only one-third of his estate, and his surviving child, Nate, was entitled to two-thirds. Marvin was not particularly well-to-do. Freida's one-third share of his estate left her facing a life of poverty. Had she received the full estate—which would have been Marvin's wish—she could have at least kept the wolf from her door. Nate blew his entire inheritance in less than one year.

* Angie lived with a longtime companion, Chris. They were not married, but their devotion to each other knew no bounds. Angie had four siblings, and had only known scorn and derision from them. When Angie contracted a fatal disease Chris spent every minute and penny available to help make Angie's life comfortable. The siblings never even came to call. Angie was too despondent to think of making a will. When death came, the *laws of intestacy* in Angie's state dictated that the siblings were entitled to everything that Angie left. Angie had little of value, except for a collection of porcelain clowns that had been lovingly accumulated over the years. Angie would have wanted Chris to have the clown collection. But the siblings took it, and there was nothing Chris could do about it.

* Matthew had prepared a will leaving everything outright to his wife, Tamara. Matthew had always handled all of the family finances, and never gave a thought as to how Tamara might do as a money manager in his absence. Matthew was well on in years when he passed away. Tamara suddenly found herself in charge of a considerable sum of money, and had no clue as to how to manage it. Most of the money was lost within two years on fraudulent investment schemes that Tamara fell prey to. She lived her remaining years in dire financial and emotional straits.

* Vivian was a wealthy woman. As a successful clothing designer she owned her own manufacturing facility and retail boutique. Over the years she had invested her profits in works of fine art. In her will she left appropriate shares to her husband and three children. When Vivian died her heirs were appalled to learn that hundreds of thousands of dollars had to be paid in federal estate taxes. Despite Vivian's wealth, she was cash-poor. Assets had to be sold to pay her estate taxes. Without her active participation in the business its profit potential was severely limited. Finding a buyer who would pay a fair price was next to impossible. Selling the art also proved difficult, as the economy was in a recession and the market for art was very soft. The family had to accept stinging losses as a result of having to sell off assets to pay the taxes. When all was said and done, Vivian's wealth was sorely depleted.

* Charlie and Emily had no financial problems because they had no finances. What little they had—modest home, small savings plans—was in joint names, with everything going to the survivor in the

event of one's death. So, they figured, there was no need in spending money on a lawyer to have a will prepared. Sadly, Charlie and Emily were both killed in a car accident. Their two small children then became the subject of horrendous family warfare as to who would be their guardian. Charlie had no brothers or sisters, and his elderly parents insisted that they should be the guardians of their grandchildren. Emily had two sisters, and they insisted that they be named joint guardians. Then the two sisters began their own battle as to how the children would be divided between them. It was an awful situation, and no one was happy when the court finally decided that one of the two sisters would be sole guardian of both children.

      *   Ned married Nancy after his first wife passed away. Ned's kids didn't like Nancy, and they urged Ned to have Nancy sign a prenuptial agreement, in which he would promise her a fixed sum of money in lieu of claiming any part of Ned's estate. Nancy did so, but reluctantly. She agreed to accept $100,000 in the prenuptial agreement. She would have received close to $300,000 from Ned's estate had she not signed the prenuptial agreement.

When Ned died Nancy hired a lawyer to represent her. The lawyer advised Nancy to contest the validity of the prenuptial agreement, claiming that she had not been properly advised of all her rights before she signed it. If she could have the agreement invalidated, she'd get $300,000, of which her lawyer would take $100,000, leaving her with $200,000. It appeared that Nancy might have a good case.

But Ned's children were determined not to let Nancy get away with this, and they hired their own lawyer to fight her claim. Early on Nancy's lawyer offered to settle the whole thing for $210,000, of which the lawyer would get $70,000, leaving Nancy with $140,000. Such a settlement would have saved Ned's kids tens of thousands of dollars in legal fees, but now principle was involved. They vowed to fight on.

Months of bickering and pretrial maneuvering went by. Ned's kids finally caved in and agreed to settle for $240,000, of which Nancy's lawyer would get $80,000 and Nancy would get $160,000. Ned's kids considered the settlement a very small victory: They had kept $60,000 from flying away had Nancy won the trial. But the whole sad affair had cost them $40,000 in legal fees. Had they taken the offer of settlement ($210,000) they would have been $90,000 better off with only minimal legal fees to pay.

* Walt and Shirley were comfortable in their retirement, and they had every intention of leaving a tidy sum to their children. They were intrigued by an advertisement touting "living trusts" as the ideal way to resolve all estate planning matters. They went to a free seminar and listened to a lot of confusing, but very smooth, talk about the benefits of a living trust.

When the seminar was concluded Walt and Shirley couldn't act fast enough: They hired the lawyers who were conducting the seminar to prepare a living trust for them, and the documents were signed and paid for within three days. Walt and Shirley told their children what they had done, and the children reacted with deep concern. "Shouldn't you have consulted your own lawyers before you dealt with these strangers?" the children asked. Walt and Shirley were totally content that they had done the right thing, and were peeved that their kids had questioned their judgment. The matter was soon forgotten.

A few years later Walt and Shirley died within a few months of each other. That's when the children learned to their deep dismay that the lawyers who had prepared the living trust had been named in that document as trustees of, and lawyers for, the estates. The fees that the lawyers paid themselves took a huge slice out of the estate. Walt and Shirley's children quickly found out that it would cost them dearly to challenge the matter in court, and that their chances of winning were slim.

*
**   *
**   *
**

I could go on for another 100 pages describing other situations that arose as a result of faulty or incomplete estate planning, or total lack thereof. But I think the point is clear: There are more potential problems than you can imagine that can arise out of failure to do proper estate planning.

With respect to the cases involving the state *laws of intestacy* you must be aware of the fact that each of the fifty states has its own laws that determine who gets what if a person dies *intestate*, that is without a will or some other valid form of estate distribution. If you don't know how your own state's laws of intestacy work, you'd best get cracking and find out. You might be in for a shock when you find out how your state's legislature has created a plan for the distribution of your estate. If you don't like what your state has in store for you, you must take steps on your own to develop a plan that does suit you.

As the other brief case histories illustrate, distribution is not the only matter that should concern you.

* Matt and Tamara's case illustrates problems that can arise with respect to *asset management.*

* Vivian's case illustrates problems relative to *liquidity* and *estate tax liability.*

* Charlie and Emily's case illustrates the potentially devastating effects of *guardianship* issues.

* Ned and Nancy's case illustrates the dangerous waters that can swirl around *remarriages* and *prenuptial agreements.*

* Walt and Shirley's case illustrates how *scoundrels* can play havoc with even the best-intentioned people. (Living trusts *might* be good for some people, but not for all people. Some of the aggressive marketing of these plans by some lawyers raise troublesome issues.)

This chapter is definitely *not* intended to be a substitute for proper estate planning. It *is* intended to stimulate you to take all necessary and proper steps toward developing a proper estate plan.

I know, estate planning is not a fun thing. Most people's attitudes toward it are shaped by fear, by superstition ("If I sign a will today, I'll be struck by lightning tomorrow."), and by a natural aversion to lawyers. Those attitudes can cause you the problems that our cast of characters in this chapter have suffered. Those problems represent only the tip of the iceberg of possible difficulties that can be encountered.

Yes, estate planning will cost some money.

Yes, you can just copy someone else's will, putting in your own names, and avoid getting a bill from a lawyer. That's just plain dumb.

Yes, you can buy various do-it-yourself fill-in-the-blanks will "kits" from various sources, but I strongly recommend against this as your final estate planning step. There are too many personal and technical variations in each individual case; the kits can't possibly contemplate or deal with all of your own specific individual needs and desires.

Yes, you can just spend all the money you have while you're still alive, so that most of the above-noted problems couldn't possibly occur. But what if you die before you've spent it all? Or what if the money runs out before it's your time to call it quits?

The only proper way to develop a proper estate plan is with an attorney who is skilled in that area of the law. If your own family lawyer isn't specialized in that field, he or she can recommend someone who is. Seek recommendations from friends, family, co-workers, or clergy. Most local bar associations can refer you to specialists in that (or any other) field.

Have an initial interview with the lawyer to determine if you feel comfortable with his or her demeanor, background, and expertise. Ask that such a preliminary interview be without cost (or at minimal cost) to you. (Rosefsky's Rule #738b again.)

At the outset of an estate planning relationship the lawyer should inquire about all your personal and financial interests that may have a bearing on the final documents. You must divulge all of this information if the plan is to accomplish all that you want it to.

The lawyer should tell you, in *clear, understandable, jargon-free terms* just exactly what options are open to you, and what the implications of each option are. If need be, ask the lawyer to draw simple charts showing how the estate assets would be distributed under the various options (including, of course, to the estate tax collector, should that be an issue in your case). Above all, the lawyer should clearly make the fee schedule known: how much is to be paid, and at what times.

The relationship with the estate planning lawyer doesn't end with the signing of the will or trust documents. Both you and the attorney must be vigilant to changes in circumstances that might dictate the need for changes in your estate plan. These circumstances could include modifications in your family membership (births, deaths, marriages, divorces); moving to another state whose laws could affect the validity or specific details of your existing estate plan; modifications in the law—particularly federal estate tax law—that could impact on your existing plan; and, overall, simply changing your mind about any of the elements already written into your estate plan. *Any* changes to estate documents should be made in the proper legal fashion; *any* attempts to make changes without proper legal advice can produce undesired results.

What can a proper estate plan accomplish? Distribution, liquidity, and management of assets; guardianship arrangements to suit you, as needed; tax savings; minimizing of squabbles, bickering, and legal warfare; and, overall, peace of mind for yourself and your family.

Do it right. Make it a fitting ending.